Reading Engagement

MOTIVATING READERS
THROUGH
INTEGRATED INSTRUCTION

John T. Guthrie
Allan Wigfield

National Reading Research Center
University of Maryland at College Park
College Park, Maryland, USA

Editors

INTERNATIONAL

Reading Association
800 Barksdale Road, PO Box 8139
Newark, Delaware 19714-8139, USA

The International Reading Association attempts, through its publications, to provide a forum for a wide spectrum of opinions on reading. This policy permits divergent viewpoints without implying the endorsement of the Association.

Director of Publications   Joan M. Irwin
Assistant Director of Publications   Wendy Lapham Russ
Senior Editor   Christian A. Kempers
Associate Editor   Matthew W. Baker
Assistant Editor   Janet S. Parrack
Editorial Assistant   Cynthia C. Sawaya
Association Editor   David K. Roberts
Production Department Manager   Iona Sauscermen
Graphic Design Coordinator   Boni Nash
Design Consultant   Larry F. Husfelt
Electronic Publishing Supervisor   Wendy A. Mazur
Electronic Publishing Specialist   Anette Schütz-Ruff
Electronic Publishing Specialist   Cheryl J. Strum
Electronic Publishing Assistant   Peggy Mason

Library of Congress Cataloging in Publication Data
    Reading engagement: Motivating readers through integrated instruction/John T. Guthrie, Allan Wigfield, editors.
        p.   cm.
    Includes bibliographical references and index.
    1. Reading (Elementary)—United States.   2. Motivation in education—United States.   3. Active learning—United States.   4. Literacy—United States.   I. Guthrie, John T.   II. Wigfield, Allan.
    LB1573.R2787   1997   96-47428
    372.4—dc21
    ISBN 0-87207-148-0 (pbk.)

Contents

Foreword

For the past few years we have witnessed calls for increasing students' interest in reading and in learning in general. The 1992 poll of International Reading Association members by the National Reading Research Center indicated that creating interest, intrinsic desire, and motivation were in the top 10 priorities of the membership. Unfortunately, we have received little guidance in fostering the desired engagement in our students. In this regard, *Reading Engagement: Motivating Readers Through Integrated Instruction* is a timely book.

This publication also might be considered to be an "it's about time" book for the reading profession. Psychologists consider the process of motivation to be cognitively generated but with considerable impact from affective factors. Although the importance of affective factors has long been a focus of educational theorists, with a taxonomy of the affective domain presented in 1964, the same cannot be said for the field of reading education and research. Almost 20 years ago, when I edited the IRA publication *Using Literature and Poetry Affectively*, I received many comments about the misspelling of the last word in the title. It seemed that few reading professionals had affective factors in mind when they thought of reading instruction and practice.

An examination of article titles in the major reading research journals from their first volume year until the call by the NRRC for a new focus on motivation and other affective factors indicated that only about nine percent were devoted to the various affective factors. Since 1992 the figure has actually declined to approximately seven percent. The benchmark publications of the past decade fare no better: *Becoming a Nation of Readers*, the *Handbook of Reading Research, Volume II*, and the oft-quoted *Beginning to Read: Thinking and Learning About Print* are virtually silent on the various components of the affective dimension and motivation.

Before 1992 less than three percent of the total journal articles published were identified by practitioners as being primarily concerned with this important area, and there were only five IRA books published, all prior to 1986. Times have changed and we are now paying more than just lip service to issues relating to reading engagement. The International Reading Association has accepted the challenge by its membership: since 1992 we have seen nine percent of *The Reading Teacher* articles and seven percent of the *Journal of Adolescent & Adult Literacy* dealing with motivation and/or affective factors, and *Reading Engagement: Motivating Readers Through Integrated Instruction* is the second IRA title dealing with this domain to be published since 1994.

In this book the reader will find a wonderful union of theory and practice. The contributors to the first section provide both practitioners and researchers with the theoretical and research base for understanding reading engagement and its underlying processes. The authors in Section II build upon this foundation by giving us solid ideas for improving student reading engagement in our classrooms. The editors, John Guthrie and Allan Wigfield, have provided us with a timely and "it's about time" book that will foster the goal of creating engaged and interested readers.

Jon Shapiro
The University of British Columbia
Vancouver, British Columbia, Canada

Contributors

Kathryn H. Au
Associate Professor, College of Education
University of Hawaii
Honolulu, Hawaii

Roger Bruning
Velma Warren Hodder Professor of Educational Psychology
University of Nebraska–Lincoln
Lincoln, Nebraska

Lyn Corno
Professor of Education and Psychology
Teachers College, Columbia University
New York, New York

Linda B. Gambrell
Professor and Associate Dean, College of Education
University of Maryland at College Park
College Park, Maryland

John T. Guthrie
Professor, Department of Human Development
Codirector, National Reading Research Center
University of Maryland at College Park
College Park, Maryland

Barbara Ann Marinak
Reading Consultant
Central Dauphin School District
Harrisburg, Pennsylvania

Ann Dacey McCann
Graduate Research Assistant, National Reading Research Center
University of Maryland at College Park
College Park, Maryland

Judi Randi
Adjunct Professor, Graduate School
University of New Haven
West Haven, Connecticut

JoyLynn Hailey Reed
Lecturer, Department of Speech Communication
University of Texas
Austin, Texas

Robert B. Ruddell
Professor and Chair, Division of Language, Literacy, and Culture
Graduate School of Education
University of California at Berkeley
Berkeley, California

Carol Minnick Santa
Language Arts Coordinator
Kalispell Public Schools
Kalispell, Montana

Diane Lemonnier Schallert
Professor, Department of Educational Psychology
University of Texas
Austin, Texas

Dale H. Schunk
Professor and Head, Department of Educational Studies
Purdue University
West Lafayette, Indiana

Barbara M. Schweiger
Supervisor, Reading Services and Director of Elementary Summer School
Omaha Public Schools
Omaha, Nebraska

Anne P. Sweet
Federal Monitor, National Reading Research Center
Office of Educational Research and Improvement, U.S. Department of Education
Washington, DC

Julianne C. Turner
Assistant Research Professor, Psychology Department
University of Notre Dame
Notre Dame, Indiana

Norman J. Unrau
Associate Professor, Division of Curriculum and Instruction
Charter School of Education
California State University, Los Angeles
Los Angeles, California

Allan Wigfield
Associate Professor, Department of Human Development
University of Maryland at College Park
College Park, Maryland

Barry J. Zimmerman
Distinguished Professor of Educational Psychology
Graduate School and University Center
City University of New York
New York, New York

Introduction

Reading Engagement: A Rationale for Theory and Teaching

John T. Guthrie and Allan Wigfield

T he purpose of this book is to present research findings that illuminate reading engagement. These findings are drawn from two areas: theoretical research on how cognition and motivation intersect in reading and classroom-based inquiries into learning contexts that encourage long-term engagement. These two sources merge to form a growing body of knowledge. The point of this knowledge base, and the purpose of this book, is to understand reading engagement, to account for it, to be able to recognize it, and to learn how to help students develop their own forms of engagement. In addition, some authors in this volume address the broader concept of literacy engagement by discussing both reading and writing in their chapters.

To introduce the notion of reading engagement, we offer an example of two engaged readers. The following vignette of a fifth-grade classroom is from videotapes of actual classroom interactions. After presenting this example, we briefly sketch the profile of the students as engaged readers. We describe their cognitive strategies, motivational goals, social dispositions, and social interaction patterns. This vignette raises questions: How do we depict engagement? How do we create long-term engagement in classrooms? Several research trends are converging to address these questions. In this opening chapter, we identify these trends, and we briefly note how they can inform our understanding of reading engagement.

A Vignette of Reading Engagement

Our students are fifth graders in a low-income school near an urban center. The class is multicultural, with minority students and second-language learners well represented. Several students who receive help from a resource teacher are included. The class is studying environmental science in a 16-week unit that will integrate language arts with science. A conceptual theme of adaptation—including survival, feeding, breeding, shelter, and defense—will provide focus for reading, writing, and science learning. As the class begins the unit, students gather on the hillside behind the school building to do some observational work.

Embarking on a cricket hunt, students work in small teams to capture a specimen. One of the boldest class members, Robert, quickly exclaims, "I caught one! I got it!" His teammate, Kantu, does not want to touch the cricket and says, "Put it in the box, but don't put it in with the spider." Robert and Kantu are elated with their discovery and note the cricket's behavior, color, and habitat. Taking the cricket into the classroom in its box, the students begin drawing their specimen and writing a chronicle of their hunt. As the students draw and write, they focus their attention on the physical features of the cricket and its environment. After several days of observational activities, the students are bursting with questions.

To help students build on their sense of wonder, the teacher guides them in forming their questions. Along with the rest of the class, Robert and Kantu place their questions on a wall chart displaying their curiosities. These questions will guide the science and literacy learning of the unit. As goals for the learning activities, the questions are personal to the students because they involve their experience of discovery and are expressed in their own words. The teacher helps the students direct their questions toward the conceptual theme of adaptation. Robert's question is "I want to know whether crickets have a brain," and Kantu asks, "Why do crickets live here in the summer and where do they go in the winter?"

Having posed their questions, Robert and Kantu begin a quest for answers. During class time, they are encouraged to browse the 40 to 50 trade books in the classroom library. With the teacher's guidance, Robert finds a science book about insects. Over several days he compares his specimen with the text and illustrations, entering his insights in his science journal. Kantu learns search strategies from the teacher's instruction, and he finds a diagram of the cricket's life cycle in one of the trade books. Kantu becomes absorbed in recording the cricket's life cycle in his science journal. Meanwhile, Robert shares his drawing with everyone. As the students become more proficient in finding information, they proudly exchange their techniques for combining information from pictures and texts.

After several days, the teacher asks each team to decide how it will learn about crickets. To avert chaos in the classroom, the teacher helps the teams compose rules for talking and working together. With experience, the teams improve their rules to make their work more fair to everyone, fun, and productive. Some teams choose to conduct more observations, while others choose to read. Robert and Kantu decide to conduct an experiment. They compose a plan, collect data, and graph the results. The team concludes that crickets prefer lettuce to popcorn and hamburger.

In the middle of the unit, the teacher introduces literature relevant to the theme. The students are intrigued by *Tuck Everlasting* by Natalie Babbitt, a novel in which the characters discover water that makes people live forever. Robert and Kantu disagree about whether living forever would be desirable. In his literary journal, Kantu states that "living forever wouldn't be natural because everything dies," but Robert prefers the fantasy of the book because "it would be fun to see the future." After the novel, students read poems about the theme. Robert finds a poem about spiders that portrays their patience as predators, and Kantu is captivated by a poem that compares the life span of an insect to that of a star.

To parallel the literary reading, the teacher invites each team to choose its own insect or animal and compose a concept web of its adaptation. In each team, individual members select subtopics of feeding, breeding, shelter, and defense. Over a 15-day period, students retrieve information from multiple texts, illustrations, and references. After collecting information in journals, teams collaborate to construct a large poster of their findings. Researching the feeding habits of the monarch butterfly, Robert exclaims, "I've found the best information about how they eat." Kantu decides to study the reproductive cycle of the monarch. Robert and Kantu become more invested in learning about adaptation as they share ideas and challenge each other's thinking.

Each team decides how to express its understanding of adaptation to the other students. One team designs a poster with explanations, which is placed on a bulletin board in the hall. Another composes a narrative, weaving the gathered information into a story, which they illustrate and print on the classroom computer. Robert and Kantu design and produce a 10-minute videotape of themselves as experts explaining the life cycle of the monarch butterfly. After showing the video to a fourth-grade class in their school, Robert and Kantu shake hands as the class applauds.

Interpretation of This Vignette

Many perspectives can be taken to describe what is happening in this vignette. We see, first, that students are using their minds as they interact with text to learn. They are locating helpful sources, composing, and reading. They are understanding texts in different genres, including informational books and poems. They are integrating ideas and building understanding. In brief, the students are using cognitive strategies for learning with text, including identifying relevant texts, summarizing, locating details, fusing ideas, and building concepts that can explain what they see. However, these students are doing more than gaining cognitive expertise.

Robert and Kantu are excited. They want to learn. Their motivational qualities are central to their strategy learning. Robert and Kantu have powerful reasons for reading and writing that are vital motivations for learning literacy skills. Without these motivations, the difficult work of cognitive learning does not occur rapidly, if it occurs at all. Because these motivations are so valuable, we want to understand them. Where do these motivations come from? How can teachers initiate and sustain the development of motivations in classrooms? How can long-term curiosity and desire to read be nourished? These questions are addressed by different authors in this book.

Multiple lines of inquiry have provided a base for research on the motivational aspects of reading. These inquiries begin with the historical emphasis on cognitive research. For example, Huey (1908/1968) provides an early psychological perspective on reading.

And so to completely analyze what we do when we read would almost be the acme of a psychologist's achievements, for it would be to describe very many of the most intricate workings of the human mind, as well as to unravel the tangled story of the most remarkable specific performance that civilization has learned in all its history. (p. 6)

More recently, from the perspective of literary criticism rather than psychology, Rosenblatt (1978) defines two forms of reading stances: the efferent, which refers to knowledge gained from reading, and the aesthetic, which refers to the cognitive and affective experience during reading. Although Rosenblatt's definition of reading is substantially mentalistic, a small role for affect is provided. However, this role does not relate to motivational goals or purpose for engaging in reading. Huey and Rosenblatt are only two of the psychological and literary sources of the 20th century who illustrate that reading has been defined as a cognitive, mental occurrence.

The traditional view of reading acquisition has been centered on cognitive processes. Since the 1880s learning to read has been viewed widely as a process of learning to recognize words (Huey, 1908/1968; Juel, Griffith, & Gough, 1986). To learn rapid word recognition, it is necessary to acquire phonemic awareness and an understanding of letter-sound correspondences and orthography (Chall, 1983; Ehri, 1994). In addition, although the emergent literacy movement (Sulzby & Teale, 1991) underscores the social roles of books as communication systems, learning is substantially cognitive and linguistic in the emergent literacy perspective.

Complementing these definitional orientations toward reading, empirical studies of the reading process have been overwhelmingly cognitive. In the 1960s, linguists, psycholinguists, cognitive psychologists, and reading researchers explored complex models of reading as a cognitive and language process. Compilations of research on reading, *Handbook of Reading Research, Volume II* (Barr et al., 1991) and *Theoretical Models and Processes of Reading* (4th edition; Ruddell, Ruddell, & Singer, 1994) contain extensive work on the processes of cognition but little on the processes of motivation for reading. Although attitudes toward reading have been recognized by a few investigators more recently (Mathewson, 1994), reading research has been bound paradigmatically as a cognitive or linguistic process. Because researchers have been following these definitional perspectives and beliefs, motivation for reading has been underrepresented in reading research during much of the 20th century.

At least four lines of inquiry in the 1990s have led to the need to understand motivation for reading more fully. First, studies of cognitive strategy development for reading have emphasized the deliberate, conscious, effortful nature of strategies (Pintrich & Schrauben, 1992). Such a demanding cognitive system does not operate frequently and automatically; it requires effort, persistence, and desire. These demands on the reader have led investigators to ask questions about motivation. The issue of why students choose (or do not choose) to use strategies they have learned for reading is a motivational question.

A second line of research emphasizes the positive contribution of the amount of reading to reading achievement. Various investigations have documented that the amount and breadth of reading are the single largest factor contributing to reading achievement. Diary studies (Anderson, Wilson, & Fielding, 1988), measures of print exposure (Stanovich & Cunningham, 1991), and questionnaire data (Guthrie et al., 1995) conclude that high frequency, amount, and diversity of reading activity increase reading achievement. Further, these influences occur when crucial background factors including the amount of schooling, mental ability, gender, and economic level are held constant.

Recognizing the potent contribution of the amount of reading activity to reading achievement, we naturally ask, "What accounts for amount of reading?" This is essentially a question of motivation. As explained in this book, motivation theorists define motivation in terms of the beliefs, values, needs, and goals that individuals have. The authors in the first section of this book address this issue, but they discuss different motivational constructs. The practical question "What are the types of classroom conditions that can cultivate the hopes, desires, and expectations of students to become active readers?" is the focus of this volume's second section.

In a third line of research that has influenced our perspective, motivation theorists have explored how motivation and cognition intersect to enhance achievement. As shown by expectancy-value theory (Wigfield & Eccles, 1992), self-determination models (Deci, 1992), goal-oriented research (Dweck & Leggett, 1988), and studies of interest in text (Alexander, Kulikowich, & Schulze, 1994; Shraw, Bruning, & Svoboda, 1995), motivation is increasingly linked to academic achievement. Yet, few of these researchers have explicitly addressed motivation for reading. Extending the connection of motivation to academic achievement more explicitly to reading, writing, and literacy achievement is one of the purposes of this volume.

Fourth, social constructivists have argued that literacy is a sociolinguistic interaction (Bloome & Green, 1992; Heath, 1983). The role of interpersonal interaction surrounding literacy is to encourage the growth of intrapersonal cognitive and language functions. Within this framework, the roles of motivations have not been highlighted or formally explicated. The acquisition of motivational goals through social mediation promises to be a fruitful area for inquiry.

In concert with these lines of research, the National Reading Research Center (NRRC) was funded by the Office of Educational Research and Improvement based on a proposal emphasizing the centrality of literacy engagement, which refers to the joint functioning of motivation with knowledge, strategies, and social interactions in literacy. This volume contains extensive reports of teacher collaborative research and the findings of individual researchers pursuing the engagement perspective.

Organization of the Book

In a practical sense, the aim of this book is to account for the literacy interactions of Robert and Kantu. In the classroom vignette presented, not only are these students gaining cognitive expertise, but they also are increasing their motivations. For Robert and Kantu, comprehension is accompanied by motivation. But "accompanied" is too weak a term;

perhaps better terms are "fueled" or "driven." Because wanting to read—motivation—is so useful for learning to read, we believe it will be valuable to explore the existing bodies of theory and research on motivations. To account for the reading and writing of these students, we need to describe their desires for reading, to discuss the origins of their reasons for reading, and to map the connections of their cognitions and motivations during their literacy activities. We also address the classroom contexts that enhance individual engagement. The interplay between individual engagement and classroom contexts is depicted in the figure below.

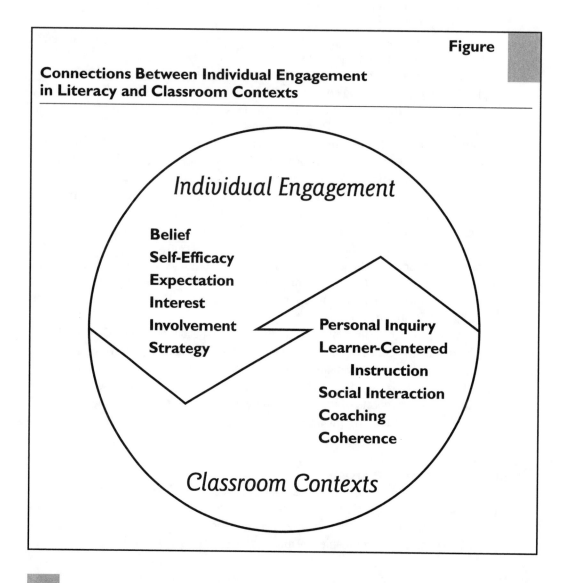

Figure

Connections Between Individual Engagement in Literacy and Classroom Contexts

Individual Engagement

Belief
Self-Efficacy
Expectation
Interest
Involvement
Strategy

Personal Inquiry
Learner-Centered Instruction
Social Interaction
Coaching
Coherence

Classroom Contexts

Guthrie & Wigfield

Section I Motivations, Beliefs, and Self-Efficacy in Literacy Development

Authors of chapters in the first section of this book provide overviews of several prevailing theories of motivation. Explanatory ideas of motivation developed in psychological and educational research are illustrated with examples from classroom literacy tasks. Basic concepts are emphasized along with their relation to the development of reading and writing.

In Chapter 1, Wigfield explains prevailing fundamental concepts of motivation called *motivation constructs* such as ability beliefs, expectancy for success, and achievement values. He describes expectancy-value theory and the ways in which this theory relates to intrinsic and extrinsic motivations for learning. Schunk and Zimmerman in Chapter 2 explicate social cognitive theory in terms that connect the basic theoretical ideas to literacy development. They emphasize self-efficacy as a contributor to the development of literacy competence and illustrate their points by reviewing intervention work designed to enhance self-efficacy and reading and writing performance. Corno and Randi's Chapter 3 emphasizes how motivational and volitional constructs are linked to strategies for literacy and literacy teaching. In particular, they discuss how volitional strategies such as management of resources and processes of self-direction and self-control are needed to continue motivational intentions. They describe volitional styles such as conscientiousness and persistence that are grounded in motivations for literacy. In addition, they discuss ways to enhance motivation and volition through collaborative innovations among teachers, administrators, and researchers. In Chapter 4, Schallert and Reed review research on text-based interest. They discuss studies that suggest that interest enhances the use of prior knowledge; these studies are contrasted with others that indicate that interest increases attention and involvement during reading. The authors consider alternative causal models along with implications of these models for classroom instruction.

Teacher orientations, beliefs, and perceptions about literacy motivation are addressed in the final two chapters of Section I. In Chapter 5, Sweet describes teacher perceptions about literacy. She illustrates that the self-determination theory articulated by Deci and colleagues (1991) is at least partially implicit in teachers' theories about student engagement. In Chapter 6, Ruddell and Unrau propose a broad model of reading motivation that depicts the multiple influences on the intentions of learners. Aspects of the classroom environment also are included in this model.

Section I Themes and Principles

Motivations for literacy are multifaceted and complex. Nearly all the authors in the first section argue that motivation cannot be reduced to a single factor that readers have or do not have. Rather, it is multidimensional and influences reading performance in complex ways. In their chapters on student motivation, Wigfield and Ruddell and Unrau develop this theme most extensively. In her chapter on teacher perceptions, Sweet discusses the multifaceted views teachers have of student motivation. The crucial implication of this theme is that children approach (or avoid) reading for many different reasons and in many different ways. The chapters in this section help explain these various motivations.

Motivation is characterized as beliefs. Historically, motivation often was characterized as a drive or as being based on the reinforcement of behavior. In contrast, current views of motivation describe it as readers' beliefs about themselves, such as their sense of self-efficacy, expectancies for reading success, and sense of self as a reader. Schunk and Zimmerman emphasize readers' self-efficacy in their chapter; Sweet discusses teachers' sense of children's competence and autonomy; Wigfield discusses readers' expectancy and competence beliefs; and Ruddell and Unrau discuss a broad set of self-beliefs and relate them to readers' motivation. All the authors contend that when these beliefs are positive, children and adults are more likely to engage in complex, meaningful activities.

Motivation is described as affect, involvement, and interest. Another important aspect of reading motivation is the affect and enjoyment associated with reading. Affect and enjoyment are involved in constructs such as the value of reading, intrinsic motivation for reading, and interest in reading. When individuals value reading, and when they are interested in the subject they are reading about, engagement is enhanced. This principle is emphasized in the chapters on student motivation by Wigfield, Schallert and Reed, and Ruddell and Unrau, and in Sweet's chapter on teacher perceptions of student motivation.

Motivation and strategies interact during reading. Motivation theorists increasingly are considering how motivation and cognition work together during reading. This relation is clearly illustrated in two of the chapters in Section I: Schunk and Zimmerman discuss how self-efficacy, goal setting, and strategy use influence children's reading and writing; and Corno and Randi explain how motivation can lead an individual to perform an activity such as reading and how volitional and cognitive strategies can sustain involvement in the activity.

Reading motivations can be enhanced. Another theme in Section I is that reading motivations can be enhanced through different kinds of interventions. These interventions range from working with individual children in programs such as those discussed by Schunk and Zimmerman, to focusing on teacher beliefs about children as Sweet does in her chapter. In Section II authors discuss classroom programs designed to enhance the motivation of many children; thus, this theme connects the two sections.

Reading motivations vary across different classroom contexts. Finally, motivation should not be thought of just as a characteristic of the learner; rather, it is influenced by the learner's setting. Crucial aspects of this setting include the kinds of teacher beliefs about students that Sweet discusses and the classroom variables that Ruddell and

Unrau include in their model. The authors in the second section of the book emphasize further how different settings influence children's reading motivations.

Section II Classroom Contexts That Promote Literacy Engagement

Our view is that literacy engagement is the aim of education. We want students to be able to read and want to read. The practices of a literate society depend on positive motivational dispositions as well as highly developed competencies. Further, we believe that literacy engagement cannot be acquired unless it is experienced. Our expectation is that extensive opportunities for engagement in literacy practices in school are the optimal means for reaching the goal of literacy engagement for all.

The second section in this volume is dedicated to describing contexts that are designed to influence learners' motivations. Section II contains several substantially independent programs that have been designed and implemented to enhance literacy engagement. In Chapter 7, Guthrie and McCann convey a classroom-based reading program called Concept-Oriented Reading Instruction (CORI) designed to accelerate the development of reading engagement for elementary students through integrating language arts and science. In Chapter 8, Bruning and Schweiger describe their collaborative program to enhance the literacy engagement of at-risk students. Their program combines observations of nature with activities such as note taking, text searches, interpretive discussion, and self-expression of students. Au, in Chapter 9, represents anthropological perspectives on becoming literate and portrays an educational framework that is culturally responsive. She also describes the influence of the program on children and the ownership of their literacy activity.

Education for younger children is emphasized by Turner in Chapter 10. She describes classroom contexts at the primary level that contrast "open" and "closed" task environments. She illustrates that open situations focusing on student choice, control, challenge, and collaboration enhance intrinsic motivation for literacy pursuits. Gambrell and Marinak extend this line of thinking in Chapter 11. They discuss the variety of incentives, both extrinsic and intrinsic, that are used to spur reading and writing in the primary grades. Finally, in Chapter 12, Santa addresses enhancing literacy engagement from the viewpoint of a school district in change. She reports a retrospective on a five-year program of districtwide transformation to develop contexts for promoting literacy engagement. Several themes have been identified by the instructional and educational developers involved and have been incorporated into programs at the classroom, school, and district levels.

Section II Themes

The authors in Section II composed their chapters and the projects on which the chapters are based independently. Despite this distinctiveness, the authors have devised remarkably similar themes for promoting literacy engagement, which are outlined next.

Engagement as an aim of teaching. Engagement in reading and writing is the expressed goal of the CORI program described by Guthrie and McCann and the districtwide initiative in language arts described by Santa. Similarly, Bruning and Schweiger place equal priority on motivational development and skill acquisition in their integrated teaching. In addition, ownership is the primary aim of literacy instruction in the program for Native American Hawaiian children described by Au. To motivate these ethnically diverse students to increase learning and using literacy, Au portrays her approach to culturally responsive teaching. The merger of motivational and cognitive goals has led these authors to formulate new frameworks for classroom learning.

Personal inquiry. Conducting in-depth inquiry into issues of personal significance is a cornerstone to several contextual models provided in the chapters in Section II. In their classroom intervention projects, Bruning and Schweiger emphasize investigative goals, and Guthrie and McCann underscore observational activity in science and literature resources. Inquiry also is the center of Santa's process of district-level change. Teachers and administrators who aim toward teaching for engagement rely on teacher questioning, innovating, and reflecting as vehicles for growth.

Learner-centered instruction. Au proposes that if teachers are to foster ownership of literacy, they must support the cultural identities and peer relationships of learners. This can be reflected in self-selected reading and writing among other activities. Turner emphasizes learner centeredness in her description of "open" classroom tasks in which students choose their texts and literacy processes. She points to the importance of supporting student choice for enhancing motivation, which is similar to Guthrie and McCann's principle of self-direction.

Social interaction. Most of the authors in Section II emphasize varied social structures in the classroom. Au underscores the need to build on the interrelationships of peers in the classroom, and Turner and Guthrie and McCann point to the need to initiate collaboration between partners and teams. All the authors concur that social processes undergird motivational development. Bruning and Schweiger assert that creating a climate of shared learning is vital to an investigative classroom, and Santa underscores the need for collaboration among teachers who are embarking on a long-term process of schoolwide change.

Teacher support for cognitive learning. Bruning and Schweiger suggest that learning should be directed by the teacher, referring to teacher guidance as needed by students. Guthrie and McCann recommend that direct strategy instruction is needed to help students learn the searching, comprehending, and composing strategies that are important in CORI. According to Turner, strategy learning is supported by tasks that are challenging; optimal challenge, in which tasks are neither too difficult nor too easy, leads students to want to learn useful strategies and creates a poignant opportunity for teaching. Most authors suggest that learner-based strategy teaching will increase engagement.

Coherence and accountability. Au suggests that if literacy engagement is not emphasized in evaluation, it is neglected in teaching. When teachers believe they will be rewarded for enhancing ownership, students will become committed to their own literacy development. Guthrie and McCann agree, recommending that learners should not be required to meet criterion-referenced standards but should be expected to communicate their understanding of self-selected topics in forms of drawing, writing, and performing. Rewards for successfully engaging in reading and writing can encourage some students, especially those who are not intrinsically motivated, according to Gambrell and Marinak. In Santa's view, the hallmark of progress in systemic reform is the involvement of teacher teams who promote literacy engagement in the classroom. When the aims and accountabilities of classrooms are coordinated and centered on engagement, the classroom becomes a place of coherence.

A Look Ahead

The themes of this book represent ways of thinking about Robert and Kantu in the vignette at the beginning of this introduction. How do we talk about the scenario in which they were central players? How do we discuss their interests, desires, and accomplishments? We invite you to construct your own replies to these questions as you read the first section of the book in which other researchers offer their viewpoints. We educators are interested in creating and sustaining classrooms in which students become engaged, and learn how to engage themselves, in a wide range of literacy actions and interactions.

As you read the second section of this book, ask yourself, "How do I initiate and maintain a motivating environment in the classroom?" We invite you to consider these chapters as part of the discussion about how motivational needs of students can be addressed. How do we coordinate motivational factors with students' cognitive competencies and social depositions to foster the growth of literacy?

References

Alexander, P.A., Kulikowich, J.M., & Schulze, S.K. (1994). How subject-matter knowledge affects recall and interest. *American Educational Research Journal, 31*, 313–337.

Anderson, R.C., Wilson, P.T., & Fielding, L.G. (1988). Growth in reading and how children spend their time outside of school. *Reading Research Quarterly, 23*, 285–303.

Barr, R., Kamil, M.L., Mosenthal, P., & Pearson, P.D. (Eds.). (1991). *Handbook of reading research, Volume II*. White Plains, NY: Longman.

Bloome, D., & Green, J.L. (1992). Educational contexts of literacy. *Annual Review of Applied Linguistics, 12*, 49–70.

Chall, J.S. (1983). *Learning to read: The great debate* (2nd ed.). New York: McGraw-Hill.

Deci, E.L. (1992). The relation of interest to the motivation of behavior: A self-determination theory perspective. In K.A. Renninger, S. Hidi, & A. Krapp (Eds.), *The role of interest in learning and development* (pp. 43–70). Hillsdale, NJ: Erlbaum.

Deci, E.L., Vallerand, R.J., Pelletier, L.G., & Ryan, R.M. (1991). Motivation and education: The self-determination perspective. *Educational Psychologist, 26*, 325–346.

Dweck, C.S., & Leggett, E.L. (1988). A social-cognitive approach to motivation and personality. *Psychological Review, 95,* 256–273.

Ehri, L.C. (1994). Development of the ability to read words: Update. In R.B. Ruddell, M.R. Ruddell, & H. Singer (Eds.), *Theoretical models and processes of reading* (4th ed., pp. 323–358). Newark, DE: International Reading Association.

Guthrie, J.T., Schafer, W.D., Wang, Y.Y., & Afflerbach, P. (1995). Relationships of instruction to amount of reading: An exploration of social, cognitive, and instructional connections. *Reading Research Quarterly, 30,* 8–25.

Heath, S.B. (1983). *Ways with words: Language, life and work in communities and classrooms.* Cambridge, England: Cambridge University Press.

Huey, E.B. (1968). *The psychology and pedagogy of reading.* Cambridge, MA: MIT Press. (Original work published 1908)

Juel, C., Griffith, P.L., & Gough, P.B. (1986). Acquisition of literacy: A longitudinal study of children in first and second grade. *Journal of Educational Psychology, 78,* 243–255.

Mathewson, G.C. (1994). Model of attitude influence upon reading and learning to read. In R.B. Ruddell, M.R. Ruddell, & H. Singer (Eds.), *Theoretical models and processes of reading* (4th ed., pp. 1131–1161). Newark, DE: International Reading Association.

Pintrich, P.R., & Schrauben, B. (1992). Students' motivational beliefs and their cognitive engagement in classroom academic tasks. In D.H. Schunk & J.L. Meese (Eds.), Student perceptions in the classroom (pp. 149–184). Hillsdale, NJ: Erlbaum.

Rosenblatt, L.M. (1978). *The reader, the text, the poem: The transactional theory of the literary text.* Carbondale, IL: Southern Illinois University Press.

Ruddell, R.B., Ruddell, M.R., & Singer, H. (Eds.) (1994). *Theoretical models and processes of reading* (4th ed.). Newark, DE: International Reading Association.

Shraw, G., Bruning, R., & Svoboda, C. (1995). Sources of situational interest. *Journal of Reading Behavior, 27*(1), 1–17.

Stanovich, K.E., & Cunningham, A.E. (1991). Studying the consequences of literacy within a literate society: The cognitive correlates of print exposure. *Memory & Cognition, 20*(1), 51–68.

Sulzby, E., & Teale, W. (1991). Emergent literacy. In R. Barr, M.L. Kamil, P. Mosenthal, & P.D. Pearson (Eds.), *Handbook of reading research, Volume II* (pp. 727–758). White Plains, NY: Longman.

Wigfield, A., & Eccles, J.S. (1992). The development of achievement task values: A theoretical analysis. *Developmental Review, 12,* 265–310.

Section I Motivations, Beliefs, and Self-Efficacy in Literacy Development

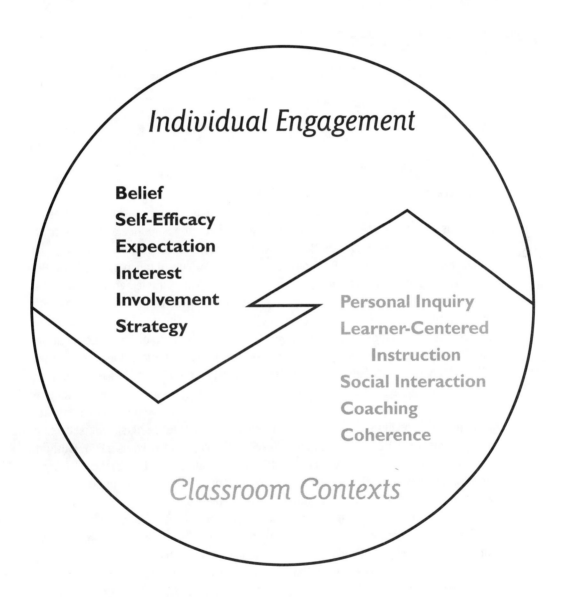

Individual Engagement

Belief
Self-Efficacy
Expectation
Interest
Involvement
Strategy

Personal Inquiry
Learner-Centered
Instruction
Social Interaction
Coaching
Coherence

Classroom Contexts

Children's Motivations for Reading and Reading Engagement

Allan Wigfield

Research on children's reading has a long and rich history, and much has been learned about how children learn to read. As discussed in the introduction, the focus of most of the research on reading has been the *cognitive* aspects of reading; the volumes by Adams (1990); Barr, Kamil, Mosenthal, and Pearson (1991); and Ruddell, Ruddell, and Singer (1994) provide important reviews of much of that work. Because reading is an effortful activity that involves choice (for example, when a child asks, "Am I going to read or watch television?"), *motivation* is involved in reading, along with cognition. Motivation deals with the *whys* of behavior; motivation theorists try to understand the choices individuals make about which activity to do or not to do, their degree of persistence at the chosen activities, and the amount of effort they exert as they do the activity (Eccles, Wigfield, & Schiefele, in press; Pintrich & Schunk, 1996; Weiner, 1992). Purely cognitive models of reading do not address these issues, so they do not provide a complete picture of reading. For instance, a purely cognitive perspective on reading cannot explain why some children read infrequently despite being skillful readers. In the *engagement* perspective on reading (Baker, Afflerbach, & Reinking, 1996; Guthrie, 1996; Guthrie, McGough, Bennett, & Rice, 1996) both cognitive and motivational aspects of reading are considered. This perspective provides a more complete account of how children learn to read and become engaged in literacy activities.

Work done within the engagement framework by my colleagues and me has focused on delineating the nature of children's reading motivations. We have used constructs, or concepts, from research on children's general achievement motivation and from work on motivation for reading. We believe that there are a variety of possible reading motivations that can influence children's engagement in reading and their reading performance (see Guthrie, 1996; Oldfather & Wigfield, 1996; Wigfield & Guthrie, 1995, for further discussion). The following vignettes describe children with different reading motivations.

A fifth-grade student (whom I will call Jamal) reads in his free time an unusual mix of books, ranging from poetry books to manuals describing how to repair cars. When asked about his reading, he says that unfamiliar and difficult words sometimes stump him and threaten to disrupt his reading, but he continually strives to improve his reading. When he understands the new words and phrases, he knows his reading skills are improving. His growing skills and confidence in them help him continue to pursue his reading interests and read increasingly complex books.

Cheryl, another fifth grader, reads avidly in class, keeping a book by her side to read when there are breaks in classroom activities. She often reads late into the night at home, a practice her family accepts. In explaining her interest in reading, she said she becomes very absorbed in the characters and the plot of the stories she reads. She keeps turning the pages because she wants to see what happens to the characters with whom she has become so involved. This excitement sparked by books keeps Cheryl reading even when other activities are available to her.

Bill is a fifth-grade student who will read only when others around him are reading or when he is in a group. But when peer support is removed, he stops reading. His teacher reports that much of the work Bill begins does not get finished because he does not get personally involved with his work. Although Bill keeps books around him to read in his spare time, he rarely continues his reading unless directed to by his teacher.

In these vignettes, children read to master new material, because of interest in the characters and plot in a story, for social reasons, and to comply with the teacher's directions. Each of these motivations can enhance children's reading engagement, but some of them also might interfere with children's reading engagement, a problem which will be discussed later. Further, two of the children (Jamal and Cheryl) appear to be very motivated to read, whereas Bill is not. How are these different motivations depicted in the vignettes conceptualized by motivation theorists?

Defining Motivational Constructs

Researchers who study motivation have defined a number of important motivational constructs and have assessed how these constructs relate to different achievement behaviors. However, most of their work has been on motivation in general rather than motivation for specific areas such as reading and writing. Reading researchers study the processes by which children and adults become engaged in reading but have not yet fully incorporated the constructs defined by motivation researchers (see Oldfather & Wigfield, 1996, for further discussion). I begin this section with a brief overview of the motivation constructs prominent in current motivation theories and then discuss how we have adapted them to the reading field. Some of these constructs are discussed in more detail by other authors in the first section of this volume.

Many motivation theorists propose that individuals' beliefs, values, and goals for achievement play a crucial role in their achievement-related behavior (see, for example, Bandura, 1977; Eccles et al., 1983; Nicholls, 1990; Pintrich & Schunk, 1996; Stipek & Mac Iver, 1989; Weiner, 1992; Wigfield & Eccles, 1992). Eccles, Wigfield, and Schiefele (in press; see also Eccles & Wigfield, 1985) state that the beliefs, values, and goals studied by motivation theorists can be conceptualized as different questions students can ask themselves. The questions most directly relating to motivation are "Can I succeed?" and "Do I want to succeed and why?" In terms of reading, these questions are "Can I be a good reader?" and "Do I want to be a good reader and why?"

Constructs Relating to the Question "Can I Succeed?"

The primary constructs relating the question "Can I succeed?" are children's *ability beliefs*, *expectancies*, and *efficacy beliefs*. Ability beliefs are children's evaluations of their competence in different areas. Researchers have documented that children's and adolescents' ability beliefs relate to and predict their achievement performance in domains such as reading and math (Eccles et al., 1983; Meece, Wigfield, & Eccles, 1990; Nicholls, 1979a; Stipek & Mac Iver, 1989; Wigfield et al., 1995). Expectancies refer to children's sense of how well they will do on an upcoming task, instead of their general belief of how good they are at the task (see Stipek, 1984). These beliefs also predict children's performance on different tasks.

Bandura's (1977; see also Schunk, 1991b) construct of self-efficacy also deals with individuals' expectancies about being able to do tasks; however, Bandura defines self-efficacy as a generative capacity in which different subskills are organized into courses of action. He proposes that individuals' *efficacy expectations*, or their beliefs that they can accomplish a given task or activity, are a major determinant of activity choice, willingness to expend effort, and persistence. When they think they can accomplish a task, people are more likely to choose to do it, continue working on it when they encounter difficulty, and ultimately complete the task. In work with school-aged children, Schunk and his colleagues (1991b) demonstrated that students' sense of efficacy relates to their academic performance (see also Zimmerman, Bandura, & Martinez-Pons, 1992), including their reading achievement (Schunk & Rice, 1993). They showed that training students both to be more efficacious and to believe they are more efficacious improves children's achievement in subject areas such as reading and math. An important implication of this research for motivation for reading is that when children believe they are competent and efficacious at reading they should be more likely to engage in the activity. In Chapter 2 of this volume, Schunk and Zimmerman present a detailed review of the work on self-efficacy and reading comprehension.

There are several examples of ability and efficacy beliefs in the vignettes presented earlier. In the vignette in the introduction, Robert and Kantu are described as becoming more efficacious at finding information, which leads them to share their techniques with each other and experience pride in their success. Their growing skills and efficacy facilitate their continued engagement in the classroom activities. In the vignettes in this chapter, Jamal's competence and efficacy beliefs are most clearly apparent. As he successfully masters difficult words and topics, his sense of his own reading competence and efficacy increases, which leads him to read even more complicated books.

Constructs Relating to the Question "Do I Want to Succeed and Why?"

Answering the question "Do I want to succeed and why?" affirmatively and with a clear reason is critical to motivation. Even if individuals believe they are competent and efficacious at an activity, they may not engage in it if they have no reason or incentive for doing so. One construct relating to the first part of this question is *subjective task values*. Subjective task values refer broadly to individuals' incentives for doing different activities.

Eccles and I and our colleagues have done recent work on the nature of children's and adolescents' subjective task values and how their values relate to their performance and choice of different activities. We defined different components of subjective task values, including *interest value*, how much the individual likes or is interested in the activity; *attainment value*, the importance of the activity; and *utility value*, the usefulness of an activity (see Eccles et al., 1983; Wigfield, 1994; Wigfield & Eccles, 1992, for reviews of this work and further discussion of the different components of subjective task values). A major finding from this work, as mentioned earlier, is that students' ability beliefs and expectancies for success predict their performance in mathematics and language arts, whereas their subjective task values predict both intentions and actual decisions to continue taking mathematics and language arts courses (Eccles et al., 1983; Meece, Wigfield, & Eccles, 1990). This finding suggests that students' valuing of reading may be one of the more important predictors of their engagement in reading activities.

Another major construct relating to the question "Do I want to succeed?" is *intrinsic and extrinsic motivation*. Intrinsic motivation refers to being motivated and curious to do an activity for its own sake, and extrinsic motivation means being motivated for external reasons such as receiving a reward or being told to do the activity (Deci & Ryan, 1985; Harter, 1981; see Chapter 11 in this volume for further discussion of intrinsic and extrinsic motivation for reading). Intrinsic motivation has some parallels with the interest value construct defined by Eccles et al. (1983). One indicator of intrinsic motivation is total involvement in an activity. Many readers have experienced what Csikszentmihalyi (1978) describes as the "flow experience," losing track of time and self-awareness when becoming completely involved in an activity such as reading a book. Maehr's (1976) concept of continuing motivation is another important aspect of intrinsic motivation; he defines continuing motivation as individuals' engagement in a learned activity outside the context in which it was learned. He argues that schools focus too much on learning in school and not enough on promoting children's continuing motivation to learn outside the school setting.

Building on this work, Oldfather (1992) presents a social constructivist view of intrinsic motivation for learning identified as the continuing impulse to learn, an ongoing participation in learning that is motivated by the learner's thoughts and feelings that emerge from his or her processes of constructing meaning. It is characterized by intense involvement, curiosity, and a search for understanding, as the individual experiences learning as a deeply personal and continuing agenda. An important implication of Oldfather's and other theorists' work for reading is that individuals' engagement in reading will be greatly facilitated when they are intrinsically motivated to read and find personal meaning in the reading that they do. Chapter 4 in this volume provides further discussion of how involvement with one's own reading fosters reading engagement.

Intrinsic and extrinsic motivation constructs are illustrated in the vignettes presented earlier. As Robert and Kantu hunt for crickets and then learn more about them, they become very absorbed in the topic and show a great deal of interest in finding out more about it. Their interest and wonder promote engagement with the various activities they do to learn more about crickets. Cheryl also is a very intrinsically motivated, interested reader; she loses herself in books and becomes deeply involved with them. In contrast, Bill reads more for extrinsic reasons, such as to comply with the teacher or to be part of a group.

The second part of the question posed, "*Why* do I want to succeed?", can be categorized primarily by two constructs, *achievement goals* and *subjective values*, just discussed. Achievement goals refer to the purposes children have for achievement in different areas; they deal directly with the "whys" of behavior. Researchers study different kinds of achievement goals. Some (Ames, 1992b; Dweck & Leggett, 1988; Nicholls, 1979b; Nicholls et al., 1989) define different broad goal orientations toward achievement, with two goal orientations deemed most prominent: the goal to learn an activity and the goal to outperform others. These goal orientations have important consequences for motivation. When students focus on outperforming others, they are more likely to choose to do tasks and activities they know they are able do. In contrast, children focusing on learning choose challenging tasks and are more concerned with their own progress than with outperforming others. Researchers who study children's goals argue further that children who have learning goals will be more likely to maintain positive motivation in school. An important implication of this work for reading instruction is that learning goals should be emphasized in reading instruction.

Mastery goals are evident in Robert and Kantu's study of crickets. They generate many questions, develop particular goals to pursue, and work together to achieve them. Competing against each other does not seem to occur to them; instead, the focus is on mastering the subject. Similarly, Jamal's continuing work with difficult and challenging materials shows a strong learning goal orientation; his major focus is improving his own reading.

These broad goal orientations or patterns are not the only ways researchers study goals. Some researchers (see, for example, Schunk, 1991a) look at more particular aspects of goals, such as whether they are distal or proximal, or general or specific; this work is discussed in more detail by Schunk (1991b) and in Chapter 2 by Schunk and Zimmerman in this volume. Still others (such as Wentzel, 1991, in press) propose that students have multiple achievement goals, including both academic and social goals (see also Urdan & Maehr, 1995).

Table 1 summarizes the different motivational constructs described in the previous two sections. The constructs listed are organized in two columns by the questions "Can I succeed?" and "Do I want to succeed and why?" The constructs in the third column under the heading "What do I need to do to succeed?" are explained in the next section.

	Table	I

Defining Motivation Constructs and Dimensions of Reading Motivation

Can I Succeed?	Do I Want to Succeed and why?	What Do I Need to Do to Succeed?
Motivation Construct	**Motivation Construct**	**Motivation-Related Construct**
Ability beliefs	Subjective task values	Strategy use
Expectancies	Interest value	Self-Regulation
Efficacy beliefs	Attainment value	Volition
	Utility value	Help seeking
	Intrinsic and extrinsic motivation	
	Achievement goals	
	Mastery goals	
	Competitive goals	
	Other academic goals	
	Social goals	
Reading Motivation	**Reading Motivation**	
Reading efficacy	Reading curiosity	
Reading challenge	Involvement	
Reading work avoidance	Importance of reading	
	Reading for recognition	
	Reading for grades	
	Competition in reading	
	Social reasons for reading	
	Reading compliance	

Another Question Relating to Motivation: "What Do I Need to Do to Succeed?"

My colleagues and I (Eccles, Wigfield, & Schiefele, in press) pose the question "What do I need to do to succeed?" as a way to conceptualize constructs such as *strategy use*, *volition*, *self-regulation*, and *help seeking*. These constructs link cognition and motivation together. Because we have not measured these constructs in our work on children's reading motivations, I will not discuss them in detail here. However, they are mentioned because of their importance to reading achievement and because they are featured by authors of Chapters 2 and 3 in this volume; also, several of the chapters in the second section discuss strategy instruction in the classroom.

These constructs are illustrated in the vignette in the introduction. Robert and Kantu's interest in crickets must be followed with effective strategy use for them to learn more about crickets. Their teacher helps them pose reasonable questions and set goals for what they want to accomplish, which are prerequisites for effective learning. Robert and Kantu learn how to search materials effectively to find more information about insects and how to work in cooperative groups to learn more and to make presentations to the class about what they learn. In these ways their initial curiosity leads to quality learning about the topic; without the strategies for learning they may have become frustrated as they tried to learn more about crickets, perhaps losing their initial interest in the topic.

Relations Among Motivational Constructs

Because researchers often have focused on only one or two motivational constructs, we still do not have much information about how they relate to one another. However, we do know that competence beliefs, achievement values, and intrinsic motivation relate positively to one another (Eccles & Wigfield, 1995; Harter & Connell, 1984). Thus, when children think they are competent, they are more likely to be motivated for intrinsic reasons. Further, positive competence beliefs, intrinsic motivations, and learning goals lead to greater persistence, choice of more challenging activities, and higher level of engagement in different activities (Ames, 1992b; Dweck & Leggett, 1988). Similarly, if children have positive efficacy beliefs, they are likely to set more challenging goals for themselves (Schunk, 1991b).

Information about links between motivation and strategy use is beginning to emerge as well. We know that learning goals relate to the use of deeper processing strategies (elaboration) and metacognitive, self-regulatory strategies, such as planning and comprehension monitoring (Pintrich & De Groot, 1990; Pintrich, Marx, & Boyle, 1993). These links have been demonstrated in both correlational and laboratory studies. Positive efficacy beliefs relate to better strategy use and more cognitive engagement (Pintrich & De Groot, 1990; Schunk, 1991b). Personal interest relates to the use of a variety of higher order strategies and deeper level processing of material (Alexander, Kulikowich, & Jetton, 1994; Pintrich, Marx, & Boyle, 1993; Schiefele, 1991).

Pintrich and De Groot's (1990) study provides a good illustration of some of the connections between motivations and strategy use. They found that seventh-grade students' perceived self-efficacy and valuing of science and language arts learning related positively to their reported use of cognitive strategies and self-regulation in those two subject areas. Like Meece, Wigfield, and Eccles (1990), they also found that students' expectancies related more strongly to performance than did their subjective task values. However, Pintrich and De Groot note that students' cognitive strategy use and self-regulation directly predicted performance, whereas their efficacy beliefs and values did not. Pintrich and De Groot suggest that the effects of self-efficacy and values on students' performance were mediated through their use of strategies and self-regulation. They argue that students' self-efficacy may facilitate their cognitive engagement and that their subjective task values relate to their choices about whether to become engaged, but that their use of cognitive strategies and self-regulation relate more directly to performance. These results show how motivation and cognition can work together to facilitate (or impede) performance in different school subjects (see Pintrich & Schrauben, 1992, for a theoretical model describing relations between motivation and cognition). These findings suggest that students who believe they are efficacious at reading and value the activity should use more elaborate cognitive strategies as they read to become better readers.

The relations across some of the motivation and strategy constructs are evident in the vignettes in the introduction and in this chapter. Robert and Kantu's interest in crickets is followed by attempts to learn more about them. With the teacher's help and guidance, they use effective strategies to pursue this learning, which increases both their knowledge and their sense of competence about the subject. The new information they learn and their stronger sense of competence further enhance their interest in the topic, leading to even more in-depth learning. Similarly, Jamal's hard work to master difficult words increases both his reading skills and sense of competence, which allows him to pursue his reading interests in greater depth. Likewise, Cheryl's fascination with books and the time she spends reading increase her reading skills, allowing her to read more challenging and interesting materials. Through research and conversations with students we are learning much about the links among different motivations and their links to strategies, but more information about these links still is needed.

Attitudes Toward Reading and Interest in Reading

In reading research literature, some researchers discuss affective and motivational factors that can influence reading engagement. These researchers look primarily at two constructs: *attitudes toward reading* and *interest in reading*. *Attitudes toward reading* are defined generally as individuals' feelings about reading. Alexander and Filler (1976) state that these feelings about reading influence how much individuals involve themselves in reading and relate to individuals' motivation for reading (see also Mathewson, 1985, 1994; McKenna, 1994; and Ruddell & Speaker, 1985, for more specific models of how individuals' attitudes toward reading influence their reading engagement). Although Mathewson (1985) states that individuals' attitudes toward reading will differ across subject areas, scales designed to assess individuals' attitudes toward reading have remained rather general (McKenna & Kear, 1990). These scales to assess reading attitudes also have not included items to assess the different motivational constructs discussed in the previous section.

There also is a substantial body of research on *reading interest* and how interest influences reading comprehension (see Alexander, Kulikowich, & Jetton, 1994, for a recent review of the work on interest's effects on text comprehension). In discussing interest, Schiefele (1991) notes the important distinction between *individual interests* and *situational or text-based interests*. He defines individual interests as relatively stable feelings about different activity areas (such as reading); people generally tend to be interested in some activities and less interested in other activities. Individual interests seem similar to the intrinsic motivation construct discussed earlier. Situational interests are more activity specific and less stable; for example, situational interest is interest sparked by a particular text.

In one study, Schiefele (1991) assessed how college students' situational interest in text materials influenced their comprehension, when the students' prior knowledge of the materials and general intelligence were controlled. Schiefele found that college students who were interested in the text materials used in the study processed those materials more deeply and used more elaborate learning strategies while reading than did students less interested in the materials.

Shirey and his colleagues (1992) also examined how individuals' interest in reading materials affects their comprehension and task attention. Like Asher and Markell (1974) and Asher, Hymel, and Wigfield (1978), they found that children recalled more from interesting sentences than from noninteresting sentences (see also Anderson, Mason, & Shirey, 1984). Anderson (1982) also found that children paid more attention (as measured by duration of reading time) to interesting than to noninteresting materials. Renninger (1992) found in studies of fifth and sixth graders that interest in the materials read enhanced comprehension, even of materials that were quite difficult for the children (although there were some gender differences in these patterns). Overall, these results indicate that students' interest in the material they read relates clearly to the use of effective learning strategies, their level of attention, and their comprehension of reading materials. Thus interest in reading appears to be an important motivational variable influencing different aspects of reading performance.

Varieties of Reading Motivations

To explore the motivations more specifically in the reading domain, Wigfield and Guthrie (1995) developed a questionnaire measure of children's motivations for reading, deriving the different dimensions in large part from the work on motivation just reviewed. The Motivations for Reading Questionnaire (MRQ) originally was designed to assess 11 different possible dimensions of reading motivations (see Wigfield & Guthrie, 1995, for a more complete discussion of the development of the original version of the questionnaire, and Wigfield, Guthrie, & McGough, 1996, for administration and scoring instructions). These different dimensions are summarized in the bottom half of Table 1 under the heading "Reading Motivation." This table also shows how the dimensions of reading motivation connect to the general motivation constructs previously discussed, which are organized by questions. The first two dimensions in the first column—*reading efficacy* and *reading challenge*—are based on the competence and efficacy belief constructs and include the notion that reading often is an activity that requires hard work to accomplish. *Reading efficacy* is the belief that one can be successful at reading; and *reading challenge* is the satisfaction of mastering or assimilating complex ideas in text. These two dimensions are illustrated in Jamal's approach to reading: he works to master challenging material and feels more efficacious after doing so.

The set of dimensions assessed in the MRQ, listed in the second column of Table 1, is based on the work on intrinsic and extrinsic motivations, values, and learning and performance goals. Dimensions relating to intrinsic motivations and learning goals include *reading curiosity*, the desire to learn about a particular topic of personal interest, and *involvement*, the pleasure gained from reading a well-written book or article on an interesting topic. Although this construct is somewhat similar to intrinsic motivation, it captures something unique to reading, the involvement with particular kinds of texts. *Importance of reading* is a dimension taken from Eccles's and my work on subjective task values (Eccles et al., 1983; Wigfield & Eccles, 1992). In the earlier vignettes, Cheryl's approach to reading is characterized by her curiosity of and involvement with different topics and by the importance reading has to her. Robert's and Kantu's reading motivations can be characterized in similar, intrinsic ways.

Dimensions assessed in the MRQ that relate to extrinsic motivations for reading include *reading for recognition*, the pleasure in receiving a tangible form of recognition for success in reading, and *reading for grades*, the desire to be favorably evaluated by the teacher. *Competition in reading* is the desire to outperform others in reading, a dimension tied to the notion of performance goals. These three dimensions reflect the fact that children do much of their reading in school, where their reading performance is evaluated and where they may compare their performance to others' performance. Thus, recognition, grades, and competition may figure prominently in children's motivations for reading.

The other dimensions listed in the bottom half of Table 1 relate to social aspects of reading. These were included because reading often is a social activity. These dimensions are based on the work on social goals in the achievement motivation literature (Urdan & Maehr, 1995; Wentzel, 1991, 1996). One proposed dimension is *social reasons for reading*, or the process of sharing the meanings gained from reading with friends and family. Another is *reading compliance*—reading because of an external goal or requirement. The final dimension assessed in the MRQ, listed in the first column of Table 1, is a set of items that ask students what they do not like about reading; we call this set *reading work avoidance*. Bill's reading seems to be characterized by these three motivations; he reads when there are others to read with (social) and when told to do so by the teacher (compliance), and he also avoids reading in other circumstances.

The original MRQ contained 82 items intended to measure each of these different constructs. The questionnaire was given to approximately 100 fourth- and fifth-grade students twice during a school year (see Wigfield & Guthrie, 1995, for more details about this study). Various statistical analyses were run to assess the proposed dimensions of reading motivations and to determine whether the items had good psychometric qualities. These analyses show that a number of the proposed dimensions can be clearly identified and have adequate to good internal consistency reliabilities. The most clearly defined dimensions include social reasons for reading, reading competition, reading work avoidance, reading efficacy, reading recognition, reading challenge, reading curiosity, and involvement.

Based on the results of the first study, a revised 54-item version of the MRQ was created (see Table 2). This revised version of the questionnaire was given to approximately

Table 2

Motivations for Reading Questionnaire, Revised Version

Reading Efficacy

I know that I will do well in reading next year.

I am a good reader.

I learn more from reading than most students in the class.

In comparison to my other school subjects, I am best at reading.

Challenge

I like hard, challenging books.

I like it when the questions in books make me think.

I usually learn difficult things by reading.

If the project is interesting, I can read difficult material.

If a book is interesting, I don't care how hard it is to read.

Curiosity

If the teacher discusses something interesting, I might read more about it.

I read about my hobbies to learn more about them.

I read to learn new information about topics that interest me.

I like to read about new things.

If I am reading about an interesting topic, I sometimes lose track of time.

I enjoy reading books about people in different countries.

Involvement

I read stories about fantasy and make believe.

I make pictures in my mind when I read.

I feel like I make friends with people in good books.

I like mysteries.

I enjoy a long, involved story or fiction book.

I read a lot of adventure stories.

Importance

It is very important to me to be a good reader.

In comparison to other activities I do, it is very important to me to be a good reader.

Recognition

My friends sometimes tell me I am a good reader.

I like hearing the teacher say I read well.

I am happy when someone recognizes my reading.

My parents often tell me what a good job I am doing in reading.

I like to get compliments for my reading.

(continued)

Table 2

Motivations for Reading Questionnaire, Revised Version (*continued*)

Grades

I look forward to finding out my reading grade.

Grades are a good way to see how well you are doing in reading.

I read to improve my grades.

My parents ask me about my reading grade.

Social

I visit the library often with my family.

I often read to my brother or my sister.

I sometimes read to my parents.

My friends and I like to trade things to read.

I talk to my friends about what I am reading.

I like to help my friends with their schoolwork in reading.

I like to tell my family about what I am reading.

Competition

I like being the only one who knows an answer in something we read.

I like being the best at reading.

It is important for me to see my name on a list of good readers.

I try to get more answers right than my friends.

I like to finish my reading before other students.

I am willing to work hard to read better than my friends.

Compliance

*I do as little schoolwork as possible in reading.

*I read because I have to.

I always do my reading work exactly as the teacher wants it.

Finishing every reading assignment is very important to me.

I always try to finish my reading on time.

Reading Work Avoidance

I don't like reading something when the words are too difficult.

I don't like vocabulary questions.

Complicated stories are no fun to read.

I don't like it when there are too many people in the story.

Note: Asterisks indicate the items were not used in scale construction for that construct.

600 fifth- and sixth-grade children who were taking part in an intervention study designed to enhance their reading comprehension. Half the children participating in the project experienced the Junior Great Books curriculum, a curriculum designed to facilitate involvement with reading and reading comprehension; the other half were in control classrooms (see Wigfield et al., 1996, for a more detailed description). The revised MRQ was given in the fall of the school year, before the program was implemented.

As in the first study, different statistical analyses were done in the second study to assess the various proposed dimensions of the MRQ. Confirmatory factor analyses showed that the different proposed dimensions of motivation could be identified empirically. The internal consistency reliabilities of these dimensions were quite similar to the reliabilities in the first study. The general conclusion from both studies is that reading motivations are multidimensional.

Connections Among Reading Motivations

In both studies using the MRQ, correlational analyses were run to determine how strongly the different scales related to one another. In general, most of the relations were positive and ranged from low to moderately high, with the exception of the work avoidance scale, which related negatively to all the scales except to competition. Three conclusions can be drawn from these correlational analyses. First, the various kinds of reading motivations relate positively to one another, which shows that children have multiple motivations for reading and are not reading for exclusively intrinsic or extrinsic reasons. Second, the *negative* relations of work avoidance to the other motivation scales suggest that children who are positively motivated for many different reasons do not want to avoid difficult and challenging reading. Third, the *positive* relations of work avoidance and competition suggest that care should be taken with competitive reading activities. Although direction of causality cannot be inferred from correlational data, the positive relation of these scales means that either too much competition leads children to avoid reading, or those who avoid reading say they are motivated for competitive reasons. In either case reading engagement may be less likely to occur.

Linking Motivations to Reading Frequency and Performance

To relate the dimensions of reading motivations to reading frequency, Wigfield and Guthrie (1995) also obtained information about children's reading frequencies from two sources: (1) the Reading Activities Inventory (Guthrie, McGough, & Wigfield, 1994), a measure that asks children to list titles of different kinds of books they read recently and to indicate how often they read different kinds of books; and (2) a measure of children's reading frequency in a school-based reading program that encouraged children to read books. The dimensions of reading motivations relating most strongly include social, reading efficacy, curiosity, involvement, recognition, grades, and reading importance. Thus both intrinsic and extrinsic reasons for reading related to children's reported reading frequencies in the study, although overall it appeared that the intrinsic motivations for reading related more strongly to reading frequency than did the extrinsic motivations. Similar measures of reading frequency were obtained in the second study, and correlational analyses done in that study in general showed similar results: both intrinsic and extrinsic motivations related to reading frequency; however, the strongest relations were with the more intrinsic reading motivations and with reading self-efficacy.

From these results it can be concluded that children are more likely to read frequently when they feel efficacious about their reading skills and are intrinsically motivated to read. However, extrinsic motivations relate to reading frequency also, so their importance should not be overlooked. Researchers now need to look at how children's intrinsic and extrinsic reading motivations relate to their engagement in reading over time.

In the second study, students also completed two subtests of the Gates-MacGinitie Reading Test (vocabulary and comprehension) and two performance assessments designed for the project (see Baker, Fernandez-Fein, & Scher, 1995, for descriptions of these assessments) in the fall and spring of the school year. Relations of reading motivations to reading performance were examined by regressing reading performance on children's motivations. The results of these regression analyses showed that the motivation scales accounted for between 6 and 13% of the variance in the performance measures. The motivation scales predicting most consistently the Gates-MacGinitie (GM) scores include reading work avoidance, social reasons for reading, and reading efficacy and recognition. Both the work avoidance and social scales negatively predicted GM scores, indicating that children with higher scores on these motivation scales had lower GM scores. Reading efficacy and recognition positively predicted GM scores; children with higher scores on these scales tended to score higher on the GM measures.

The motivation scales most consistently predicting the performance assessment (PA) measures include work avoidance and social, both of which were negative predictors. The negative relations indicate that children who scored higher on these motivation scales tended to score lower on the PA measures. Reading efficacy and recognition predicted two of the PA scales positively, which means that children with higher scores on this scale tended to have higher PA scores.

In summary, results of these two studies show that there are different dimensions of reading motivations that can be measured reliably. These dimensions include some of the important constructs identified by motivation researchers: competence and challenge, intrinsic and extrinsic motivations, and different goals for reading. For the most part these reading motivations relate positively to one another (the major exception being reading work avoidance, which relates negatively to most of the other motivations). They also relate positively to children's reading frequency. Some of them (especially reading self-efficacy and recognition) predict positively children's performance on standardized tests, whereas others (especially reading work avoidance and social reasons for reading) predict these test scores negatively. There are many issues that remain to be studied regarding children's reading motivations; I close with a consideration of the issue of change in reading motivations.

Change in Reading Motivations

Promoting lifelong literacy engagement is an important goal for educators. A question linked to this issue is how do children's motivations change as they proceed through school? Findings from the general motivation literature suggest that many children's achievement motivation declines through the elementary and middle school years. Such declines have been found in children's general interest in school (Epstein & McPartland, 1976), their intrinsic motivations (Harter, 1981), their continuing impulse to learn (Oldfather, 1992; Oldfather & McLaughlin, 1993), and their ability beliefs and expectancies for success for different school subjects (Eccles, Wigfield, Harold, & Blumenfeld, 1993; Marsh, 1989; Wigfield et al., 1995; see also Eccles, Wigfield, & Schiefele, in press, for a detailed review of this work).

Do these findings apply to the literacy area? Some of the studies (Eccles, Wigfield, Harold, & Blumenfeld, 1993; Marsh, 1989) asked children about reading and found that older elementary school children have less positive ability beliefs in reading and value reading less than do younger elementary school children. Gambrell et al.'s (1993) study also shows that third graders appear to value reading more and have more positive reasons for reading than do fifth graders. In the two studies of reading motivations discussed earlier (Wigfield & Guthrie, 1995; Wigfield et al., 1996), the evidence is more mixed: some age differences in reading motivation were found in the first study, but fewer were found in the second study. This may be because these studies did not include a wide age range of children.

Several researchers suggest that the declines in motivation observed as children proceed through school are due to changes in school and classroom environments that children experience (Eccles, Wigfield, Midgley et al., 1993, and Oldfather & McLaughlin, 1993). Although motivation often is considered a personal characteristic of students, these researchers emphasize that the kinds of school and classroom environments students encounter can influence students' motivation greatly. There are major changes in school environments following children's transition to middle school that may undermine students' motivation; they include the fact that middle schools typically are larger, less personal, and more formal than elementary schools. Middle grade teachers are often subject-matter specialists, and they teach many more students than do elementary teachers. Compared to elementary school classrooms, traditional middle school classrooms place a greater emphasis on teacher control and discipline, less personal and positive teacher-student relations, and fewer opportunities for student decision making and choice (Eccles & Midgley, 1989; Eccles, Wigfield, Midgley et al., 1993). Practices such as whole-class task organization and ability grouping between classrooms also are more common in the middle grades, and grading and evaluation become more salient and have long-term consequences for students. Eccles, Wigfield, Midgley et al. (1993) discuss in detail how these changes can lessen students' competence and efficacy beliefs, reduce intrinsic motivation for learning, and lead children to focus more on rewards and grades than on curiosity and learning.

The effect of these kinds of school and classroom environment changes on motivations for literacy should be assessed further. If similar declines are found in reading motivations (which seems likely, when the findings in the general motivation literature are considered), educators need to think of ways to redesign classrooms to continue to foster positive reading motivations. There are exciting new classroom curricula and district-based programs being designed to foster children's engagement in reading; several of these programs are described in chapters in the second half of this book. These programs are having positive effects on children's reading motivations and reading engagement. For instance, Guthrie, Van Meter et al. (1996) found that nearly all the third- and fifth-grade children experiencing Concept-Oriented Reading Instruction, explained in Chapter 7, increased in intrinsic motivation, use of volitional strategies, and reading engagement and frequency.

Motivation theorists also have suggested ways to change classroom environments to facilitate motivation. Ames (1992a) developed one of the most influential of these programs. She uses the acronym TARGET to describe the program because it focuses on the following six aspects of the classroom: tasks, authority, rewards, grouping, evaluation, and time. She also has worked extensively with teachers to develop this program. One goal of TARGET is to focus children more on learning rather than on competitive goals. Another goal is to help both teachers and children shift the focus from ability and outcome to effort and improvement. Some of the ideas included in the program, such as making classroom activities more meaningful and authentic, using heterogeneous and cooperative classroom grouping, and allowing students choice and autonomy, are contained in the reading programs described in the second part of this book (see also Guthrie, Van Meter et al., 1996).

Conclusion

Our studies of children's reading motivations show that there are different dimensions of these motivations that correspond to constructs that are now well established in the motivation literature. These reading motivations can be measured reliably, and they relate to both children's reading frequency and their reading performance. Thus we have an emerging picture of children motivated to read for various reasons, some of which may promote lifelong literacy engagement. These motivations are psychological in nature and are greatly influenced by school and classroom contexts.

Author's Notes

I would like to thank Ann McCann for providing the vignettes of children's reading motivations used in this chapter, which she obtained through interviews with elementary school children.

The studies on reading motivation discussed in this chapter are from National Reading Research Projects of the Universities of Georgia and Maryland. They were supported under the Educational Research and Development Centers Program (PR/AWARD No. 117A2007) as administered by the Office of Educational Research and Improvement, U.S. Department of Education. The findings and opinions expressed here do not necessarily reflect the position or policies of the National Reading Research Center, the Office of Educational Research and Improvement, or the U.S. Department of Education.

References

Adams, M.J. (1990). *Beginning to read: Thinking and learning about print*. Cambridge, MA: MIT Press.

Alexander, J.E., & Filler, R.C. (1976). *Attitudes and reading*. Newark, DE: International Reading Association.

Alexander, P.A., Kulikowich, J.M., & Jetton, T.L. (1994). The role of subject-matter knowledge and interest in the processing of linear and nonlinear texts. *Review of Educational Research, 64,* 201–252.

Ames, C. (1992a). Achievement goals and the classroom motivational climate. In D.H. Schunk & J.L. Meece (Eds.), *Student perceptions in the classroom* (pp. 327–348). Hillsdale, NJ: Erlbaum.

Ames, C. (1992b). Classrooms: Goals, structures, and student motivation. *Journal of Educational Psychology, 84,* 261–271.

Anderson, R.C. (1982). Allocation of attention during reading. In A. Flammer & W. Kintsch (Eds.), *Discourse processing* (pp. 292–305). New York: North-Holland.

Anderson, R.C., Mason, J., & Shirey, L.L. (1984). The reading group: An experimental investigation of a labyrinth. *Reading Research Quarterly, 20,* 6–38.

Asher, S.R., Hymel, S., & Wigfield, A. (1978). Influence of topic interest on children's reading comprehension. *Journal of Reading Behavior, 10,* 35–47.

Asher, S.R., & Markell, R. (1974). Sex differences in comprehension of high- and low-interest reading material. *Journal of Educational Psychology, 66,* 680–687.

Baker, L., Afflerbach, P., & Reinking, D. (1996). Developing engaged readers in home and school communities: An overview. In L. Baker, P. Afflerbach, & D. Reinking (Eds.), *Developing engaged readers in school and home communities* (pp. xiii–xxvii). Hillsdale, NJ: Erlbaum.

Baker, L., Fernandez-Fein, S., & Scher, D. (1995). *Improving children's reading through the Junior Great Books Curriculum: An intervention study*. Unpublished manuscript, University of Maryland, Baltimore County.

Bandura, A. (1977). Self-efficacy: Toward a unifying theory of behavioral change. *Psychological Review, 84,* 191–215.

Barr, R., Kamil, M.L., Mosenthal, P., & Pearson, P.D. (Eds.). (1991). *Handbook of reading research, Volume II*. White Plains, NY: Longman.

Csikszentmihalyi, M. (1978). Intrinsic rewards and emergent motivation. In M. Lepper & D. Greene (Eds.), *The hidden costs of reward: New perspectives on the psychology of motivation* (pp. 205–216). Hillsdale, NJ: Erlbaum.

Deci, E.L., & Ryan, R.M. (1985). *Intrinsic motivation and self-determination in human behavior*. New York: Plenum.

Dweck, C.S., & Leggett, E.L. (1988). A social-cognitive approach to motivation and personality. *Psychological Review, 95,* 256–273.

Eccles, J.S. et al. (1983). Expectancies, values and academic behaviors. In J.T. Spence (Ed.), *Achievement and achievement motives* (pp. 75–146). San Francisco, CA: W.H. Freeman.

Eccles, J.S., & Midgley, C. (1989). Stage-environment fit: Developmentally appropriate classrooms for young adolescents. In C. Ames & R. Ames (Eds.), *Research on motivation in education* (Vol. 3, pp. 139–186). San Diego, CA: Academic.

Eccles, J.S., & Wigfield, A. (1985). Teacher expectancies and student motivation. In J.B. Dusek (Ed.), *Teacher expectancies* (pp. 185–226). Hillsdale, NJ: Erlbaum.

Eccles, J.S., & Wigfield, A. (1995). In the mind of the achiever: The structure of adolescents' academic achievement-related beliefs and self-perceptions. *Personality and Social Psychology Bulletin, 21,* 215–225.

Eccles, J.S., Wigfield, A., Harold, R., & Blumenfeld, P.C. (1993). Age and gender differences in children's self- and task perceptions during elementary school. *Child Development, 64,* 830–847.

Eccles, J.S., Wigfield, A., Midgley, C. et al. (1993). Negative effects of traditional middle schools on students' motivation. *The Elementary School Journal, 93,* 553–574.

Eccles, J.S., Wigfield, A., & Schiefele, U. (in press). The development of achievement motivation. In N. Eisenberg (Ed.), *Handbook of child psychology* (Vol. 4, 5th ed.). New York: Wiley.

Epstein, J.L., & McPartland, J.M. (1976). The concept and measurement of the quality of school life. *American Educational Research Journal, 13,* 15–30.

Gambrell, L.B. et al. (1993). *Elementary students' motivation to read.* Unpublished manuscript, University of Maryland, National Reading Research Center.

Guthrie, J.T. (1996). Educational contexts for engagement in literacy. *The Reading Teacher, 49,* 432–445.

Guthrie, J.T., McGough, K., Bennett, L., & Rice, M.E. (1996). Concept-oriented reading instruction: An integrated curriculum to develop motivations and strategies for reading. In L. Baker, P. Afflerbach, & D. Reinking (Eds.), *Developing engaged readers in school and home communities* (pp. 165–190). Hillsdale, NJ: Erlbaum.

Guthrie, J.T., McGough, K., & Wigfield, A. (1994). *Measuring reading activity: An inventory* (Instructional Resource No. 4). Athens, GA: National Reading Research Center.

Guthrie, J.T., Van Meter, P., et al. (1996). Growth of literacy engagement: Changes in motivations and strategies during concept-oriented reading instruction. *Reading Research Quarterly, 31,* 306–333.

Harter, S. (1981). A new self-report scale of intrinsic versus extrinsic orientation in the classroom: Motivational and informational components. *Developmental Psychology, 17,* 300–312.

Harter, S., & Connell, J.P. (1984). A model of children's achievement and related self-perceptions of competence, control, and motivational orientation. In J.G. Nicholls (Ed.), *Advances in motivation and achievement: Vol. 3. The development of achievement motivation* (pp. 219–250). Greenwich, CT: JAI Press.

Maehr, M.L. (1976). Continuing motivation: An analysis of a seldom considered educational outcome. *Review of Educational Research, 46,* 443–462.

Marsh, H.W. (1989). Age and sex effects in multiple dimensions of self-concept: Preadolescence to early adulthood. *Journal of Educational Psychology, 81,* 417–430.

Mathewson, G.C. (1985). Toward a comprehensive model of affect in the reading process. In H. Singer & R.B. Ruddell (Eds.), *Theoretical models and processes of reading* (3rd ed., pp. 841–856). Newark, DE: International Reading Association.

Mathewson, G.C. (1994). Model of attitude influence upon reading and learning to read. In R.B. Ruddell, M.R. Ruddell, & H. Singer (Eds.), *Theoretical models and processes of reading* (4th ed., pp. 1131–1161). Newark, DE: International Reading Association.

McKenna, M.C. (1994). Toward a model of reading attitude acquisition. In E.H. Cramer & M. Castle (Eds.), *Fostering the love of reading: The affective domain in reading education* (pp. 18–40). Newark, DE: International Reading Association.

McKenna, M.C., & Kear, D.J. (1990). Measuring attitude toward reading: A new tool for teachers. *The Reading Teacher, 43,* 626–639.

Meece, J.L., Wigfield, A., & Eccles, J.S. (1990). Predictors of math anxiety and its consequences for young adolescents' course enrollment intentions and performances in mathematics. *Journal of Educational Psychology, 82,* 60–70.

Children's Motivations for Reading and Reading Engagement

Nicholls, J.G. (1979a). Development of perception of own attainment and causal attributions for success and failure in reading. *Journal of Educational Psychology, 71,* 94–99.

Nicholls, J.G. (1979b). Quality and equality in intellectual development: The role of motivation in education. *American Psychologist, 34,* 1071–1084.

Nicholls, J.G. (1990). What is ability and why are we mindful of it? A developmental perspective. In R.J. Sternberg & J. Kolligian (Eds.), *Competence considered* (pp. 11–40). New Haven, CT: Yale University Press.

Nicholls, J.G., Cheung, P., Lauer, J., & Patashnick, M. (1989). Individual differences in academic motivation: Perceived ability, goals, beliefs, and values. *Learning and Individual Differences, 1,* 63–84.

Oldfather, P. (1992, December). *Sharing the ownership of knowing: A constructivist concept of motivation for literacy learning.* Paper presented at the 42nd Annual Meeting of the National Reading Conference, San Antonio, TX.

Oldfather, P., & McLaughlin, J. (1993). Gaining and losing voice: A longitudinal study of students' continuing impulse to learn across elementary and middle school contexts. *Research in Middle Level Education, 17,* 1–25.

Oldfather, P., & Wigfield, A. (1996). Children's motivations to read. In L. Baker, P. Afflerbach, & D. Reinking (Eds.), *Developing engaged readers in school and home communities* (pp. 89–114). Hillsdale, NJ: Erlbaum.

Pintrich, P.R., & De Groot, E. (1990). Motivational and self-regulated learning components of classroom academic performance. *Journal of Educational Psychology, 82,* 33–40.

Pintrich, P.R., Marx, R.W., & Boyle, R.A. (1993). Beyond cold conceptual change: The role of motivational beliefs and classroom contextual factors in the process of conceptual change. *Review of Educational Research, 63,* 167–199.

Pintrich, P.R., & Schrauben, B. (1992). Students' motivational beliefs and their cognitive engagement in classroom academic tasks. In D.H. Schunk & J.L. Meece (Eds.), *Student perceptions in the classroom* (pp. 149–183). Hillsdale, NJ: Erlbaum.

Pintrich, P.R., & Schunk, D.H. (1996). *Motivation in education: Theory, research, and application.* Englewood Cliffs, NJ: Prentice Hall.

Renninger, K.A. (1992). Individual interest and development: Implications for theory and practice. In K.A. Renninger, S. Hidi, & A. Krapp (Eds.), *The role of interest in learning and development* (pp. 361–396). Hillsdale, NJ: Erlbaum.

Ruddell, R.B., Ruddell, M.R., & Singer, H. (Eds.). (1994). *Theoretical models and processes of reading* (4th ed.). Newark, DE: International Reading Association.

Ruddell, R.B., & Speaker, R. (1985). The interactive reading process: A model. In H. Singer & R.B. Ruddell (Eds.), *Theoretical models and processes of reading* (3rd ed., pp. 751–793). Newark, DE: International Reading Association.

Schiefele, U. (1991). Interest, learning, and motivation. *Educational Psychologist, 26,* 299–323.

Schunk, D.H. (1991a). Goal setting and self-evaluation: A social cognitive perspective on self-regulation. In M.L. Maehr & P.R. Pintrich (Eds.), *Advances in achievement and motivation* (Vol. 7, pp. 85–113). Greenwich, CT: JAI Press.

Schunk, D.H. (1991b). Self-efficacy and academic motivation. *Educational Psychologist, 26,* 233–262.

Schunk, D.H., & Rice, J.M. (1993). Strategy fading and progress feedback: Effects on self-efficacy and comprehension among students receiving remedial reading services. *The Journal of Special Education, 27,* 257–276.

Shirey, L.L. (1992). Importance, interest, and selective attention. In K.A. Renninger, S. Hidi, & A. Krapp (Eds.), *The role of interest in learning and development* (pp. 281–296). Hillsdale, NJ: Erlbaum.

Stipek, D.J. (1984). Young children's performance expectations: Logical analysis or wishful thinking? In J.G. Nicholls (Ed.), *Advances in motivation and achievement: Vol. 3. The development of achievement motivation* (pp. 33–56). Greenwich, CT: JAI Press.

Stipek, D.J., & Mac Iver, D. (1989). Developmental change in children's assessment of intellectual competence. *Child Development, 60,* 521–538.

Urdan, T.C., & Maehr, M.L. (1995). Beyond a two-goal theory of motivation and achievement: A case for social goals. *Review of Educational Research, 65,* 213–244.

Weiner, B. (1992). *Human motivation: Metaphors, theories, and research.* Newbury Park, CA: Sage.

Wentzel, K.R. (1996). Social goals and social relationships as motivators of school adjustment. In J. Juvonen & K.R. Wentzel (Eds.), *Social motivation: Understanding school adjustment* (pp. 226–247). New York: Cambridge University Press.

Wentzel, K.R. (1991). Social and academic goals at school: Motivations and achievement in context. In M.L. Maehr & P.R. Pintrich (Eds.), *Advances in motivation and achievement* (Vol. 7, pp. 185–212). Greenwich, CT: JAI Press.

Wigfield, A. (1994). Expectancy-value theory of achievement motivation: A developmental perspective. *Educational Psychology Review, 6,* 49–78.

Wigfield, A., & Eccles, J.S. (1992). The development of achievement task values: A theoretical analysis. *Developmental Review, 12,* 265–310.

Wigfield, A. et al. (1995). *Change in children's competence beliefs and subjective task values across the elementary school years: A three-year study.* Manuscript submitted for publication.

Wigfield, A., & Guthrie, J.T. (1995). *Dimensions of children's motivations for reading: An initial study* (Research Report No. 34). Athens, GA: National Reading Research Center.

Wigfield, A., Guthrie, J.T., & McGough, K. (1996). *A questionnaire measure of children's motivations for reading* (Instructional Resource No. 22). Athens, GA: National Reading Research Center.

Wigfield, A., Wilde, K., Baker, L., Fernandez-Fein, S., & Scher, D. (1996). *The nature of children's reading motivations, and their relations to reading frequency and reading performance* (Research Report No. 63). Athens, GA: National Reading Research Center.

Zimmerman, B.J., Bandura, A., & Martinez-Pons, M. (1992). Self-motivation for academic attainment: The role of self-efficacy beliefs and personal goal setting. *American Educational Research Journal, 29,* 663–676.

Developing Self-Efficacious Readers and Writers: The Role of Social and Self-Regulatory Processes

Dale H. Schunk and Barry J. Zimmerman

From toddlers' first experiences with written text, their sense of personal efficacy in understanding and using this strange system of symbols plays a key role in their development of reading and writing competence. According to social cognitive theory, youngsters' decoding and encoding of meaning initially is learned from the modeled use of this complex orthographic system by family members, peers, and teachers. As children gain confidence in their symbolic competence, they are motivated increasingly to take charge of their learning by setting personal reading and writing goals and by evaluating their progress toward them. Children's mastery of text comprehension shifts gradually from social to self-regulatory processes as motivated by their growing sense of self-efficacy.

Previous research on social and self-regulatory processes used by learners to acquire reading and writing skills focused on the effects of students' domain-specific knowledge of reading and writing, but these factors were insufficient to explain motivation and continued textual mastery. More recent research has shown that self-beliefs about factors such as one's learning capabilities, the content to be learned, and the setting in which learning occurs are essential in motivating personal mastery of knowledge (Schunk & Zimmerman, 1994). One of the most potentially important self-beliefs that has been studied is perceived self-efficacy. *Self-efficacy* refers to beliefs a person has about his or her capabilities to learn or perform behaviors at designated levels (Bandura, 1986, in press). Research shows that self-efficacy predicts students' motivation for learning as well as their use of self-regulatory processes (Schunk, 1996).

This chapter discusses how observing social models, participating in goal setting, and engaging in self-evaluation influence self-efficacy, motivation, and orthographic learning. *Modeling* refers to patterning thoughts, beliefs, strategies, and actions after those displayed by one or more models—teachers or peers who explain and demonstrate skills. An example of modeling is a child emulating an adult's pronunciation of a word written on a sign. A *goal* is an outcome that a person is consciously trying to accomplish, such as learning to read a list of key words accurately. Goals are important for self-regulation because they provide standards against which people can gauge their progress (Schunk, 1990). The *self-evaluation* process involves comparing self-judgments of present performance with a goal and reacting to those judgments, such as when students stop searching for information after they realize that they have enough material to write a report. *Self-reactions* involve valuing or emotional responses and include evaluations of a person's reading performance as noteworthy, unacceptable, and so forth. Recent research demonstrates the effectiveness of goal setting and self-evaluation in students' achievement in various academic areas (Schunk, 1996).

Modeling, goal setting, and self-evaluating are illustrated in the vignette in the introduction involving Robert and Kantu. Initially the teacher serves as a model by demonstrating how to form questions. Students then act as models for one another as they share drawings, information, and explanations. Goals are established when teams select the projects they will work on, and Robert and Kantu decide to conduct an experiment. Teams also have supplemental goals (such as producing a videotape). Self-evaluations occur throughout the project: for example, when students decide if they have gathered sufficient information, share ideas, challenge others' thinking, and record information and explanations to present to others. Collectively these activities help build Robert's and Kantu's self-efficacy and motivation for continued learning (Schunk, 1987, 1990, 1996).

The next section discusses social cognitive theory and focuses on the roles of self-efficacy, modeling, goal setting, and self-evaluation in academic learning settings.

Theoretical Background

Social Cognitive Theory

According to Bandura (1986), human behavior depends on reciprocal interactions among thoughts and beliefs, behaviors, and environmental factors. In regard to the link between achievement beliefs and behaviors, research shows that students' self-efficacy beliefs influence behaviors such as choice of tasks, effort, persistence, and achievement (Bandura, 1986, in press; Schunk, 1990; Zimmerman, 1995). Also, students' behaviors can alter efficacy beliefs. As students read, they note their progress toward their learning goals, such as knowing the meaning of certain scientific words. Goal accomplishments (behaviors) convey to students that they are capable of performing well, which enhances perceived self-efficacy for continued learning.

Students' behaviors and classroom environments also are related. Consider a teacher who directs students' attention to printed material through eye-catching displays. Social environment influences behavior when students attend to the material without much conscious deliberation. Students' behaviors also can alter their instructional environments. For example, when students answer comprehension questions incorrectly, the teacher may reteach the lesson differently rather than continue with the original material.

Thoughts and beliefs and environmental factors affect each other. As an example of how beliefs can affect the environment, consider different students with high and low self-efficacy for learning Spanish vocabulary. Those with high efficacy may view the task as a challenge and work diligently to master it, thereby creating a productive classroom environment to include positive teacher expectations for their learning. Those with low efficacy may attempt to avoid studying the vocabulary, which might disrupt the classroom. The influence of environment on student thoughts and beliefs is evident when teachers give students feedback (such as, "That's right. You really are getting good at reading these science materials") that raises self-efficacy and sustains motivation for skill improvement.

Self-Efficacy

Sources and consequences. As mentioned, self-efficacy has been shown to influence task choice, effort, persistence, and achievement. Compared with students who doubt their learning capabilities, those who have a sense of efficacy for acquiring orthographic skill or performing well on a reading or writing task participate more readily, work harder, persist longer when they encounter difficulties, and achieve at a higher level. In the vignette in the introduction Robert and Kantu seem to have a strong sense of self-efficacy for learning because they display these achievement behaviors.

Learners obtain information to appraise their self-efficacy from their actual performances, vicarious experiences, forms of persuasion, and physiological reactions. Students' own reading or writing performances can offer reliable guides for assessing efficacy. In general, successes raise efficacy and failures lower it. Students acquire efficacy information socially by comparing their overt performances with those of others, such as when they compare a written essay with that of a similar performing classmate (Schunk, 1987). The amount of group interaction in the introductory vignette provides ample opportunities for students to socially compare themselves to similar others and believe that if others can perform well, they can too.

Learners often receive information from parents, teachers, and peers that conveys to them that they are capable of performing a task (for example, "I know that you can write this report"). Positive persuasive information increases efficacy, although this increase will be temporary if students begin to perform poorly. Students also acquire efficacy information from physiological indicators such as sweating and increased heart rate. For example, if a student experiences symptoms that signal high anxiety about reading aloud in front of the class, this may convey that the student lacks skills for reading aloud; conversely, if the student experiences lower anxiety, this may raise his or her self-efficacy.

Self-efficacy is important, but it is not the only influence on achievement. Other important influences are skills and knowledge, outcome expectations, and perceived value of learning. High self-efficacy will not produce a competent performance when requisite knowledge and skills are lacking. Outcome expectations, or beliefs about the anticipated consequences of actions, are important because students do not engage in activities they believe will lead to negative outcomes. Perceived value (of the importance of learning or of the use that will be made of what is learned) affects behavior because learners show little interest in activities they do not value. These influences on achievement are addressed in the introductory vignette. Teacher modeling and class activities are designed to provide students with knowledge and skills. Teams expect that their efforts to produce the poster and projects will be rewarded by the teacher and appreciated by students. Also, students understand the value of the learning by knowing how it fits into the integrated curriculum.

Self-efficacy and the development of literacy competence. As shown in the figure on page 38, effective learning requires that learners have a sense of self-efficacy for being able to use their skills to acquire new knowledge (Bouffard-Bouchard, Parent, & Larivee, 1991; Zimmerman, 1989, 1990). As students work on a task they observe their performances and compare them to their goals. Self-evaluations of progress enhance efficacy and maintain motivation. Students who feel efficacious about reading or writing well are apt to concentrate on the task, use proper procedures, manage time effectively, seek assistance as necessary, monitor performance, and adjust strategies as needed (Schunk, 1994; Zimmerman, 1994). The model portrays the reciprocal influences discussed by Bandura (1986): enhanced self-efficacy, motivation, and achievement sustain students' self-efficacy for learning and lead them to set new goals when they master their present ones.

Although low self-efficacy is detrimental for learning, effective learning does not require that efficacy be extremely high. At overly high levels, students may feel overconfident and become slack in their efforts, which can retard learning (Salomon, 1984). If learners feel efficacious about overcoming difficulties in achieving their goals, their doubts about whether they will succeed can increase effort and lead to better use of strategies than will feelings of overconfidence.

Many students suffer from low self-efficacy for improving their literacy skills such as oral reading, reading comprehension, essay writing, and spelling proficiency. In areas such as comprehension and writing it is difficult for a student to ascertain how much he or she is improving. Students typically rely on teacher feedback for progress information, and they may not be able to reliably gauge progress on their own. Later in this chapter there are examples of interventions designed to improve students' acquisition of literacy skills and self-efficacy for learning and performing those skills.

Modeling

Modeling can serve the functions of inhibition and disinhibition, response facilitation, and observational learning (Schunk, 1987). Inhibition or disinhibition occurs when a model strengthens or weakens an observer's behavioral inhibitions. Observing a model performing a feared activity without negative consequences—such as giving a dramatic reading in class—may lead observers to believe there is little to fear and to perform the task themselves. Response facilitation occurs when modeled actions serve as social prompts

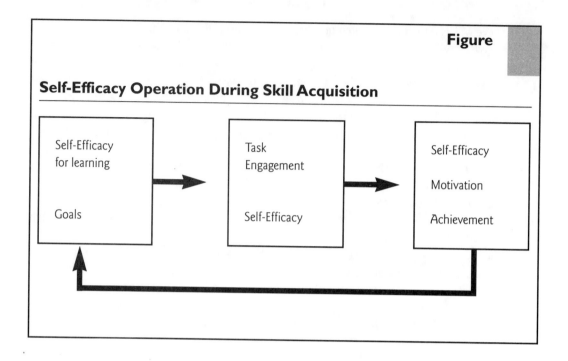

Figure

Self-Efficacy Operation During Skill Acquisition

Self-Efficacy for learning

Goals

Task Engagement

Self-Efficacy

Self-Efficacy

Motivation

Achievement

for observer behavior. Facilitation effects are evident when students do what they see others do (for example, when students read the same magazines that popular peers read).

Observational learning occurs when observers display new behaviors that they did not know before seeing them modeled (Bandura, 1986; Schunk, 1987). For example, in the opening vignette observational learning happens as a consequence of the teacher assisting students to pose questions and set rules for working together. Other observational learning occurs when students serve as models for one another. An important form of observational learning occurs through cognitive modeling, which incorporates modeled demonstrations with verbal explanations of the model's thoughts and reasons for performing the actions (Meichenbaum, 1977).

The functional value of behavior, or whether modeled actions result in success or failure or reward or punishment, has strong effects on observer modeling. Modeled behaviors are likely to be performed if they lead to rewarding outcomes but unlikely if they result in punishment. Robert and Kantu realize that their efforts in the class project have high functional value because they continue to acquire knowledge and develop interest in crickets.

In addition, modeling fulfills information and motivation functions. Modeled behavior provides information about what sequence of actions will lead to success and about which actions have undesirable consequences. Models can raise efficacy among observers who are apt to believe that they will be successful if they follow the same behavioral sequence. Models also can motivate observers to perform the same behavior or to avoid per-

Schunk & Zimmerman

forming it. For example, preschoolers begin to make comparisons of their behavior to that of models, and these comparisons exert increasingly powerful effects throughout school (Schunk, 1987).

As mentioned, perceived similarity between model and observer may be important, especially in situations when individuals have experienced difficulties and have doubts about performing well. The more alike observers are to models, the greater the probability that similar actions by observers are socially appropriate and will produce comparable results. We would expect this influence to be strong in Robert and Kantu's class because students have much interaction and are pursuing similar but new activities.

Goal Setting

Goals, which can be acquired through modeling, are integral components of academic motivation and learning. Goals motivate students to exert extra effort and persistence, focus on relevant task features, and use strategies that will help them learn (Locke & Latham, 1990). At the start of learning activities, students have goals such as acquiring skills and knowledge, finishing work, and making good grades. When learners make a commitment to attain a goal—such as improving the clarity of their writing—they are likely to compare their performance with the goal as they work on the task. Positive self-evaluations of progress increase self-efficacy and sustain motivation (Schunk, 1990). A perceived discrepancy between performance and the goal may create dissatisfaction, which can enhance effort (Bandura, 1988; Locke & Latham, 1990).

Goal-setting theory has been applied to various domains including academic, motor, work, and social (Locke & Latham, 1990). Here we focus on the academic domain in which achievement research shows that goals do not automatically enhance learning and motivation (Schunk, 1990); rather, the goal properties of specificity, proximity, and difficulty are important. Although students often have broad, general goals (for example, to become a better writer), goals that incorporate *specific* performance standards are more likely to enhance learning and activate self-evaluation than are general goals (Locke & Latham, 1990). Specific goals also promote efficacy because it is easier to evaluate progress toward an explicit goal than to a general goal. Thus, it is helpful to divide a general goal into a set of specific subgoals that focus attention and effort and enhance performance (Locke & Latham, 1990).

Goals can be distinguished by how far they extend into the future. Compared with temporally distant goals, proximal short-term goals are achieved more quickly and result in greater motivation and higher efficacy. Proximal goals are especially influential with young children who are not fully capable of conceptualizing distant outcomes (Graham & Harris, 1994). Research shows that broader, longer range goals (such as writing a term paper) are best accomplished by subdividing the task into a series of short-term, manageable subtasks (Schunk, 1990). This approach is apparent in the opening vignette, in which the 16-week unit is divided into components to be accomplished on a short-term basis.

Developing Self-Efficacious Readers and Writers

The difficulty of a goal is an important property for motivation because people expend greater effort to attain a difficult goal than an easier one (Schunk, 1990). However, people do not attempt to attain what they believe is impossible. Goals that are perceived as moderately difficult increase motivation and convey a clear sense of progress, which increases efficacy.

Goal effects also may depend on whether the goal denotes a learning or performance outcome (Meece, 1991). A learning goal refers to what knowledge and skills students seek to acquire (for example, to learn how to write active-voice sentences); a performance goal (such as to write 10 passive-voice sentences) denotes what task students are to complete (Dweck & Leggett, 1988). The questions that Robert and Kantu ask in the vignette in this book's introduction represent learning goals. Goal-setting research typically has focused on such goals as rate or quantity of performance, but educators increasingly are advocating greater emphasis on learning processes and strategies (Weinstein, Goetz, & Alexander, 1988).

To evaluate progress it is essential that learners receive goal progress feedback, especially when they cannot derive reliable information on their own. For example, students may have trouble determining whether their writing style is improving or whether they are comprehending text better. Goal progress feedback increases self-efficacy and motivation when it conveys that students are competent and can continue to improve by working diligently. It is probable that the students in the opening vignette received goal progress feedback from their teacher and from peers because there is much class sharing.

As mentioned earlier, the goal principles described in this section are applicable to domains other than academic skill learning. Because of this, it is common to have multiple goals operating at the same time, which may conflict (Wentzel, 1992). For example, students might believe that academic progress can be gained only at some social cost (such as peer disapproval). Nonetheless, the generality of goal principles and those involving self-efficacy, modeling, and self-evaluation has been established in diverse contexts.

Self-Evaluation

Of critical importance in maintaining a sense of self-efficacy is the process of self-evaluation of capabilities and progress in skill acquisition. Positive self-evaluations lead students to feel efficacious about learning and motivate them to continue to work diligently because they believe they are capable of making further progress (Schunk, 1990). Aspiring writers are willing to continue writing as long as they believe they are improving their craft. The opening vignette shows that students engage often in self-evaluation.

Negative self-evaluations will not diminish self-efficacy and motivation if students believe they are capable of succeeding but that their present approach is ineffective (Bandura, 1986). These students may work harder, persist longer, adopt a better strategy, or they may seek help from teachers and peers (Schunk, 1990). These and other achievement strategies are likely to lead to success (Bouffard-Bouchard, Parent & Larivee, 1991; Zimmerman & Martinez-Pons, 1992).

Beginning around the third grade, children can make reasonably accurate evaluations of their capabilities (Assor & Connell, 1992). However, students usually do not self-evaluate without prompting. They should be prompted to record their progress periodically. The large poster constructed by Robert, Kantu, and their classmates is a tangible indicator of their progress. Such explicit self-evaluations constitute a type of self-monitoring because students can compare their present work with their prior accomplishments. By making performance improvements salient, self-monitoring increases self-efficacy, sustains motivation for learning, and promotes skills. Students not proficient in self-evaluation initially may need to be taught cues for assessing performance and gauging goal progress. In addition, self-evaluation is easier when the task lends itself to quantification and more difficult when progress is qualitative—often the case in literary domains. Thus, students may wonder if their writing really is improving. The use of feedback by teachers and through peer conferences is especially helpful in this case (DiPardo & Freedman, 1988).

Literacy Research

In this section we discuss research on reading and writing that highlights the important roles played by self-efficacy, modeling, goal setting, and self-evaluation. We focus on studies that have implemented interventions designed to improve students' literacy skills or that sought to clarify processes in their acquisition. (See Pajares & Johnson, 1994; Shell, Murphy, & Bruning, 1989; and Zimmerman & Martinez-Pons, 1990, for nonintervention research that highlights the central role of self-efficacy in reading and writing motivation and achievement.)

Reading Achievement

Goal setting. As mentioned, research attests to the effectiveness of specific, short-term, and moderately difficult goals in increasing students' motivation, self-efficacy, and achievement. Studies have found that goal setting is beneficial for a variety of reading skills. Gaa (1973) assigned first- and second-grade students to one of three conditions: conferences with goal setting, conferences without goal setting, and no conferences. Youngsters who attended goal-setting conferences met with the researcher weekly when they received feedback on the previous week's attainment, were given a list of reading skills, and selected those they would try to master the following week. In the conferences without goal setting, children received general information about material covered previously and what would be covered next. No-conference students received instruction comparable to that given to the other students. Children in all three conditions set goals at the end of the study. Children in the goal conferences demonstrated the highest reading achievement and the smallest discrepancy between goals set and mastered, which shows that proximal goal setting promoted accurate self-evaluations of capabilities. Gaa (1979) replicated these results with 10th-grade students in English language arts classes and found that students who attended goal conferences took greater responsibility for their successes.

Tollefson et al. (1984) taught goal setting to seventh- and ninth-grade students with learning disabilities. Students set weekly goals (spelling words or math problems) from a list of moderately difficult tasks to master. The goal and a study plan were stated in a written contract, which was designed to help students take responsibility for their learning and to highlight that effort enhances achievement. Compared with students in a no-treatment control group, students who set goals considered effort to be an important cause of success and set more realistic goals.

Schunk and Rice (1989) explored the effects of fourth- and fifth-grade students' process (learning) and product (performance) goals on their self-efficacy and reading comprehension. The students had low reading skills as indicated by standardized reading test vocabulary and comprehension scores that were at or below the 20th percentile (roughly equivalent to third grade). Students were taught a strategy for finding main ideas by an adult who cognitively modeled the strategy. Some students received a process goal of learning to use the strategy; others were given a product goal of answering questions; those in a group that was given general goals were advised to work productively. Compared with students in the general-goal group, children with process and product goals judged self-efficacy for finding main ideas to be high, and children with process goals demonstrated better comprehension.

In a follow-up study (Schunk & Rice, 1991), fifth-grade students whose scores on standardized reading tests were at or below the 20th percentile were given a product goal of answering questions, a process goal of learning to use the strategy for finding main ideas, or a process goal plus progress feedback. The feedback linked performance with strategy use and conveyed that students were making progress toward the learning goal. Students who received the goal plus feedback demonstrated higher self-efficacy and comprehension than did learners with process and product goals. These results show that remedial readers benefit from explicit feedback on their progress toward attainment of a process (learning) goal.

Perceived strategy effectiveness. Studies show that strategy instruction with feedback influences reading achievement, strategy use, and self-efficacy. Teaching students to use learning strategies enhances achievement outcomes, motivation, and perceptions of capabilities (Borkowski, Johnston, & Reid, 1987; Paris, Cross, & Lipson, 1984; Weinstein & Mayer, 1986); however, instruction does not ensure that children maintain strategy use over time or generalize, or transfer, it to other tasks or settings (Garner, 1990; Pressley et al., 1990). There are many reasons for nontransfer; one is that students believe the strategy is not as important for success as are other factors such as time availability or teacher assistance. To promote strategy transfer, teachers may need to inform students about the uses of a strategy and how it helps improve performance (Borkowski, 1985; Paris, Wixson, & Palincsar, 1986).

Two studies showed that multiple sources of information about the value of a strategy improve achievement outcomes (Schunk & Rice, 1987). Participants were fourth- and fifth-grade children who had scored at or below the 20th percentile on standardized reading tests. In the first study, children received a goal of learning to use a strategy for finding main ideas and were given general strategy information, specific strategy information, specific plus general information, or no strategy information. General information emphasized the value of the strategy for all reading tasks; specific information conveyed the value of using the strategy to identify main ideas. In a follow-up study, children received strategy-effectiveness feedback, specific strategy information, or specific information plus feedback that linked children's performances with strategy use. In both studies, the combined treatment best promoted self-efficacy and comprehension. This treatment may have engendered in children a sense of control over their reading success, which increases self-efficacy.

Further evidence on the importance of information on strategy usefulness comes from studies by Schunk and Rice (1992). Fourth- and fifth-grade students whose scores on standardized reading tests were in the lowest 30th percentile in the school district received instruction on finding main ideas. In the first study, some students were taught a comprehension strategy; others received strategy instruction by observing an adult model and were given feedback linking strategy use with improved performance; and those in a control group received instruction without the strategy. In the second study, fourth- and fifth-grade children were taught the strategy or received instruction without strategy training; then they were given instruction on locating details. Some were taught how to modify the strategy for the new task; others did not employ the strategy on locating details. Children who received feedback about strategy value (in the first study) and instruction on strategy modification (in the second study) demonstrated the highest self-efficacy, comprehension, strategy use, and transfer of the strategy to the new comprehension task.

Research supports the idea that students who receive remedial reading instruction benefit from procedures that require extensive cognitive activity and inform them of strategy usefulness (Schunk & Rice, 1993). Fifth-grade children who had scored in the lowest 30th percentile on standardized reading tests received instruction on locating main ideas and were taught to verbalize a strategy while applying it. Some were taught to fade their verbalizations to silent (inner) speech. Half of the children in the fading and no-fading conditions periodically received feedback linking strategy use with better performance. The no-fading and no-feedback condition scored lower on self-efficacy, skill, and self-reported strategy use than the other three conditions. Fading plus feedback led to higher strategy use compared with the fading-only and feedback-only conditions and to better comprehension than did feedback only. Results from a statistical (regression) analysis showed that experimental condition, self-efficacy, and strategy use were the best predictors of achievement.

In the studies cited in this section, self-efficacy typically was a dependent variable affected by experimental conditions (such as goals and strategy feedback) and reading instruction and practice. The figure on page 38 shows that self-efficacy also functions as a variable that affects motivation and achievement. This reciprocal influence is hypothesized to occur during task engagement, although the studies cited were not designed to assess the bidirectional influence. The Schunk and Rice (1993) study supports the predictive utility of self-efficacy for reading achievement. Research in other achievement domains (such as writing and mathematics) has shown that self-efficacy influences learning of cognitive skills (Schunk, 1981; Zimmerman & Bandura, 1994).

Writing Achievement

There is less research on writing than on reading achievement, but study results are remarkably consistent in showing that self-efficacy relates to learning and that modeling, goal setting, and self-evaluation exert desirable effects. For example, Schunk and Swartz (1993a, 1993b) explored the effects of learning goals and progress feedback on children's self-efficacy, achievement, and use of writing strategies. Average ability (fifth grade) and gifted (fourth grade) students received writing instruction over 20 days that covered four types of paragraphs: descriptive, informative, narrative story, and narrative descriptive. Children were taught a five-step writing strategy (for example, choose a topic to write about, pick the main idea, and so forth) through cognitive modeling by an adult, which was followed by guided and independent practice. Children also shared feedback with one another on their essays.

Students were assigned to one of four conditions: process (learning) goal, process goal plus progress feedback, product (performance) goal, or general goal (instructional control). Students who received the process goal and the process goal plus progress feedback were advised by the adult that their goal was to learn to use the strategy to write paragraphs. Product-goal students were told their goal was to write paragraphs; general-goal students were advised to do their best. The verbal progress feedback, given by the adult, linked strategy use with improved writing performance (for example, the adult commented, "You're doing well because you followed the steps in order").

The condition of the process goal plus feedback was the most effective, but there were some benefits of providing only a process goal. Students who received the process goal plus feedback generally outperformed students with product and general goals on self-efficacy and writing achievement; they evaluated the strategy positively; and they demonstrated the highest strategy use. Their gains were maintained after six weeks and were generalized to types of paragraphs on which they had received no instruction. Statistical (regression) analyses showed that experimental condition and self-efficacy were significant predictors of writing achievement.

Graham and Harris (1989a, 1989b; Sawyer, Graham, & Harris, 1992) showed that teaching fifth- and sixth-grade students (normally achieving and those with learning disabilities) a strategy for writing essays or stories improves self-efficacy and composition skill. They also showed that gains are maintained and can generalize to other content and settings. The strategy was taught through a cognitive modeling procedure; the models also conveyed strategy value by emphasizing that strategy use would help students attain their learning goals. Other critical components of the procedure were self-monitoring of performance and self-evaluation of progress by comparing goals with achievement.

Zimmerman and Bandura (1994) assessed the influence of self-efficacy, goal setting, and self-evaluation on the development of first-year college students' writing proficiency. Students were enrolled in either advanced or regular classes based on advanced placement test scores. At the beginning of the semester, students were tested on self-efficacy, goal setting, and self-evaluative processes. At the end of the semester, students' final grades served as the writing proficiency measure.

Two self-efficacy scales were used in this study: a scale for writing self-regulatory efficacy assessed students' perceived capabilities to perform self-regulatory behaviors associated with writing such as planning, revising, generating good topics, managing time, and maintaining motivation for writing; a scale for self-efficacy for academic achievement required that students rate their beliefs for achieving each of 12 possible grades (A, A-, B+...F) in the writing course they were taking.

For the goal-setting measure, subjects indicated which of 12 academic grades they were striving for in the course. The self-evaluation instrument asked students to rate how satisfied they would be to attain each of the 12 possible final grades.

The researchers explored causal relations among variables using statistical techniques (path analysis). Students' enrollment in advanced or regular class was linked to their verbal aptitude scores, but neither of these variables directly influenced course grades. Instead, verbal aptitude influenced writing outcome indirectly through its effects on self-evaluative standards, which influenced grade goals. Students' self-regulatory efficacy for writing affected both academic self-efficacy and self-evaluative standards, which influenced grade goals. Academic self-efficacy and grade goals had the greatest impact on writing proficiency.

Implications for Practice

The ideas presented in this chapter suggest many potential implications for teaching reading and writing. Some suggestions are given in the table on page 46, along with ideas on how they are implemented in the vignette in the introduction involving Robert and Kantu.

One suggestion is to use models in the classroom. Especially important are cognitive models who verbalize their actions as well as their thought processes as they read or write (Zimmerman & Kleefeld, 1977). At times it may be important to use coping models who initially portray learning difficulties and express low self-efficacy for learning; these models show by displaying perseverance, effort, and effective strategy use and by verbalizing coping statements (such as, "I have to pay better attention") that they improve their performance (Schunk, Hanson, & Cox, 1987). Coping models contrast with mastery models, who perform the task flawlessly from the outset. Students who typically learn easily in school may benefit from being exposed to mastery models, but those who often have difficulty may perceive themselves more similar in competence to coping models.

In cooperative groups, where students work jointly on a task, group members serve as models for others. Responsibilities are divided so each group member is responsible

Implications for Teaching Practice

1. Use Models

   Examples: Robert and Kantu explain and demonstrate to peers the process they used to gather information on their topic; older students who participated in the project in prior years come to class to discuss their topics and how they conducted the research.

2. Build Self-Efficacy

   Examples: The teacher ensures that Robert and Kantu's project is reasonable and can be completed in the time frame; teacher and peers provide Robert and Kantu with feedback indicating that they are making progress.

3. Develop Goal-Setting and Self-Evaluation Skills

   Examples: The teacher asks Robert and Kantu to plan the steps in the project, the approximate time frame, and ways to monitor progress; Robert and Kantu periodically evaluate their progress using a rating scale or by writing a short progress report.

4. Teach Effective Learning Strategies

   Examples: The teacher models use of strategies to the class; the value of strategies is demonstrated when Robert and Kantu discuss with other students how strategy use is improving performance on tasks.

for some part of the task (Cohen, 1994). During writing instruction, peers often confer, critique one another's writing, and offer suggestions for improvement (Fitzgerald, 1987).

A second suggestion is to build self-efficacy by having students experience learning progress and success, exposing them to successful models, and providing encouraging feedback that is substantiated by success. Teachers can incorporate these sources of efficacy information into the classroom by teaching effective strategies, employing social models, and providing progress feedback (such as, "You are getting better"). Although actual successes exert strong effects on self-efficacy, the vicarious and persuasive sources also are effective.

Third, teachers need to help students develop goal-setting and self-evaluation skills. For example, they might be asked to set the goal of varying the structure of adjacent sentences to achieve more sophisticated prose. Instruction on goal setting may be necessary until students can set accurate goals. Students also may need to be taught self-evaluative strategies. One strategy is to have students complete a self-report scale where they rate their progress and discuss these ratings with the teacher who provides feedback. In addition, students can be taught to use outcome cues to evaluate progress.

Finally, teachers need to teach effective learning strategies through modeling, guided practice, independent practice, and peer conferences. For example, an important component of writing is revising. Compared with average writers, better writers spend more time revising what they have written (Stallard, 1974). Many students are reluctant to revise, which may reflect low motivation (the belief that revising will not improve writing) and a lack of knowledge of how to evaluate writing quality and what to revise. Teachers can demonstrate a strategy for assessing the clarity of writing by stating their purpose in writing. As they read aloud what they have written, they can evaluate whether it is focused on the purpose, clearly stated, and comprehensible to readers. Peer conferences also can be used to provide feedback and suggested revisions to classmates' writing.

Teaching students strategies helps build self-efficacy. When students know what to do to perform competently, their expectations for performing well increase. Further, the use of peer models provides an important source of efficacy information that predicts motivation and achievement.

A Final Word

It is important to develop a resilient sense of self-efficacy in students as competent readers and writers. There is substantial evidence indicating that students' efficacy beliefs can be enhanced by social interventions such as modeled use of strategies and feedback emphasizing learning progress and by deliberate self-regulatory efforts involving goal setting and self-evaluation. Teachers who incorporate these social and self-regulatory experiences into their classrooms will observe improvements in their students' literacy proficiency and motivation and will witness a transformation in their students' identities and aspirations as readers and writers.

References

Assor, A., & Connell, J.P. (1992). The validity of students' self-reports as measures of performance affecting self-appraisals. In D.H. Schunk & J.L. Meece (Eds.), *Student perceptions in the classroom* (pp. 25–47). Hillsdale, NJ: Erlbaum.

Bandura, A. (1986). *Social foundations of thought and action: A social cognitive theory*. Englewood Cliffs, NJ: Prentice Hall.

Bandura, A. (1988). Self-regulation of motivation and action through goal systems. In V. Hamilton, G.H. Bower, & N.H. Frijda (Eds.), *Cognitive perspectives on emotion and motivation* (pp. 37–61). Dordrecht, The Netherlands: Kluwer Academic.

Bandura, A. (in press). *Self-efficacy: The exercise of control*. New York: Freeman.

Borkowski, J.G. (1985). Signs of intelligence: Strategy generalization and metacognition. In S. Yussen (Ed.), *The growth of reflection in children* (pp. 105–144). New York: Academic.

Borkowski, J.G., Johnston, M.B., & Reid, M.K. (1987). Metacognition, motivation, and controlled performance. In S.J. Ceci (Ed.), *Handbook of cognitive, social, and neuropsychological aspects of learning disabilities* (Vol. 2, pp. 147–173). Hillsdale, NJ: Erlbaum.

Bouffard-Bouchard, T., Parent, S., & Larivee, S. (1991). Influence of self-efficacy on self-regulation and performance among junior and senior high-school age students. *International Journal of Behavioral Development, 14*, 153–164.

Cohen, E.G. (1994). Restructuring the classroom: Conditions for productive small groups. *Review of Educational Research, 64,* 1–35.

DiPardo, A., & Freedman, S.W. (1988). Peer response groups in the writing classroom: Theoretic foundations and new directions. *Review of Educational Research, 58,* 119–149.

Dweck, C.S., & Leggett, E.L. (1988). A social-cognitive approach to motivation and personality. *Psychological Review, 95,* 256–273.

Fitzgerald, J. (1987). Research on revision in writing. *Review of Educational Research, 57,* 481–506.

Gaa, J.P. (1973). Effects of individual goal-setting conferences on achievement, attitudes, and goal-setting behavior. *Journal of Experimental Education, 42,* 22–28.

Gaa, J.P. (1979). The effects of individual goal-setting conferences on academic achievement and modification of locus of control orientation. *Psychology in the Schools, 16,* 591–597.

Garner, R. (1990). When children and adults do not use learning strategies: Toward a theory of settings. *Review of Educational Research, 60,* 517–529.

Graham, S., & Harris, K.R. (1989a). Components analysis of cognitive strategy instruction: Effects on learning disabled students' compositions and self-efficacy. *Journal of Educational Psychology, 81,* 353–361.

Graham, S., & Harris, K.R. (1989b). Improving learning disabled students' skills at composing essays: Self-instructional strategy training. *Exceptional Children, 56,* 201–214.

Graham, S., & Harris, K.R. (1994). The role and development of self-regulation in the writing process. In D.H. Schunk & B.J. Zimmerman (Eds.), *Self-regulation of learning and performance: Issues and educational applications* (pp. 203–228). Hillsdale, NJ: Erlbaum.

Locke, E.A., & Latham, G.P. (1990). *A theory of goal setting and task performance.* Englewood Cliffs, NJ: Prentice Hall.

Meece, J.L. (1991). The classroom context and students' motivational goals. In M.L. Maehr & P.R. Pintrich (Eds.), *Advances in motivation and achievement* (Vol. 7, pp. 261–285). Greenwich, CT: JAI Press.

Meichenbaum, D. (1977). *Cognitive behavior modification: An integrative approach.* New York: Plenum.

Pajares, F., & Johnson, M.J. (1994). Confidence and competence in writing: The role of self-efficacy, outcome expectancy, and apprehension. *Research in the Teaching of English, 28,* 313–329.

Paris, S.G., Cross, D.R., & Lipson, M.Y. (1984). Informed strategies for learning: A program to improve children's reading awareness and comprehension. *Journal of Educational Psychology, 76,* 1239–1252.

Paris, S.G., Wixson, K.K., & Palincsar, A.S. (1986). Instructional approaches to reading comprehension. In E.Z. Rothkopf (Ed.), *Review of research in education* (Vol. 13, pp. 91–128). Washington, DC: American Educational Research Association.

Pressley, M. et al. (1990). A primer of research on cognitive strategy instruction: The important issues and how to address them. *Educational Psychology Review, 2,* 1–58.

Salomon, G. (1984). Television is "easy" and print is "tough": The differential investment of mental effort in learning as a function of perceptions and attributions. *Journal of Educational Psychology, 76,* 647–658.

Sawyer, R.J., Graham, S., & Harris, K.R. (1992). Direct teaching, strategy instruction, and strategy instruction with explicit self-regulation: Effects on the composition skills and self-efficacy of students with learning disabilities. *Journal of Educational Psychology, 84,* 340–352.

Schunk, D.H. (1981). Modeling and attributional effects on children's achievement: A self-efficacy analysis. *Journal of Educational Psychology, 73,* 93–105.

Schunk, D.H. (1987). Peer models and children's behavioral change. *Review of Educational Research, 57,* 149–174.

Schunk, D.H. (1990). Goal setting and self-efficacy during self-regulated learning. *Educational Psychologist, 25*, 71–86.

Schunk, D.H. (1994). Self-regulation of self-efficacy and attributions in academic settings. In D.H. Schunk & B.J. Zimmerman (Eds.), *Self-regulation of learning and performance: Issues and educational applications* (pp. 75–99). Hillsdale, NJ: Erlbaum.

Schunk, D.H. (1996). Goal and self-evaluative influences during children's cognitive skill learning. *American Educational Research Journal, 33*, 359–382.

Schunk, D.H., Hanson, A.R., & Cox, P.D. (1987). Peer model attributes and children's achievement behaviors. *Journal of Educational Psychology, 79*, 54–61.

Schunk, D.H., & Rice, J.M. (1987). Enhancing comprehension skill and self-efficacy with strategy value information. *Journal of Reading Behavior, 19*, 285–302.

Schunk, D.H., & Rice, J.M. (1989). Learning goals and children's reading comprehension. *Journal of Reading Behavior, 21*, 279–293.

Schunk, D.H., & Rice, J.M. (1991). Learning goals and progress feedback during reading comprehension instruction. *Journal of Reading Behavior, 23*, 351–364.

Schunk, D.H., & Rice, J.M. (1992). Influence of reading-comprehension strategy information on children's achievement outcomes. *Learning Disability Quarterly, 15*, 51–64.

Schunk, D.H., & Rice, J.M. (1993). Strategy fading and progress feedback: Effects on self-efficacy and comprehension among students receiving remedial reading services. *Journal of Special Education, 27*, 257–276.

Schunk, D.H., & Swartz, C.W. (1993a). Goals and progress feedback: Effects on self-efficacy and writing achievement. *Contemporary Educational Psychology, 18*, 337–354.

Schunk, D.H., & Swartz, C.W. (1993b). Writing strategy instruction with gifted students: Effects of goals and feedback on self-efficacy and skills. *Roeper Review, 15*, 225–230.

Schunk, D.H., & Zimmerman, B.J. (Eds.). (1994). *Self-regulation of learning and performance: Issues and educational applications*. Hillsdale, NJ: Erlbaum.

Shell, D.F., Murphy, C.C., & Bruning, R.H. (1989). Self-efficacy and outcome expectancy mechanisms in reading and writing achievement. *Journal of Educational Psychology, 81*, 91–100.

Stallard, C.K. (1974). An analysis of the writing behavior of good student writers. *Research in the Teaching of English, 8*, 206–218.

Tollefson, N., Tracy, D.B., Johnsen, E.P., Farmer, A.W., & Buenning, M. (1984). Goal setting and personal responsibility training for LD adolescents. *Psychology in the Schools, 21*, 224–233.

Weinstein, C.E., Goetz, E.T., & Alexander, P.A. (Eds.). (1988). *Learning and study strategies: Issues in assessment, instruction, and evaluation*. San Diego, CA: Academic.

Weinstein, C.E., & Mayer, R.E. (1986). The teaching of learning strategies. In M.C. Wittrock (Ed.), *Handbook of research on teaching* (3rd ed., pp. 315–327). New York: Macmillan.

Wentzel, K.R. (1992). Motivation and achievement in adolescence: A multiple goals perspective. In D.H. Schunk & J.L. Meece (Eds.), *Student perceptions in the classroom* (pp. 287–306). Hillsdale, NJ: Erlbaum.

Zimmerman, B.J. (1989). A social cognitive view of self-regulated academic learning. *Journal of Educational Psychology, 81*, 329–339.

Zimmerman, B.J. (1990). Self-regulating academic learning and achievement: The emergence of a social cognitive perspective. *Educational Psychology Review, 2*, 173–201.

Zimmerman, B.J. (1994). Dimensions of academic self-regulation: A conceptual framework for education. In D.H. Schunk & B.J. Zimmerman (Eds.), *Self-regulation of learning and performance: Issues and educational applications* (pp. 3–21). Hillsdale, NJ: Erlbaum.

Zimmerman, B.J. (1995). Self-efficacy and educational development. In A. Bandura (Ed.), *Self-efficacy in changing societies* (pp. 202–231). New York: Cambridge University Press.

Zimmerman, B.J., & Bandura, A. (1994). Impact of self-regulatory influences on attainment in a writing course. *American Educational Research Journal, 29*, 663–676.

Zimmerman, B.J., & Kleefeld, C. (1977). Toward a theory of teaching: A social learning view. *Contemporary Educational Psychology, 2*, 158–171.

Zimmerman, B.J., & Martinez-Pons, M. (1990). Student differences in self-regulated learning: Relating grade, sex, and giftedness to self-efficacy and strategy use. *Journal of Educational Psychology, 82*, 51–59.

Zimmerman, B.J., & Martinez-Pons, M. (1992). Perceptions of efficacy and strategy use in the self-regulation of learning. In D.H. Schunk & J.L. Meece (Eds.), *Student perceptions in the classroom* (pp. 185–207). Hillsdale, NJ: Erlbaum.

Motivation, Volition, and Collaborative Innovation in Classroom Literacy

3

Lyn Corno and Judi Randi

I n the introduction, Guthrie and Wigfield define student literacy engagement as the joint functioning of motivation and strategies for literacy. They illustrate how improvements in reading and writing can result from the "engagement perspective on literacy"—when students put their goals, interests, and growing self-confidence to use in the context of a rich, integrated curriculum. Among other things, this perspective encourages students to use strategies for managing tasks and for effectively processing information.

However, the classroom scene that Guthrie and Wigfield depict in the vignette in the introduction is not yet routine, nor is it a likely scenario in the absence of careful, collaborative work between teachers and researchers. This work, or process of *collaborative innovation*, between teachers and researchers undergirds what the fifth graders in the classroom did and ultimately learned. This process relates to the variety of motivational and volitional factors that underlie the engagement of the teachers and students involved. If it is beneficial to engage students with curricula and enable them to work collaboratively and as self-regulated learners, similar benefits should result with teachers. Teachers gain when they are engaged with their work, continually upgrade the quality of their curricula, and regularly appraise their own teaching and that of their peers. The collaborative innovation that is undertaken by the teacher and the researchers depicted in the vignette affects the teacher as the engagement perspective on literacy affects the students in the classroom.

This chapter characterizes the collaborative innovation process for use by teacher-researcher teams working toward an engagement perspective on literacy. Collaborative innovation between teachers and researchers is not typically used in staff development, despite considerable evidence that it should be (Randi & Corno, in press). To introduce collaborative innovation, we first discuss underlying aspects of motivation and volition. Then we offer examples from research to illustrate how teachers, parents, and others who work with children might better address the motivational and volitional aspects of literacy engagement in classrooms and in other achievement tasks.

What Motivational and Volitional Aspects Underlie a Literacy Engagement Perspective?

Most students enter school motivated to learn. How often have we heard students say, "I really meant to do well on that assignment"? But intentions to succeed often are not enough. The attainment of academic success requires voluntary sustained effort—effort despite numerous classroom distractions. Students also are plagued by conflicting priorities that tax their attention spans further. The ability to focus despite distractions requires diligence that is more than simple motivation—it requires the voluntary sustained effort that psychologists call *volition*.

Motivation and volition have long been understood to work in conjunction with two other important psychological functions, cognition and emotion, to promote long-term success in school (Snow, Corno, & Jackson, 1996). Just as studies have shown that aspects of students' school-related cognition underlie their effective processing of academic information, it has become clear that certain aspects of students' motivation and volition work together with emotions to support their long-term accomplishments in school and beyond.

Aspects of Motivation

As several authors in this volume demonstrate, among the most important aspects, or constructs, of student academic motivation are goals and expectations regarding school learning and performance. Goals and expectations are complemented by students' values, interests, self-evaluations, and growing concepts of themselves as young readers and writers (Zimmerman & Schunk, 1989). Research shows that these constructs of motivation affect the level and kind of effort students put forth in school and, through effort, their achievement and other accomplishments. Knowing what the underlying constructs of motivation are and how they function increases teachers' understanding of ways to improve students' engagement with the material they encounter in their learning. Also, teachers who become familiar with both the motivational and volitional aspects of literacy engagement are more likely to foster such engagement in their students' work lives and in their own. Because other chapters in this volume target the definitions and constructs of motivation, we discuss volition in more detail.

Aspects of Volition

How do we identify volition in students? What kinds of verbal and nonverbal behavior and what patterns of response do we look for? Among the most important aspects of volition are *volitional strategies*. Alternatively referred to as *action controls*, these strategies are thoughts and actions that enhance attentiveness or focus on tasks to support the pursuit of goals. When researchers look at what it is that successful students do in school, they often find a wide array of action controls—time management, self-monitoring, and skillful use of resources, among other things. Action controls or volitional strategies underlie the effortful behavior that leads to school success (Corno, 1993).

The routine use of volitional strategies over time is believed to lead students toward a stylistic tendency to be conscientious, or diligent, in their work. Institutions such as schools and work settings encourage these tendencies by defining a "work ethic" to which participants conform. A conscientious work orientation is another important aspect of volition, which is obtained in part through environmental influences in school and elsewhere. Conscientiousness is highly predictive of success in the workplace and in school (Barrick & Mount, 1991).

Just as modern theory finds motivation to be more than wishes or wants, so does it distinguish volition from colloquial conceptions of individual willpower or strength of will. Theory also defines a range of different categories of volitional strategies that function to enhance motivation by directing effort. We have grouped these categories into three broad areas (more specific categorizations are presented elsewhere; see, for example, Corno & Kanfer, 1993). First, strategic thinking and behavior can be used to control motivation-related cognitions such as conflicting goals. Second, strategies that involve careful self-monitoring aid in handling emotions that can undermine motivation. Third, apart from these strategies that control the internal aspects of thinking (cognition) and feeling (emotion), strategies also may be used to minimize distractions and control aspects of the external (task) environment. Consider some school-related examples from each of the following three categories.

Control of motivation-related cognition. Students often have multiple goals that need prioritizing. It is not uncommon, for example, for a student to want to get the most from a classroom activity (a cognitive goal) with minimal effort (an emotional goal). These two goals conflict. The student who strategically raises the cognitive goal's priority on important tasks exhibits highly volitional behavior. Similarly, a student who can finish homework (a cognitive goal) when he or she would rather be watching television (an emotional goal), is strategically prioritizing competing goals.

Another form of conflict can occur when a teacher's stated objectives differ from what students seek to accomplish on classroom tasks. For example, teachers often expect written assignments to be formatted a certain way and to contain specific content. However, beginning writers may pay less attention to formatting concerns than the teacher prefers. Finding a way to prioritize these conflicting goals so that both can be accomplished is an example of strategic volition. Teachers who are aware of such competing goals and how these conflicts can impede students' writing progress can work with students to help them set priorities.

Students' motivation-related thinking or cognition also involves their learning and performance expectations and self-evaluations. In the elementary grades, classroom projects and tasks often include incentives (the promise of reward or opportunity for work done well). When students learn to raise the value of incentives in their mind, or when they begin to anticipate satisfaction with work done well, they are controlling motivation-related thinking. Similarly, students need to learn to handle constructive criticism from teachers when their work is imperfect. Many students have the tendency to say they "can't solve problems" or "aren't good spellers" when they make mistakes; but negative self-evaluations like these can affect negatively students' future motivation in math, spelling, or whatever area they define as their weakest (Weiner, 1990).

It is more productive for students to learn that they can evaluate their imperfect work in a balanced fashion that preserves self-worth by statements such as, "The work was a challenge and help wasn't always available," or "I ought to congratulate myself for trying hard under these circumstances." Teachers can help students view imperfect work more accurately by stating that it is simply "unfinished," rather than "wrong." Accurate self-evaluations recognize that tasks vary in difficulty and support and attribute some of the students' imperfect work to these external factors beyond student control. They also recognize what the student did right, reinforcing a second try. Deliberate efforts to control self-evaluations and other motivation-related cognitions represent a "take-charge" approach to difficult tasks that many young children need to be taught. Learning how and when it is important to use stronger initiative can help a student carry out intentions to succeed in school.

Control of emotion. Another general category of action control involves the strategic management of both negative and positive emotions. As with negative self-evaluations, students also associate anxious, self-debilitating emotions with particular subject areas or tasks they find difficult (for example, "math anxiety" or "test anxiety"). When feelings of self-defeat are noted by a student and then deliberately set aside to focus attention on the task at hand, that student is handling negative emotion strategically (Tobias, 1985).

As another example, consider what can happen when students become aware when their interest wanes during a science lesson. They might seek ways to make the material more personally engaging. Many teachers try to make lessons more interesting for students, but when *students* can make themselves more interested in a subject—when they can alter a science task by using a computer, working with a classmate, or finding a new medium for testing a hypothesis—their volitional behavior adds value to the teacher's best intentions. When teachers instruct students in emotion-control strategies and encourage them to find their own ways to become interested, students can play an important role in the instructional process.

Students also have positive emotions in school, pleasurable feelings that can be capitalized on when they occur. For example, research has shown that students who learn to visualize themselves successfully completing difficult tasks promote their own feelings of efficacy (Schunk, 1994). When these successes are visualized, a student can intentionally bring about the pleasurable experience of "flow" (Csikszentmihalyi, 1975)—an emotion so pleasurable, people want to continually experience it. Testimonials from successful writers, scientists, and statesmen suggest that many of these individuals have linked pleasurable feelings to their school efforts (Zimmerman, 1990).

Control of environment. More rudimentary than the previous two "strategies that engage the mind" (Pressley et al., 1989), the action control strategies in a third category include the basic ways in which students can mobilize external resources to help structure and simplify their work environments. As with the other two categories, students use these control strategies to direct their efforts toward goals.

Gathering reference materials and conducting interviews before writing about a subject is an example of mobilization of external resources, as are the use of organizing tools such as maps and outlines to collect written thoughts; finding work materials, partners, and quiet locations to study; and planning time requirements carefully. Teachers often teach students to plan and organize environmental resources in the early grades; teachers report that helping students learn these strategies is a large part of the curriculum through third grade. This basic category of volitional control provides a stepping stone toward mastery of the more sophisticated volitional strategies just described. Other, more subtle, examples of environmental control strategies include deliberately dividing tasks into smaller clusters of sequential steps, expertly seeking information from a more knowledgeable adult or peer, and pressing beyond the explicit bounds of a task to probe into hidden meanings of actions and events.

Considering the last of these subtle environmental manipulations, we know, for example, that tacit (or untaught) information can be acquired from skillful resource manipulation in tasks. What happens when students deliberately ask questions about things not explicitly taught in a lesson? They are trying to uncover important cues for optimal performance of a task, which is a very sophisticated environmental manipulation. In literature or in social studies, for example, such careful attention can help students learn the most important information.

Identifying crucial conditions in the social, political, or historical context—the subtext of written work—often inspires precisely the kinds of deeper interpretations that teachers wish for students to reach. Students can learn to push beyond the bounds of school assignments to look for information not contained in history textbooks, to look for ways that narratives reflect the times in which they were written, and to question the rules of culture and convention that underlie the practice of even science and mathematics. By routinely asking, "What is *not* being taught here?" a student can gain tacit knowledge about school subjects. Tacit knowledge has been shown to make the difference between average and exceptional performance in various activities outside school (Sternberg & Wagner, 1993). Future research might investigate how teachers can more actively promote such skillful resource manipulation so that all students can learn how to acquire tacit knowledge.

Summary. The examples of volitional strategies demonstrate that the early acquisition of volitional control will support students' mental engagement with their work. Each category of strategies we have defined can enhance student engagement and persistence with tasks. When tasks are successfully completed by students, the experience becomes self-reinforcing; students are more likely to experience future successes (Bandura, 1977).

Although we have described each category of volitional control strategies separately, it is important to emphasize that volition involves more than learning lists of strategies. Theory and research argue that the most successful students develop a "conscientious workstyle" through the display of similar behavior across different situations (Messick, 1989). Both effective and ineffective workstyles can become stereotypes for students. Teachers observe students' stylistic preferences and begin to describe them in stylistic terms: "She is a good worker" or "He has trouble completing tasks." If students internalize these labels, they can ultimately influence their future expectations and choices (Weiner, 1990).

More Conclusions from Research

What else has research discovered about the role of volition in education? It has been found that students who report using action control strategies in academic situations also display learning that is more efficient, more codified, and deeper (see Zimmerman & Schunk, 1989, or Pintrich, 1990, for reviews of this research). Action control supports school *learning* as well as engagement. In addition, students who display productive follow through as a workstyle in high school do better on a number of indicators of success in college—including student leadership and nonacademic accomplishments (Willingham, 1985). As mentioned, a conscientious work orientation is one of the best predictors of success in the workplace (Barrick & Mount, 1991). Perhaps most important, the routine combination of learning and volitional strategies has been shown to enable students to become self-regulated—to do what they say they want to do in most any circumstance (Schunk & Zimmerman, 1994).

Empirical studies have documented a number of different ways that students can direct learning and volitional self-management strategies toward success in different subject areas (see, for example, Dole et al., 1991, in reading; Mandinach & Cline, 1994, in science and mathematics; and Harris & Graham, 1992, and Zellermayer et al., 1991, in writing). And yet, research also has shown that both in and outside school self-regulated learning is the exception rather than the rule. Even when students know how to self-regulate, they do not always do it. Self-regulated learning is not the easiest way to learn (Butler & Winne, 1995). Because many students experience effort as aversive, they need to learn how to voluntarily control the tendency to do less work (Eisenberger, 1992). The strategic use of self-regulated learning according to perceived need is considered the highest demonstration of volitional capability (Heckhausen & Kuhl, 1985).

Researchers also have attempted to teach various learning and volitional control strategies to students who need to learn them. This work has found that, particularly in the early grades, it is important to discuss with students when and under what conditions strate-

Corno & Randi

gies ought to be applied (Pressley et al., 1985). Strategies also have been taught in courses for college preparation and special education, and several more-to-less direct approaches to strategy instruction have been tried (Pintrich, 1995; Sawyer, Graham, & Harris, 1992).

The most intriguing research with elementary and middle school students recognizes the important interrelations among four psychological functions: the ways that student cognition, emotion, motivation, and volition promote one another in appropriate situations (Snow, Corno, & Jackson, 1996). Guthrie and Wigfield's vignette in the introduction to this volume provides an example of this kind of research. These authors describe the teaching of cognitive and volitional strategies through integrated science and literature activities. The students, including Robert and Kantu, become better scientists and readers through direct application of the strategies they learn in this context.

One interpretation of Guthrie and Wigfield's vignette is that target students are encouraged by the teacher to ask pointed questions, which guide their comprehension and help them form conjectures (cognitive strategies). They collectively establish rules for careful data gathering and cross-checking in small groups (volitional strategies). Ultimately, the students come to understand some fundamental and enduring relations between literature and science (learning outcomes). All of these objectives are addressed in the context of activities that the teacher knows will be fun, interesting, and reinforcing (motivating and emotionally engaging) for the students. By developing a tailored and integrated (engaging) curriculum, the teacher handles the twin demons of tedium and taxing effort. Without the interference of boredom or frustration, and with the possibilities of choice and cooperation, the students are able to tackle the learning and management strategies that will deepen their knowledge of science and literary content. The classroom environment supports the application of taught strategies so students cannot easily avoid their appropriate application. Guthrie and Wigfield's vignette represents an engagement perspective on literacy that differs from a traditional approach to fifth-grade reading and language arts.

The relations among the four psychological functions in education—cognition, emotion, motivation, and volition—should be clear. It is difficult to stimulate deep cognition without addressing aspects of motivation and emotion, but these qualities alone do not ensure that students will follow through on their best intentions. The implementation of intentions is volitional. The more a student engages cognition, emotion, motivation, and volition in school pursuits, the more likely he or she will develop a personally productive workstyle. It is critical to note again that school environments need to afford students opportunities to engage these functions.

It might be tempting to ask, why would there be any need for students to exert strategic action control when there is a rich and engaging school environment, or to argue that students cannot be expected to do the work that teachers should be doing to make school environments engaging. Engaging environments are created by everyone concerned, and rich, integrated, or theme-based curricula that embed learning and volitional strategies within classroom instruction do not in any way minimize academic challenge. Some students more than others inevitably will feel burdened by academic challenge. Even in an engaged literacy curriculum, some students will need to learn strategic action control. Moreover, action control remains a highly useful skill under other classroom circumstances: for example, when the goals are vague or the work is not engaging. As Guthrie and Wigfield also note, the average classroom environment does not reflect an engagement perspective on literacy. Volition is critical to the accomplishment of other life tasks that demand sustained effort despite distractions and competing goals (see Corno & Kanfer, 1993).

What does research say about when and how volition develops in children? Current evidence suggests that few students begin to display strategic volition naturally before age 7 (Kuhl & Kraska, 1989). Children develop action control capabilities as they do other meta-level capabilities—through exposure to various situations that afford opportunities for assuming responsibility, self-monitoring, and executive control (Brown et al., 1983). Adult and peer guidance and scaffolding play key roles in establishing any child's particular developmental trajectory.

However, developmental accomplishments vary with opportunities. Most young children will benefit from direct or embedded strategy instruction in school, beginning with basic ways to manage the task environment, and gradually moving toward the more sophisticated strategies we have described. They also will benefit from implicit teachings in task situations designed to afford self-regulatory opportunities: for example, homework and group projects include tacit knowledge about effective work strategies that can be extracted for future use (Xu, 1994). Structured activities outside school also can teach volitional strategies implicitly; these include some jobs, community group, or club programs (Corno, 1995; McLaughlin, Irby, & Langman, 1994).

There is more than one way for students to develop self-regulated learning. Many situations have the potential to afford opportunities for developing volition. Part of the agenda for ongoing research in this area is to characterize classes of situations that have essentially similar or functionally equivalent effects. Teachers and researchers need to work together to determine the range and classes of situations that might develop rudimentary to sophisticated volitional and self-regulatory knowledge and skills in children.

Summary

Before considering how educators can be made more aware of how to develop volitional skills in children, let us summarize the aspects of motivation and volition previously discussed (see the figure on pages 59–61).

The set of targeted questions in the Reference Guide for Addressing Motivational and Volitional Goals in Educational Settings could be used by teachers, parents, or others who work with children to plan curriculum for subject areas, interdisciplinary projects, materials, or assessment tools. This guide provides questions that can be used to include motivational and volitional goals in various designated activities. For example, teachers could design a curriculum unit or lesson that attends to the questions listed here, or they could take a favorite lesson and modify it to address the questions. This set of questions also could be used as an evaluation instrument, a checklist, for examining the motivational

A Reference Guide for Addressing Motivational and Volitional Goals in Educational Settings

Motivation: Promoting Commitments in Education
How does the proposed curriculum address the aspects of learners' motivation?

Values, Attitudes, Interests, and Beliefs
1. What do learners already know, believe, or feel about the topics and goals of instruction?
2. In what way does the instruction require learners to use previous knowledge or to modify previously held knowledge or beliefs?
3. In what way do materials and instruction reflect learners' values and interests or capitalize on available knowledge about a subject?

Expectations for Success
1. To what extent do learners believe they can succeed in this setting, in learning this material?
2. In what ways does the instruction encourage learners to expect success and feel good about themselves as learners? How are tasks presented in manageable segments, and how are benchmarks for progress noted?
3. How does the instruction link to learners' prior successes in similar tasks or demonstrate how previous unsuccessful experiences differ from the learner's experiences with this task?

Learning and Performance Expectations
1. What are learners' own reachable goals for this effort, and to what extent do these goals fit with curricular goals? Are both sets of expectations neither too high nor too low?
2. How do the curriculum, the reward system, and the instruction help students toward accomplishment of these goals? In what ways do they promote deep and intentional learning, rather than simply trying to get the work done?
3. What are the opportunities for learners to display their best performance without pressure?
4. How can learners receive valued reinforcement for accomplishments? What types of rewards are inherent in accomplishing the task itself? How are learners encouraged to revise their work to meet standards?
5. In what ways are learners encouraged to equate success with their own efforts?

Self-Evaluations
1. What are learners telling themselves about their effort and performance as they work toward goals?
2. In what ways are learners' self-evaluations either corrected (if negative) or reinforced (if positive)? How do corrections emphasize what the student did right? How do corrections make it clear that outcomes are sometimes beyond personal control? How do corrections signal a second try?
3. What opportunities are there for learners to compare work with others who are working toward competence, coping with difficulties? Once mastery occurs, what opportunities are there for learners to compare their work with more competent performers?

(continued)

A Reference Guide for Addressing Motivational and Volitional Goals in Educational Settings *(continued)*

Volition: Protecting Commitments in Education

How does the proposed curriculum address the aspects of learners' volition?

I. In what ways are volitional strategies taught—modeled by the teacher and labeled for learners, both when the teacher does the modeling and when learners use the strategies? How are volitional strategies also taught implicitly through the curriculum (for example, as themes in literature, as a context for historical events, or as part of the process of doing science)?

Control of Motivation-Related Cognition

1. What strategies are learners given to prioritize and handle competing goals?

2. How are learners helped to check their own work and give themselves credit as progress is made toward goals?

3. What procedures are learners shown for instructing themselves when temporarily stopped and for imagining themselves doing work well?

Emotion Control

1. What signs are learners asked to observe in monitoring their emotional states while they learn? What are learners instructed to tell themselves when interest wanes, anxiety arises, the mind wanders, or fatigue sets in?

2. What opportunities are learners given to think of ways to complete tasks that will make them more fun, challenging, or reassuring about eventual success?

3. How are learners encouraged to visualize themselves doing successful work?

Control of the Environment

1. How are learners encouraged to streamline and personalize tasks as an aid to concentration and minimizing distractions?

2. What sort of discussion is there of various ways to cope with difficult tasks in the curriculum? —to push beyond the bounds of a task?

3. How does the curriculum provide choices for learners in how and at what pace to complete tasks? How are learners allowed to make choices about different but equally acceptable ways to accomplish the same tasks?

4. How are learners encouraged to use available teacher, peer, and material resources for accomplishing goals? In what ways are learners helped to view the search for resources as a positive way to approach tasks, and not as a mark of cheating or failing to do the work on their own?

5. To what extent are learners free to express disappointment with scarce resources and to find alternative ways to garner resources for their work? To what extent are learners encouraged to question the assumptions and conventions of work they are asked to complete or lessons they are taught? To what extent are learners helped to raise questions about the social, political, and historical contexts of their work?

(continued)

A Reference Guide for Addressing Motivational and Volitional Goals in Educational Settings *(continued)*

II. In what ways are learners encouraged to adopt a conscientious workstyle?

1. How is a well-defined work ethic formally conveyed to students and evaluated?
2. How are learners helped to avoid impulsive actions and plan their work?
3. In what ways are learners taught that reflection and careful planning aid in the eventual accomplishment of almost every task?
4. What are learners told to tell themselves to avoid procrastination, continue to persist, and delay the gratification for desired rewards?
5. In what ways are learners taught to check and revise their work? What other strategies are offered for learning how to persist if there is difficulty?
6. What opportunities for mental rehearsal are provided to help learners visualize themselves inhibiting behavior not conducive to success or taking risks and following through on tasks?
7. What techniques (such as checklists or self-reinforcement) are learners shown to help support follow through?
8. How is conscientiousness noted, rewarded, or appreciated by teachers, peers, and learners themselves?

and volitional aspects of commercially developed curricula. It could be used similarly to analyze videotapes of classroom lessons in which the quality of student engagement may be an important consideration.

Collaborative Innovation

In the beginning of this chapter, we stressed that teachers play a critical role in moving students toward an engagement perspective on literacy in their classrooms. However, it is unlikely that teachers can provide their students appropriate opportunities unless they themselves experience similar opportunities for self-regulated learning and guided practice in acquiring and using motivational and volitional strategies. How many schools afford teachers legitimate opportunities to alter teaching tasks in ways that make them more interesting, or permit faculty members to manage their own time and resources? How have teachers been encouraged to evaluate their own work in ways that preserve self-worth and dignity rather than focus on their own personal or professional deficiencies? In a craft as contextual and varied as teaching, the ability to acquire tacit knowledge may be critical to exceptional performance (Sternberg & Wagner, 1993). *Collaborative innovation,* a form of teacher-researcher collaboration, affords both teachers and researchers opportunities to manage their own learning and to infer theory from practice to enable them to offer students similar opportunities.

Historically, teacher professional development has encouraged replication of research-based practices. In the tradition of instructional systems or programs, staff development intended to move students toward an engagement perspective on literacy would provide teachers with materials and instructional procedures for implementing the engagement perspective and "train" the teachers in how to use them (Joyce & Showers, 1980). Teachers would be told that the trainer's goal is to help them reach the closest possible approximations to an ideal model (Southern, Jones, & Stanley, 1993). Two underlying assumptions in this approach are that researchers know best what is good classroom practice with this perspective and that teachers need to be "trained" through participant modeling (Bandura, 1977).

New understandings of how teachers learn have shed a critical light on this version of teacher professional development. These understandings have led to a "more expanded view of teacher development that encourages teachers to involve themselves as learners—in much the same way as they wish their students would" (Lieberman, 1995, p. 592). Staff development now affords teachers opportunities for their own self-regulated learning. The recognition from modern psychological theory that students actively coconstruct knowledge from task environments, according to their aptitudes and other predispositions, has demanded alternatives to whole-group, teacher-centered classroom instruction. As described by others in this volume, these alternatives include engaging activities and materials attuned to student interests, conversational dialogues as a primary vehicle for curricular delivery, and the provision of multiple and varied opportunities for all students to learn and to display what they know (see also Presidential Task Force on Psychology in Education, American Psychological Association, 1993). Schools are now being viewed as professional communities; teachers, researchers, and administrators are all continual learners, who learn in ways not unlike the ways their students learn (Lieberman, 1992, 1995). And teachers are now being viewed as innovators who may legitimately replace externally developed innovations with their own ideas (Randi & Corno, in press).

A Definition of Collaborative Innovation

Collaborative innovation can be defined as the process whereby teachers work together with a larger school community that includes researchers to construct, assess, and describe new classroom practices consistent with conceptual underpinnings of changing curricular standards, instructional models, and the changing needs of students. Research suggests that the introduction of any novel perspective in classrooms, including an engagement perspective on literacy, benefits greatly from collaborative innovation (Randi, 1996).

Collaborative innovation may have been practiced by some teachers before researchers labeled it "collaborative innovation." Some teachers have adapted research-based curriculum innovations to the particular needs of their students, adjusting them until they worked (see, for example, Hawthorne, 1992). Still others, some in classrooms with their students and others with colleagues, invented their own instructional practices, abstracting principles from the models they were encouraged to imitate (Connelly & Clandinin, 1988; Randi, 1996). These teachers may be said to have engaged in a collaborative innovation process with the instructional innovations provided them.

Formal opportunities are now available for teachers to engage in collaborative innovation with researchers who can personally play a role in helping teachers as they struggle to integrate findings into their own curricula. Such collaborations can result in the development of new instructional practices and assessments when research-based concepts are embedded directly into curriculum content. They ultimately should make teachers more motivated and volitional about their teaching, just as an engagement perspective on literacy should make students more motivated and volitional about their schoolwork.

How Collaborative Innovation May Promote Teacher Motivation and Volition

The collaborative innovation process has a set of assumptions and methods consistent with an engagement perspective on literacy. First, it is assumed that participants will be co-constructing knowledge about how to change identified classroom curricula and instruction and will be gathering a diverse array of complex information that can be used to provide meaningful interpretation of results. Thus, teachers' own motivation will be addressed. Second, teachers as learners will be offered the same kind of supportive scaffolds for following through on their innovations that they are being asked to provide for their students. Extending the time period for collecting information permits the kind of adjusting of materials and lessons that teachers use to maximize student response (Bullock, 1995). When documentation takes the form of qualitative narrative—a form of research that has been developing in recent years—the results are readily available to other teachers as well. So far, evidence suggests that participating teachers can be described as engaged with the material and the effort, invested in positive outcomes, and engaged in generating creative lessons, similar to how students have been described when classrooms adopt an engagement perspective on literacy.

Collaborative innovation is motivated by a view of teaching as a task involving situated learning by students—learning dependent on a host of contextual and individual difference factors and constraints (Greeno, 1989). It is assumed that teachers are knowledgeable professionals who aim to do their best for students in given settings (Lieberman & Miller, 1992). Collaborative innovation reflects the adaptive invention by teachers of fresh practices consistent with innovative theories of education yet personally attuned to the unique and varied contexts of their own classrooms. It is this kind of creative adaptation of classroom situations that is called for in promoting literacy engagement and in developing self-regulatory capabilities in children.

The tension between this new and the more traditional conceptions of teacher professional development parallels that of literacy engagement with more traditional teaching of reading and writing in the elementary grades. Interestingly, the roots of both collaborative innovation and the engagement perspective on literacy stretch back to Dewey, who has written extensively about both motivation and volition (Dewey, 1904).

An Example from Research

An example from research can be used to illustrate how collaborative innovation promotes and supports teachers' taking an engagement perspective on literacy. Duffy (1993) carried out a study designed to help elementary teachers incorporate comprehension strategy instruction into their literacy curricula. Instead of providing teachers with curriculum kits, Duffy's teachers were asked to construct their own lessons. In monthly work sessions, teachers and researchers discussed the growing body of research on elaborative reading and comprehension strategies, including theory that supported classroom implications. Duffy and his colleagues visited teachers' classrooms twice a month to provide models, suggestions, and assistance. Their intent was not to rate the teachers' approximation to a model, but to observe and offer suggestions. Their data include observations of the classrooms, interviews with the teachers, and interviews with students targeted for intensive instruction. Cases constructed for 11 teachers in four districts document teachers' progress toward adaptive expertise in comprehension strategy instruction.

Most important, Duffy found that no two teachers were alike in their adaptations of the research on strategy instruction. As a group, their progress was nonlinear: teachers worked on their strategy instruction in fits and starts, with each new effort incorporating knowledge learned previously. At times teachers were confident or confused, faithful or tentative, and stable or unstable. As teachers progressed, Duffy defined a point of "creative invention," at which time his teachers no longer followed a predefined list of strategies. Instead, they decided at that point what strategies to use, revised those strategies, and invented new strategies based on cues from their students. These teachers made the innovation their own.

This study involves a new kind of professional development with teachers, and reflects research conducted on practice. As suggested by Richardson (1994), practical research helps "describe what it means to think like a teacher and what is entailed in teacher change" (p. 8). Such research offers a new respect for teachers, and this may explain the effectiveness of collaborative innovation for bringing about classroom change that is reflective of developing theory and research.

Conclusion

The chapters in this volume address students' growth in literacy engagement with appropriate kinds of teaching, how an engagement perspective on literacy appears in teaching practice, and how to document students' engagement in literacy in the early grades. This chapter has described some underlying aspects of literacy engagement, with particular emphasis on volition as it relates to constructs of motivation and school accomplishment. The intent was to illustrate the generality and reach of these concepts—to show how the constructs of motivation and volition have equal meaning for the work of teachers and students, and equal meaning for work in and out of school. Students ultimately become active contributors to society as employees and members of community service organizations that demand voluntary sustained effort. And teachers are perhaps the most important students of innovative educational practices; their voluntary sustained efforts help continue education.

We also have argued in this chapter that the widespread adoption of an engagement perspective on literacy in classrooms appears dependent on collaborative work with practicing teachers. Collaborative innovation is not traditional staff development for teachers, so it is used fittingly with an engagement perspective on literacy and with other instructional innovations. Among the important outcomes of collaborative innovation are engaged workstyles by teachers who view themselves as educational innovators, practitioners who are self-regulated learners with a disposition for incorporating research into their teaching, and documented models of innovative practice for use by others.

References

Bandura, A. (1977). *Social learning theory*. Englewood Cliffs, NJ: Prentice Hall.

Barrick, M.R., & Mount, M.D. (1991). The big five personality dimensions and job performance: A meta-analysis. *Personnel Psychology, 44,* 1–26.

Brown, A.L., Bransford, J.D., Ferrara, R., & Campione, J. (1983). Learning, remembering, and understanding. In J. Flavell & E. Markman (Eds.), *Carmichael's manual of child psychology* (Vol. 5, pp. 77–166). New York: Wiley.

Bullock, M. (1995). What's so special about a longitudinal study? *Psychological Science Agenda, 8*(4), 9–10.

Butler, D.L., & Winne, P.H. (1995). Feedback and self-regulated learning: A theoretical synthesis. *Review of Educational Research, 65,* 245–282.

Connelly, F.M., & Clandinin, J. (1988). *Teachers as curriculum planners*. New York: Teachers College Press.

Corno, L. (1993). The best-laid plans: Modern conceptions of volition and educational research. *Educational Researcher, 22*(2), 14–22.

Corno, L. (1995). Working toward foresight and follow-through. *Mid-Western Educational Researcher, 8,* 2–10.

Corno, L., & Kanfer, R. (1993). The role of volition in learning and performance. In L. Darling-Hammond (Ed.), *Review of research in education* (pp. 301–341). Washington, DC: American Educational Research Association.

Csikszentmihalyi, M. (1975). *Beyond boredom and anxiety*. San Francisco, CA: Jossey-Bass.

Dewey, J. (1904). The relation of theory to practice in the education of teachers. In C. McMurry (Ed.), *The relation of theory to practice in the education of teachers* (Third Yearbook of the National Society for the Scientific Study of Education, Part I, pp. 9–30. Chicago, IL: University of Chicago Press.

Dole, J.A., Duffy, G.G., Roehler, L.R., & Pearson, P.D. (1991). Moving from the old to the new: Research on reading comprehension instruction. *Review of Educational Research, 61,* 239–264.

Duffy, G.G. (1993). Teachers' progress toward becoming expert strategy teachers. *The Elementary School Journal, 94*, 109–120.

Eisenberger, R. (1992). Learned industriousness. *Psychological Review, 99*, 248–267.

Greeno, J. (1989). Situations, mental models, and generative knowledge. In D. Klahr & K. Kotovosky (Eds.), *Complex information processing: The impact of Herbert A. Simon* (pp. 285–318). Hillsdale, NJ: Erlbaum.

Harris, K.R., & Graham, S. (1992). *Helping young writers master the craft: Strategy instruction and self-regulation in the writing process.* Cambridge, MA: Brookline.

Hawthorne, R.K. (1992). *Curriculum in the making.* New York: Teachers College Press.

Heckhausen, H., & Kuhl, J. (1985). From wishes to action: The dead ends and short cuts on the long way to action. In M. Frese & J. Sabini (Eds.)., *Goal directed behavior: The concept of action in psychology* (pp. 134–160). Hillsdale, NJ: Erlbaum.

Joyce, B., & Showers, B. (1980). Improving inservice training: The messages of research. *Educational Leadership, 37*, 379–385.

Kuhl, J., & Kraska, K. (1989). Self-regulation and metamotivation: Computational mechanisms, development, and assessment. In R. Kanfer, P.L. Ackerman, & R. Cudeck (Eds.), *Abilities, motivation, and methodology: The Minnesota Symposium on Individual Differences* (pp. 343–374). Hillsdale, NJ: Erlbaum.

Lieberman, A. (1992). The meaning of scholarly activity and the building of community. *Educational Researcher, 21*(6), 5–12.

Lieberman, A. (1995). Practices that support teacher development: Transforming conceptions of professional learning. *Phi Delta Kappan, 76*, 591–596.

Lieberman, A., & Miller, L.. (1992). The professional development of teachers. In M.C. Alkin (Ed.), *Encyclopedia of educational research* (Vol. 3, 6th ed., pp. 1045–1053). New York: Macmillan.

McLauglin, M.W., Irby, M.A., & Langman, J. (1994). *Urban sanctuaries: Neighborhood organizations in the lives and futures of inner-city youth.* San Francisco, CA: Jossey-Bass.

Mandinach, E.B., & Cline, H.T. (1994). *Classroom dynamics: Implementing a technology-based learning environment.* Hillsdale, NJ: Erlbaum.

Messick, S. (1989). *Cognitive style and personality: Scanning and orientation toward affect* (Research Memo No. 89-16). Princeton, NJ: Educational Testing Service.

Pintrich, P.R. (1990). Implications of psychological research on student learning and college teaching for teacher education. In W.R. Houston (Ed.), *Handbook of research on teacher education* (pp. 826–857). New York: Macmillan.

Pintrich, P.R. (Ed.). (1995). *Understanding self-regulated learning.* San Francisco, CA: Jossey-Bass.

Presidential Task Force on Psychology in Education, American Psychological Association. (1993). *Learner-centered psychological principles: Guidelines for school redesign and reform.* Denver, CO: Mid-Continental Regional Laboratory.

Pressley, M., Forrest-Pressley, D., Elliott-Faust, D., & Miller, G. (1985). Children's use of cognitive strategies, how to teach strategies, and what to do if they can't be taught. In M. Pressley & C.J. Brainerd (Eds.), *Cognitive learning and memory in children* (pp. 1–47). New York: Springer-Verlag.

Pressley, M., Goodchild, F., Fleet, J., Zajchowski, R., & Evans, E. (1989). The challenges of classroom strategy instruction. *The Elementary School Journal, 89*, 301–342.

Randi, J. (1996). *From imitation to invention: The nature of innovation in teachers' classrooms.* Unpublished doctoral dissertation, Teachers College, Columbia University, New York, NY.

Randi, J., & Corno, L. (in press). Teachers as innovators. In B.J. Biddle, T.L. Good, & I.F. Goodson (Eds.), *International handbook of teachers and teaching.* New York: Kluwer.

Richardson, V. (1994). Conducting research on practice. *Educational Researcher, 23*(5), 5–10.

Sawyer, R., Graham, S., & Harris, K.R. (1992). Direct teaching, strategy instruction, and strategy instruction with explicit self-regulation: Effects on learning disabled students' compositions and self-efficacy. *Journal of Educational Psychology, 84,* 340–352.

Schunk, D.H. (1994). Self-regulation of self-efficacy and attributions in academic settings. In D.H. Schunk & B.J. Zimmerman (Eds.), *Self-regulation of learning and performance: Issues and educational applications* (pp. 75–100). Hillsdale, NJ: Erlbaum.

Schunk, D.H., & Zimmerman, B.J. (Eds.). (1994). *Self-regulation of learning and performance: Issues and educational applications.* Hillsdale, NJ: Erlbaum.

Snow, R.E., Corno, L., & Jackson, D. (1996). Individual differences in affective and conative functions. In R. Calfee & D. Berliner (Eds.), *Handbook of educational psychology* (pp. 243–310). New York: Macmillan.

Southern, W.T., Jones, E.D., & Stanley, J.C. (1993). Acceleration and enrichment: The context and development of program options. In K.A. Heller, F.J. Monks, & A.H. Passow (Eds.), *International handbook of research and development of giftedness and talent* (pp. 387–409). New York: Pergamon.

Sternberg, R.J., & Wagner, R.K. (1993). The g-ocentric view of intelligence and job performance is wrong. *Current Directions in Psychological Science, 2,* 1–4.

Tobias, S. (1985). Test anxiety: Interference, defective skills, and cognitive capacity. *Educational Psychologist, 20,* 135–142.

Weiner, B. (1990). History of motivational research in education. *Journal of Educational Psychology, 82,* 616–622.

Willingham, W. (1985). *Success in college.* New York: The College Board.

Xu, J. (1994). *Doing homework: A study of possibilities.* Unpublished doctoral dissertation, Teachers College, Columbia University, New York, NY.

Zellermayer, M., Salomon, G., Globerson, T., & Givon, H. (1991). Enhancing writing-related metacognitions through a computerized writing partner. *American Educational Research Journal, 28,* 373–391.

Zimmerman, B.J. (Ed.). (1990). Self-regulated learning and academic achievement [Special issue]. *Educational Psychologist, 25*(1).

Zimmerman, B.J., & Schunk, D.H. (1989). *Self-regulated learning and academic achievement.* New York: Academic.

The Pull of the Text and the Process of Involvement in Reading

4

Diane Lemonnier Schallert and JoyLynn Hailey Reed

There is a story we tell of a time when one of us lost herself so totally in the reading of a story that an entire afternoon of sessions at a conference quickly passed, unattended, while page after page of the story flew by, characters came to life, and a lived experience of another time and place transpired. There are for some texts and for some readers these kinds of occasions when text and reader create an intense experience of imaginative processes suffused with deep comprehension and vibrant emotions. Because of a turn of events or a character's plight in a story, the reader may become extremely sad, and yet the experience is sought after and described as pleasurable. How might we describe such an experience psychologically, textually, and contextually? By contrast, imagine a teacher conducting a traditional reading lesson, prodding students into replaying the facts of a story and leading them question by question to make statements that are taken to represent their understanding of the story. What is the difference between a child who approaches reading as an assigned school activity and another who loses himself or herself in stories? What is the difference between a student who reads for his or her own pleasure and the student who reads a text because his or her friends are talking about it in the literature conversation groups the teacher has incorporated in the instruction?

In this chapter, we will consider the empirical and theoretical literature that would inform an understanding of what it means to be involved in what one is reading, the antecedents of such an experience, the concomitants, and the consequences. We believe that current conceptions of motivation and emotion, mostly from the psychological and educational psychological literature, will contribute to a developing understanding of the complex interplay among readers' motivations, emotions, and the fabric of social interactions in the reading environment.

Our focus on involvement—the experience a reader has when engrossed by the author's creation of the textual world—embodies the contrast between the socioconstructivist view, a framework more widely known among and espoused by literacy researchers than among motivation researchers, and a psychological perspective, a view more familiar and prevalent among motivation researchers. The deep involvement in reading that we are considering is described as a solitary, private, almost secret experience. Yet, involvement can be portrayed to be as much socially constructed as any other literacy experience. It can be considered to result from a reader's willing surrender to the author, who offers ideas that organize the reader's emotional and cognitive responses in culturally resonant ways. In addition, involvement can be analyzed from the perspective of readers' responses to tasks, both self-initiated and imposed, that can make literacy events part of the social negotiation of meaning. In this chapter, we will consider textual, psychological, and contextual perspectives on involvement, keeping in mind the interplay between the individual, psychological nature of literacy experiences and their jointly constructed social nature. However, first we need to differentiate among terms that are often used in research literature and are closely related to the underlying psychological phenomenon of involvement.

Distinguishing Among Interest, Engagement, and Involvement

Interest and *engagement* are two constructs that are sometimes used interchangeably with each other and with *involvement*. Of the three, the term *engagement* is arguably the most widely used in current reading research literature, and it also can be described as the most general in terms of what it encompasses. Representative are the views of Guthrie, Van Meter, and their colleagues (1996), who describe engagement as "the joint functioning of motivations and strategies during reading" (p. 1). As Alvermann and Guthrie (1993) state, engaged readers

> acquire the competencies and motivations to read for diverse purposes, such as gaining knowledge, performing a task, interpreting an author's perspective, sharing reactions to stories and informational text, escaping into the literary world, or taking social and political action in response to what is read. Highly engaged readers are motivated, knowledgeable, and socially interactive. (p. 2)

Both intrinsic and extrinsic motivational states are included in the definition of engagement, and engagement refers to a set of activity-related processes rather than a psychological state.

Also widely cited in reading research literature, *interest* has been used to describe both a text characteristic, referred to as situational interest, and a person variable. Krapp, Hidi, and Renninger (1992) define individual interest as

> dispositions that develop over time...are relatively stable, and are usually associated with increased knowledge, positive emotions, and increased reference value. (p. 6)

They define situational interest as

> generated by certain stimulus characteristics (e.g., life themes, novelty) and tend to be shared among individuals. Because this type of interest may be evoked suddenly by some-

> thing in the environment, it often has only a short-term effect and marginal influence on the subject's knowledge and reference system. It may, however, have a more permanent effect and serve as the basis for the emergence of individual interest. (p. 6)

In these descriptions, interest is rarely portrayed as a reader's strategic choice or in terms of how it influences the ongoing, moment-to-moment processes of reading. In contrast to how researchers have used the term *engagement*, interest does not usually refer to types of strategic processing of the text, so it is less volitional. Rather, interest is more often described as a trigger to attention deployment with the effect of aiding memory for material.

In contrast to these two constructs, we use the label *involvement* to refer to a psychological process with the following characteristics: "when an individual is involved in a task, his or her attention is wholly concentrated on that task, making a sense of time irrelevant and coinciding with deep comprehension of the task material" (Reed et al., 1996). Involvement, a process that ebbs and flows in the accomplishment of a task, is at the juncture of the cognitive and affective processes necessary for a task. In our first investigations of involvement (Reed & Schallert, 1993), our data suggest that when involvement is deep, a coupling of comprehension and concentration occurs. For example, when we say that a student is involved in a story, we mean that he or she is focusing on the reading to the exclusion of other possible tasks. Also he or she is constructing meaning that is rich and complex and that taps wide areas of tacit and explicit knowledge without much awareness of effort and striving. The instantiation of all the knowledge a reader brings to the construction of meaning when he or she comprehends the text also happens when the reader is involved. In addition, involvement adds a focused, emotional investment in the task along with a motivational drive to continue.

In terms of the relation of involvement to engagement, we see involvement as a special type of engagement. Engagement subsumes involvement in the sense that it is possible to be engaged without experiencing much involvement in a task, but it is not possible to be involved in a task without first being engaged. This distinction supposes that engagement would either precede or occur with involvement and would be necessary but not sufficient for involvement to occur. Although engagement includes the idea of invoking strategies and making conscious choices to fulfill a literacy task, strong involvement is not likely to be associated with an awareness of striving or of willing oneself to complete a task.

We have described involvement as a characteristic of a process unfolding in context, and while we believe that involvement is a democratic process in that most people can and do experience it in at least some tasks, we also see the possibility for approaching involvement as an individual difference characteristic (Csikszentmihalyi, 1990; Nell, 1988). That is, there may be individual differences in the ability or propensity to engage deeply with text. We are interested in both approaches to involvement for many reasons, including the fact that instructional manipulations may influence both enduring individual tendencies and fluctuating differences that individuals experience when engaged in particular activities.

Schallert & Reed

Textual Considerations: The Pull of the Text

What is it about some texts that leads readers to describe their experiences in phrases such as, "I found the story riveting," "I was caught by the text," or "I couldn't put it down"? What is common among these expressions is that readers are making explicit their feeling that there are some texts, or occasions of encountering texts, that seem to pull them, causing them to surrender their own ability to disengage from the print. Leaving aside for the moment the fact that some readers may have a much more developed propensity to allow print to have this power over them, we want to consider some characteristics of the texts themselves that can be counted on to produce involvement. Of course, it is a synecdoche to speak as if the text as a separate object can produce such an effect. In all cases, a text is capable of influencing a reader only when the reader begins to read. It is an accepted view in current conceptions of reading that a reader creates the text as much as the text's author does (c.f., Pearson & Tierney, 1984). Thus, in describing how texts might "pull" readers, we are explaining how certain choices made by authors are expressed in particular textual moves that appeal to readers when they encounter the text. Following, we consider three kinds of textual moves that are associated with the experience of involvement: making texts considerate, making them interesting, and making them into narratives.

Making Texts Considerate: Texts That Do Not Put Off the Reader

Let us consider a classic analysis of writing and of what a writer must do to be understood by his or her intended audience. Nystrand (1982) begins his essay with a description of what would happen if he boarded a train in Lisbon as compared with boarding one in Chicago. In Lisbon, the words uttered by native speakers of Portuguese would be incomprehensible, and he would not be able to make sense of them, whereas in Chicago, even if he did not want to be disturbed by the conversations of those around him, he would not be able to help but understand the voices he would overhear. Nystrand notes,

> In Lisbon, speakers share a certain space from which I am effectively excluded. Though not material or physical, this space is quite real, as my exclusion from the conversation clearly shows. (p. 75)

Nystrand proposes that what creates the possibility of entering into textual space with an author is the transparency to the reader of the language used. For a particular reader at a particular time, a text may be too opaque, too uninviting, and impossible for him or her to render into meaning. Text difficulty may be rooted as much in conceptual complexity or unfamiliarity as in obscurity of language and may effectively block comprehension entirely or make it effortful and unpleasant. Like a thick veil of cobwebs that block access to a newly discovered room, opaque text impedes the reader's attempts to enter into the textual world created by the author.

Since its publication, Nystrand's construct of textual space often has been used to describe what happens when readers and authors understand each other to varying degrees.

To our knowledge, it has not often been included in reflections on the motivational and emotional consequences of such interactions; yet, there is direct and indirect evidence that comprehensibility and involvement are related. For example, Nell (1988) reports a strong, positive relation between the ability to read and amount of reading, which indirectly points to the connection between an individual's likelihood of approaching an activity and how difficult he or she finds the activity. In a recent study (Reed & Schallert, 1993), we concluded from cluster analysis that involvement has two dimensions, one of which is comprehension. Later, we (Reed, Schallert, & Goetz, 1992) found that students' ratings of their own involvement as they read a 10-page academic article fluctuated systematically with features of the prose; most students rated themselves as more involved in the sections of the article that included vignettes and illustrative examples of the ideas being discussed than in the more difficult and abstract sections presenting new theoretical concepts.

It seems reasonable to conclude that one aspect of text that can pull in the reader is its comprehensibility. Although through effort a reader may be able to inhabit the textual space created by an author who, using language that is inconsiderate of the reader's needs, has violated Grice's maxims, the author-reader connection created will be fragile at best and easily disrupted. Texts that strike readers as friendly, approachable, and considerate in Armbruster's (1984) sense of the word, will more likely lead to the sort of focused, enjoyable experience that resists disengagement from reading.

Making Texts Interesting: Texts That Satisfy Curiosity and Fit a Reader's Interests

It is possible for a text to be so predictable and so easy to understand that it offers none of the delight of discovery or fascination we are ascribing to texts that capture the reader. The author Umberto Eco said in an interview,

> People always ask me, "How is it that your novels, which are so difficult, have a certain success?" I am offended by the question.... the normal reader who does not spend his day fighting with Kant or Hegel feels respected if there is a jujitsu with a novel, a resistance, a seduction. (from Eberstadt, 1995, p. 202)

This sentiment that readers enjoy the challenge of a text is in line with many related theories of motivation, curiosity, and interest. For example, Berlyne (1960) proposes that certain characteristics of environmental stimuli, such as surprise, novelty, complexity, and ambiguity, can be counted on to produce arousal in an individual and to lead to exploration. For a text to pull in a particular reader, it must have some element of novelty and ambiguity and it must somehow intrigue the reader.

Although we previously distinguished the construct of involvement from that of interest, we can learn about textual features that might cause involvement from the substantial amount of research on interest. As mentioned, researchers on interest usually make a distinction between individual interest—an individual disposition to be interested in certain topics, domains, or activities—and situational interest—a response to external conditions that elicit interest in an immediate and across-individual way. A strong individual interest might lead a reader to consider a text as having the power to hold his or her attention, when, instead, it is the reader who may be holding the text captive. A student's individual interest in a text may be an indication of an advancing stage of acquiring expertise in a domain, signaling an optimal match between interest and knowledge (Alexander, Kulikowich, & Jetton, 1994; Alexander, Kulikowich, & Schulze, 1994). Students sometimes report that an assigned reading in an advanced graduate class that had been a terrible struggle on a first reading is now enjoyable and fascinating on a subsequent reading.

However, more often students face reading tasks for which they have little individual interest. In such circumstances, how can interest come into play in triggering a state of involvement? One way could be through the use of a type of situational interest called *text-based interest* has been found to be powerful in triggering involvement (Hidi, 1990; Hidi & Anderson, 1992; Wade, 1992). Students who are reading a required assignment are likely to be drawn into their reading by features of the text such as characters with which they can identify, words that arouse vivid imagery, and texts that say the unexpected (Anderson et al., 1987; Goetz & Sadoski, 1995; Hidi, 1990; Hidi & Baird, 1988; Wade, 1992). Certain topics relating to life themes, such as death, danger, sex, power, and destruction, enhance interest. Further, the unexpected and the personally relevant also contribute to a reader's interest in a text. Most successful novelists instantiate these text-based elements into their books.

One way that textbook authors occasionally attempt to use the interest value of topics that have consensual appeal is to include vivid examples, anecdotes, or colorful language to lead individuals to read the more mundane or abstract domain concepts. Garner, Gillingham, and White (1989) term these textual moves *seductive details* and caution against their use as potential distracters from the primary intended message. In their study, Graves and colleagues (1991) compared memorability and interest level of and affective responses to four versions of texts on the same topics: the first version comprised selections from a high school history textbook, and the other three versions were produced by three separate teams of writers (composition teachers, Time-Life editors, and text linguists) who were asked to rewrite the textbook to enhance its memorability and comprehensibility. Findings suggest that students recalled a higher proportion of material in the text revised by composition teachers because the text incorporated text-based interest elements. In contrast, the revisions by Time-Life editors relied on nontext-based interest, inserting pieces of information ("nuggets") that distracted readers' attention from the main points of the text itself (see Garner et al., 1991, for a discussion on seductive details and Goetz & Sadoski, 1995 for a criticism of the seductive details research). This is a complex literature and it needs more consideration, but at this point, suffice it to say that the phenomenon, were it to be supported, would exemplify what we mean when we say that the text "pulls" the reader.

The Pull of the Text and the Process of Involvement in Reading

Making Texts into Narratives: No Escape from Stories

If there is one feature of a text that can be counted on to produce a high degree of involvement in readers, it is the riveting sort of beginning to a story that immediately grabs the reader and lands him or her in the middle of events unfolding in the inexorable way that fiction ascribes to life. Children and adults alike generally prefer stories to informational text, especially for pleasure reading (Nell, 1988). If readers were given two texts, both of which incorporate features to enhance interest, we suspect that readers would choose the narration to read. Recall that when we asked students to read an academic article that contained narratives interspersed with theoretical interpretations (Reed, Schallert, and Goetz, 1992), it was the narrative segments that students rated as more involving, interesting, and memorable.

What is it about stories that makes them so captivating? One answer to this question comes from the approach to literary criticism that is called *reader response theory*. In Rosenblatt's (1978) formulation, mentioned in the introduction to this volume, reading involves a transaction with print from which a text is created. Thus, there is no dominance ascribed to the text in re-creating an author's meaning; rather, it is the reader who re-creates within his or her sphere of possible experiences the text's meaning at that time. The individual may read the text again later and create a slightly different meaning based on his or her subsequent thoughts about and experiences away from the text. In this view, the interaction between reader and author through the vehicle of text is dynamic and recursive. The concept of text becomes much more than the written words and expands to embrace both the reader's and the writer's experience. What captivates the reader is an author who has evoked memories of past real and imagined events.

Stories are good at ambushing a reader because they combine and re-create everyday life events in a narrative sequence that is embellished and made "larger than life." Fisher (1989) proposes that people see the world through a narrative paradigm:

> The presuppositions that undergird the narrative paradigm are the following: (1) Humans are essentially storytellers. (2) The paradigmatic mode of human decision making and communication is "good reasons," which vary in form among situations, genre, and media of communication. (3) The production and practice of good reasons are ruled by matters of history, biography, culture, and character.... (4) Rationality is determined by the nature of persons as narrative beings—their inherent awareness of narrative probability, what constitutes a coherent story, and their constant habit of testing narrative fidelity, whether or not the stories they experience ring true with the stories they know to be true in their lives.... (5) The world as we know it is a set of stories, the means by which humans realize their nature as reasoning-valuing animals. The philosophical ground of the narrative paradigm is ontology. The materials of the narrative paradigm are symbols, signs of consubstantiation, and good reasons, the communicative expressions of social reality. (pp. 64–65)

Thus, being pulled into a story is inherently human in its invitation to the reader to consult with the author in creating a narration. The story creates possible ways to see the processes of life that help legitimize experiences a reader may think are idiosyncratic. Like Narcissus, the reader finds it difficult to look away from the mirrored re-creations of himself.

Psychological Considerations: The Process of Involvement

If making a text approachable and interesting and able to capitalize on the narrative tendencies of readers were the only requirement to increase memorability, motivate readers, and enhance learning, many of the issues that reading researchers and teachers grapple with would have been resolved long ago. However, the interactions between readers and texts are not so simply prescribed by author choices alone. Reading calls on participants to mobilize their motivation and emotions as well as cognition. In this section, we explore this intertwined set of processes, the psychological experience of being engrossed in a textual encounter, that is invoked and experienced while readers meet authors through texts.

The process of involvement is a phenomenon that most have experienced in some activity, found satisfying, and hope to re-create in the future. While involved, a reader will lose track of time then emerge with positive affect and increased comprehension. In our description of the dynamic swelling and ebbing of a reader's involvement with text, we think we come closest to the constructs described by the psychologist Csikszentmihalyi (1975, 1990) and the reading researcher Nell (1988). Csikszentmihalyi has spent more than 20 years investigating what he calls "optimal experiences," occasions when individuals become so engrossed by the activity they have undertaken that they lose themselves in the task. What leads to this sense of an optimal experience, according to Csikszentmihalyi (1990),

> is order in consciousness...when psychic energy—or attention—is invested in realistic goals, and when skills match the opportunities for action. The pursuit of a goal brings order in awareness because a person must concentrate attention on the task at hand and momentarily forget everything else. (p. 6)

As mentioned by other authors in this volume, Csikszentmihalyi uses the word "flow" to describe individuals' state of mind as they are engaged in an activity that stretches and challenges their abilities and that they pursue for its own sake. Although Csikszentmihalyi did not study flow in reading, our own work with involvement has been influenced by his description of the parameters that need to be in place for flow to occur, of the experience itself, and of the deep enjoyment and increased competence that results from flow experiences.

Nell's (1988) study of avid readers, readers who profess to read for pleasure to a degree that is beyond typical, is also relevant to our description of the process by which readers experience involvement. In a remarkable series of five experiments, Nell set out to explore the factors that are associated with the experience of reading for pleasure, what he terms "ludic reading." One aspect of the findings that emerged is that, like us, Nell conceives of ludic reading as a dynamic process that is enabled by antecedents that produce particular consequences and that is always subject to a process-interrupt decision that could break the involvement with the text and redirect attention to an alternative activity, sometimes in mid-sentence.

Antecedents of Involvement

Like Csikszentmihalyi and Nell, we have found in our work on involvement that for a reading task to be involving, it must not be too difficult or too easy for the reader. Similarly, a writing task is uninvolving if it is too easy or beyond the writer's capabilities technically or rhetorically. There may be several reasons for the necessary match between an individual's ability and textual difficulty. First, if a reader believes the text to be beyond his or her capabilities for comprehension, he or she may not be able to devote the necessary amount of attention to it; instead the reader may experience anxiety about how he or she will make sense of the text while worrying about how to approach the task. Second, if a text appears too easy, the reader may not choose to devote the necessary amount of attention to it, believing that his or her attention can be divided between it and other tasks. Finally, if a reader views a text as not well matched to his or her abilities, he or she may experience negative emotional reactions to the author such as annoyance, anxiety, indignation, or boredom. Because readers who are involved in a text are wholly focused on their tasks, their approach to texts must be relatively free of extraneous and competing emotions and cognition.

An important reason that involvement happens from an optimal match between an individual's abilities and the challenges of a task is that individuals find it rewarding to have control over their own lives. Csikszentmihalyi (1990) describes flow as a process of achieving happiness by gaining control over one's own inner consciousness. This control might be achieved most easily when tasks are intrinsically rewarding. However, Csikszentmihalyi describes many instances of flow experiences in prisoners of war and individuals held in concentration camps who were not at all free to engage in whatever activity they chose. Still, it was the control over their own inner lives that led to flow experiences.

Control is also central to another motivation theory that relates to how individuals might invest themselves differently in potential tasks depending on the degree to which they identify with, endorse, and internalize the purposes of a task. Deci and his colleagues (Deci, 1992; Deci & Ryan, 1985; Deci et al., 1991) propose in their *self-determination theory* that all individuals have a strong need for autonomy and that identification and investment in a task, though moderated by such factors as the associated interpersonal context in which the task is performed, depends on the extent to which the context supports autonomy or is controlling. (Self-determination theory is discussed in more detail in Chapter 5 of this volume.) Thus, a sense that a reader is choosing *to* read and is choosing *what* to read are important conditions for deep involvement.

In addition, a clear sense of both the goal of a task and how to go about completing it seems to be an important precondition for involvement. In our work with college students who told us about the conditions that led to involvement with their academic assignments, we found that they often referred to times when they had struggled with making progress on a task until they understood what they were supposed to do. When they had formed a clear view of the task and of how it would fulfill a goal for engaging with text, their attention could begin to fall through to the deep concentration that we call involvement. Thus, another important determiner of an involvement experience seems to

Schallert & Reed

be finding a match between task and purpose. One result of making such a match is a pleasurable recognition, a sense of familiar aptness, that fades into the background as the reader becomes so engrossed by the text that he or she is oblivious at a conscious level of how his or her own goals and purposes are being fulfilled by the text. Klinger (1977) describes affect as a device that gives constantly changing and updated information on how individuals' current situations relate to their goals. We believe the dynamic process of involvement can be described in the same way, as a fluctuating barometer of how well a task is fulfilling a current concern.

However, what happens when a task or text does not have the characteristics that engender involvement? This is a situation in which we see the relevance of volitional control (Corno, 1993; see also Chapter 3 in this volume), of willing oneself to pay attention, stay focused, and get involved. Whether the task requires forcing or it is freely chosen, volitional control comprises the strategies and plans invoked after decisions to pursue various goals have been made. As Corno (1993) states, "In academic settings, volition can be characterized as a dynamic system of psychological control processes that protect concentration and directed effort in the face of personal and/or environmental distractions" (p. 17). For example, if a student decides on a goal to complete a research paper before its due date, volitional control will keep the student on track to meeting that goal. Corno (1993) suggests that one possible outcome, or consequence, of volition is involvement. We found in our previous work (Reed & Schallert, 1993) that some students reported being able to exercise volitional control to begin a dreaded task that subsequently became involving and even enjoyable. This is akin to what Corno means when she refers to a "crossing the Rubicon" effect, where an initial forcing of oneself eventually precipitates a more effortless engagement with a task.

The students we interviewed as part of our research also mentioned that they sometimes had to choose *not* to get too involved with a task. This is an often reported concern of inveterate readers. For example, Nell's (1988) sample of avid readers included a family of four ranging in age from 19 to 45 who among them typically read more than 100 books per month. One member of the family reported that he sometimes wondered if the world were not passing them by. Other avid readers we know use different tricks to make sure that they do not get "caught by print," such as hiding particularly attractive books behind work that must be done or purposefully leaving behind certain materials so they are not tempted to begin reading when other tasks must take priority.

Concomitants and Characteristics of Involvement

Imagine that the antecedents have been set, the conditions are favorable, the proper stance has been adopted, and the reader is holding a text that embodies the characteristics we have mentioned as likely to engender involvement. How might we describe the experience of "falling into" a deep state of involvement with the text? At what point does the reader lose awareness of physical surroundings and immediate past and future concerns, and find himself or herself living the virtual reality invited by the author?

Involvement occurs when the construction of meaning is going well. In a sense, the reader becomes one with the text, co-constructing with the author an elaborate and vivid textual world that takes over imagination and emotions. In our work, students reported deep involvement when they also were able to manage deep comprehension, both of the text and of their task. Similarly, Nell (1988) reports that ludic readers experience vivid imagery and a heightened physiological arousal especially at times of peak immersion in the text.

Not surprisingly, involvement is associated with effortlessness and ease with the task and little sense of any affect other than that invited directly by the author and imagined and experienced by the reader (Reed & Schallert, 1993; Reed et al., 1996). Koch (1956) characterizes his "State B" as a state of effortlessness, positive affect, absence of metacognition, and a singular focus of attention. He states, "The central and decisive mark of State B is domination of the person by the problem context...in some sense, the person is the task or vice versa...thoughts relevant to the problem context seem to well up with no apparent effort" (pp. 67–69). This statement is in line with Csikszentmihalyi's (1993) descriptions of flow experiences: "Because in flow the challenges are high enough to absorb all of a person's skills, one needs to pay complete attention to the task at hand, and there is no attention left over to process any irrelevant information" (p. 182). The synonymous phrases these researchers give for involvement—of being lost in a text or oblivious to surroundings—all hint at an acute focus of attention. In one of the experiments reported in his 1988 study, Nell commented on the ease with which ludic readers could become deeply engrossed in a story they were reading even as they were hooked up to electrodes and in the bright, unfamiliar surroundings of a laboratory. As Csikszentmihalyi (1993) states, "By creating a temporary world where one can act with total commitment, flow provides an escape from the chaos of the quotidian" (p. 184).

When individuals are involved and their attention is completely focused, the interruption of activity caused by a bell ringing or a teacher calling the end of the period often will be experienced as deeply disturbing. Students will report frustration at being stopped just as they were beginning to become engaged in a task. The contrast between the loss of a sense of time that comes from a deeply enjoyable activity and the slow, marked passage of time experienced when an activity is boring or anxiety producing is one of the most often mentioned characteristics of involvement.

Finally, returning to characteristics mentioned earlier, Koch, Csikszentmihalyi, and several of our own study participants have emphasized the absence of self-conscious metacognition about the task that co-occurs with deep involvement. It may seem surprising to claim that a lack of metacognition, of task monitoring and self-regulation, would be associated with a psychologically beneficial experience; evidence shows that self-regulation and metacognitive sophistication are characteristics that develop in mature and successful learners. However, with deep involvement, self-regulation may be needed mostly to help the reader to the point at which the task itself takes over and, directs the reader's engagement. Once the reader is lost in the task, the conscious "forcing" implied by self-regulation recedes.

One issue that concerns researchers in this area is the effect that some assessments have on the process being studied. Simply measuring involvement may disrupt it. For example, Csikszentmihalyi often has used beepers to mark for his participants a point in time when he would like them to report on their psychological involvement with whatever they are doing. It is clear that such a report procedure must interrupt the task and the experience of flow, should it be occurring. Similarly, think-aloud procedures or measures that ask the reader to report on his or her current level of involvement are incompatible with deep immersion in a task. In some of our own work (Schallert, Reed, & Goetz, 1994), we used a secondary task paradigm, a reading task during which participants respond as quickly as they can to beeps they hear, to measure the level of involvement readers were experiencing at particular points in a text. One concern we had with this approach was that our participants regularly reported splitting their attention between the two tasks they had been given, again reducing the strength of the involvement experience. Measuring states of involvement as they are occurring still represents a challenge to researchers in this area.

Consequences of Involvement

Drawing again on the work of Csikszentmihalyi (1993), we describe experiences associated with deep involvement as *autotelic*—experiences that are enjoyed for their own sake and that are sought out again and again in order to re-create the pleasure of the activity. Why is an autotelic experience so pleasurable? The opportunity to match one's abilities with the challenges of the task in a way that totally fills one's attention can make such experiences highly gratifying. Readers who have lost themselves in a story will want to re-create the experience as soon as circumstances allow. For some, nearly any type of reading will do; others will seek works written by the same author or courses taught by the same professor, expecting from them an organization of consciousness that causes the delights of a flow experience. Over time, readers who have experienced the pleasure of becoming absorbed by a text will develop a sense of the types of texts or tasks that will successfully cause involvement and of the conditions that need to be in place for them to be able to re-create the joy of autotelic experiences.

Thus, one consequence of deep involvement is to motivate readers to want to read, to find reading a rewarding, sought-after activity that can displace other recreational activities. The benefits of increased reading have been documented; because the more an individual reads, the more he or she encounters new words, new ideas, and new ways of interacting with authors, it is clearly beneficial to devise tasks, environments, and strategies that will foster involvement in all kinds of reading tasks. As Guthrie, Schafer, and colleagues (1995) state, "If schools are to succeed in enabling students to exercise choice in how they participate in the community and the workplace through literacy, schools must place a higher priority on nourishing students' capabilities and dispositions for choosing to read" (p. 21).

In addition to affective, motivational consequences that lead a reader to choose to read, involvement experiences are important because they lead to a change in the contents of consciousness. A person learns more, is more creative, and understands more deeply after a highly involving textual encounter. A reader also has a better memory for and comprehension of the ideas generated while reading, and his or her attention will be solely focused on those constructed ideas. The deeply involved reader assimilates ideas into his or her knowledge in a manner that seems almost unmediated, as though even the words used in the conversation with the author are transparent.

In sum, involvement acts as a change agent—readers are different following such an experience because they have allowed themselves to create with an author a virtual reality that was not bounded by ordinary spatial and temporal constraints. In such experiences, the reader leaves behind the stuff of everyday life and transcends into an alternate motivational pattern. In her work, which proposes that love and the experience of reading great literature share a deep similarity, Person (1988) describes how a reader enters into the consciousness of the characters and ultimately of the author and is invited to construct new ideas, to imagine a new way of seeing the world, and to come to a new understanding.

Contextual Considerations: The Role of Social Factors on Involvement

In our description of the psychological nature of involvement, we may have given the impression that "losing oneself in a story" or becoming deeply involved in an academic reading task is an experience that often, or even necessarily, removes the reader from the normal world of social relations with others and from the here and now of the cultural context in which the reader lives. In this section, we want to discuss the social nature of involvement, how involvement can be initiated in or re-created for what Eeds and Wells (1989) call "grand conversations" about literature.

Even when reading quietly in a corner, a reader is enacting a socially constructed activity. In Nepal, for example, a country in which even adult fluent readers are audible as they read, one can call attention to oneself by sitting for any length of time looking at printed materials and remaining absolutely silent (Red, 1988). Cultural sanctions surround even the most private activity, even when someone acts in ways that resist cultural norms. There are other, more immediate ways that social factors can influence whether and how involvement in reading occurs. For some readers, it is not so much the reading itself that is involving as the opportunity that reading affords to have satisfying conversations about what was read.

Current educational practices emphasize the value of discussion not just in language arts lessons but also in the content areas. From a view of discussion that was not much more than recitation, as was found for many of the teachers that Alvermann and Hayes (1989) observed, to a belief in the value of student-led literature discussions (Almasi, 1995; Raphael & McMahon, 1994), student talk is increasingly recognized as key to intellectual growth. Implicit in the rationale for incorporating literature discussion in the curriculum are the motivational consequences of such curricular choices. Under ideal circumstances and for many students, talking with peers to negotiate an understanding of what was read is highly motivating. Not only are students likely to become involved in the active interaction often associated with peer-led discussion groups, they may be more interested in what they are reading as they anticipate what will happen when they meet in groups to discuss what they have read.

We are reminded of the student who was very uninvolved while reading *Hamlet* because the language was too opaque to him, but who became excited about the play after discussing it with his group in class. As Hatano and Inagaki (1991) propose, "The presence of an audience can enhance the collective construction of knowledge for social and cognitive reasons" (p. 334). This student, motivated by Hamlet's story, did try again to read the play and subsequently became intrigued by it and by Shakespeare's language. Thus, his involvement was driven by the social interaction with classmates. Further, as Hatano and Inagaki found in their research with Japanese elementary school students, group discussion "often induces individual comprehension activity...it motivates people to collect more pieces of information about the issue of the discussion and to understand the issue more deeply" (p. 346).

Thus, the construct of socially shared cognition, and its related phenomenon of distributed cognition (Salomon, 1993) (though not often approached in terms of motivation or affect), could be useful in describing the involvement generated by social interaction. When two or more people meet and discuss their individual construction of meaning, there can occur an enlargement of everyone's understanding sparked by the contributions made to the group. The dialogues reported by Eeds and Wells (1989) show this characteristic, as do those of Almasi (1995), Hopkins and Schallert (1995), and Goatley, Brock, and Raphael (1995). The construct of socially shared cognition refers to how it can be possible for a group to construct meaning, a meaning that sometimes cannot be assigned to any one individual and that is not maintained long after the group disbands. What is interesting is the enjoyment that group participants often experience when an interaction goes well, when members feel that they have been heard and that they have gained something from the time spent with the group. We might call this phenomenon shared or distributed affect, the emotional reaction generated by the group's interaction. It is not surprising that Csikszentmihalyi and Nakamura (1989) found that adolescents were most likely to be in flow when talking to friends.

Conclusion

More than anything else, involvement while reading is pleasurable, enough so that previously involved readers will take a chance on an unknown text to repeat the experience. And, involvement is memorable enough that readers often will begin a conversation about a book they have enjoyed by commenting on their affective reactions to it and on the fact that they became lost in the text. Emotional responses to text are so important that when an individual, such as the woman interviewed by Oliver Sacks (1995), is incapable of affective reactions, comprehension of even simple stories suffers. In this way emotion brings the story events together and involvement serves as the catalyst for the kind of emotional response that supports the inferential net that, in turn, creates a story for a reader.

However, there are possible negative aspects to becoming highly involved in reading. As mentioned previously, it is possible that readers who often lose themselves in their reading separate themselves from the world to such a degree that their connections with others become damaged (Nell, 1988). A child of an avid reader once reported to one of us that he hated reading because it was what his mother did and he could never talk to her when she read. In addition, it is possible for someone to enjoy reading a text and yet construct a meaning that is not the socially accepted meaning or the teacher's objective for a lesson. Involvement and flow do not guarantee socially acceptable success.

Finally, there are many interesting aspects of involvement that could be investigated. Further work in this area will need to address how to measure involvement or any other affective reaction to text or to academic tasks. We mentioned earlier that involvement can be disrupted simply by measuring it. It is also difficult to predict exactly the conditions under which deep involvement will occur, something that is not a problem except when trying to study the experience.

Another interesting issue for future research is the pursuit of involvement not so much as a situationally generated process but as an individual propensity. A description of the cognitive and affective processes of individuals who find it easy to "fall into a text" as well as the life circumstances that may have encouraged such tendencies might yield insights to inform parents and educators interested in promoting voluntary reading (see Morrow, 1991, for some interesting preliminary suggestions).

Involvement in reading is a particularly interesting activity in which to study flow because it represents an activity during which emotions, such as extremes of fear and sadness, that are not necessarily pleasant may be experienced and enjoyed nevertheless. As Nell (1988) describes, "For many subjects, fear is an especially salient emotion, and one of the principal uses of ludic reading is to master fear by delicately controlling it, so that the reader experiences the gooseflesh of fear but not its terror" (p. 43). Thus, when we are describing flow experiences and deep involvement in a reading activity, we have the opportunity of studying the paradox of negative emotions that are sought after.

As a final suggestion for research, we offer the kind of reading activity currently experienced when children and adults "surf" the Internet. A computer laboratory teaching assistant mentioned to us that he had seen a surprisingly large group of lab users come in every day and spend four or five hours simply responding to electronic mail messages and exploring different sites and chat groups on the Internet. We are very interested in why such a reading and writing activity would be so involving. One possibility may be that the text that Internet users encounter is nonlinear in organization and requires much attention to make sense of it. Also, a hallmark of such text experiences is that they are totally self-determined, with the user choosing where to go and what to read. The many visual, graphic enhancements of text, the highly varied designs, and the high interestingness of information on the Internet are features that we would predict would at least grab attention if not hold it for long periods of time. Many text encounters in the electronic world offer possibilities for multidimensional meanings, and the response of the reader is to continue constructing meaning in a world that transcends reality.

References

Alexander, P.A., Kulikowich, J.M., & Jetton, T.L. (1994). The role of subject-matter knowledge and interest in the processing of linear and nonlinear texts. *Review of Educational Research, 64,* 201–252.

Alexander, P.A., Kulikowich, J.M., & Schulze, S.K. (1994). How subject-matter knowledge affects recall and interest. *American Educational Research Journal, 31,* 313–337.

Almasi, J.F. (1995). The nature of fourth graders' sociocognitive conflicts in peer-led and teacher-led discussions of literature. *Reading Research Quarterly, 30,* 314–351.

Alvermann, D.E., & Guthrie, J.T. (1993). *Themes and directions of the National Reading Research Center* (Perspectives in Reading Report No. 1). Athens, GA: National Reading Research Center.

Alvermann, D.E., & Hayes, D.A. (1989). Classroom discussion of content area reading assignments: An intervention study. *Reading Research Quarterly, 24,* 305–335.

Anderson, R.C., Shirey, L.L., Wilson, P.T., & Fielding, L.G. (1987). Interestingness of children's reading material. In R.E. Snow & M.J. Farr (Eds.), *Aptitude, learning, and instruction: Cognitive and affective process analysis* (pp. 287–299). Hillsdale, NJ: Erlbaum.

Armbruster, B.B. (1984). The problem of "inconsiderate text." In G.G. Duffy, L.R. Roehler, & J. Mason (Eds.), *Comprehension instruction* (pp. 202–217). New York: Longman.

Berlyne, D.E. (1960). *Conflict, arousal, and curiosity.* New York: McGraw-Hill.

Corno, L. (1993). The best-laid plans: Modern conceptions of volition and educational research. *Educational Researcher, 22*(2), 14–22.

Csikszentmihalyi, M. (1975). *Beyond boredom and anxiety.* San Francisco, CA: Jossey-Bass.

Csikszentmihalyi, M. (1990). *Flow: The psychology of optimal experience.* New York: HarperCollins.

Csikszentmihalyi, M. (1993). *The evolving self: A psychology for the third millennium.* New York: HarperCollins.

Csikszentmihalyi, M., & Nakamura, J. (1989). The dynamics of intrinsic motivation: A study of adolescents. In C. Ames & R.E. Ames (Eds.), *Research on motivation in education: Vol. 3. Goals and cognitions* (pp. 45–71). San Diego, CA: Academic.

Deci, E.L. (1992). The relation of interest to the motivation of behavior: A self-determination theory perspective. In K.A. Renninger, S. Hidi, & A. Krapp (Eds.), *The role of interest in learning and development* (pp. 43–70). Hillsdale, NJ: Erlbaum.

Deci, E.L., & Ryan, R.M. (1985). *Intrinsic motivation and self-determination in human behavior.* New York: Plenum.

Deci, E.L., Vallerand, R.J., Pelletier, L.G., & Ryan, R.M. (1991). Motivation and education: The self-determination perspective. *Educational Psychologist, 26,* 325–346.

Eberstadt, F. (1995, November). Eco consciousness. *Vogue,* 196–198.

Eeds, M., & Wells, D. (1989). Grand conversations: An exploration of meaning construction in literature study groups. *Research in the Teaching of English, 23,* 4–29.

Fisher, W.R. (1989). *Human communication as narration: Toward a philosophy of reason, value, and action.* Columbia, SC: University of South Carolina Press.

Garner, R., Alexander, P.A., Gillingham, M.G., Kulikowich, J.M., & Brown, R. (1991). Interest and learning from text. *American Educational Research Journal, 28,* 643–659.

Garner, R., Gillingham, M.G., & White, C.S. (1989). Effects of "seductive details" on macroprocessing and microprocessing in adults and children. *Cognition and Instruction, 6,* 41–57.

Goatley, V.J., Brock, C.H., & Raphael, T.E. (1995). Diverse learners participating in regular education "Book Clubs." *Reading Research Quarterly, 30,* 352–380.

Goetz, E.T., & Sadoski, M. (1995). The perils of seduction: Distracting details or incomprehensible abstractions? *Reading Research Quarterly, 30,* 500–511.

Graves, M.F., Penn, M.C., Earle, J., Thompson, M., Johnson, V., & Slater, W.H. (1991). Commentary: Improving instructional text: Some lessons learned. *Reading Research Quarterly, 2,* 110–122.

Guthrie, J.T., Schafer, W.D., Wang, Y.Y., & Afflerbach, P. (1995). Relationships of instruction to amount of reading: An exploration of social, cognitive, and instructional connections. *Reading Research Quarterly, 30,* 8–25.

Guthrie, J.T., Van Meter, P., et al. (1996). Growth of literacy engagement: Changes in motivations and strategies during concept-oriented reading instruction. *Reading Research Quarterly, 31,* 306–333.

Hatano, G., & Inagaki, K. (1991). Sharing cognition through collective comprehension activity. In L.B. Resnick, J.M. Levine, & S.D. Teasley (Eds.), *Perspectives on socially shared cognition* (pp. 331–348). Washington, DC: American Psychological Association.

Hidi, S. (1990). Interest and its contribution as a mental resource for learning. *Review of Educational Research, 60,* 549–571.

Hidi, S., & Anderson, V. (1992). Situational interest and its impact on reading and expository writing. In K.A. Renninger, S. Hidi, & A. Krapp (Eds.), *The role of interest in learning and development* (pp. 215–238). Hillsdale, NJ: Erlbaum.

Hidi, S., & Baird, W. (1988). Strategies for increasing text-based interest and students' recall of expository texts. *Reading Research Quarterly, 23,* 465–483.

Hopkins, L.F., & Schallert, D.L. (1995). *How fifth-grade students' and their teacher's views of the purposes of "book club" time are reflected in their conversations.* Paper presented at the 45th Annual Meeting of the National Reading Conference, New Orleans, LA.

Klinger, E. (1977). *Meaning and void.* Minneapolis, MN: University of Minnesota Press.

Koch, S. (1956). Behavior as "intrinsically" regulated: Work notes towards a pre-theory of phenomena called "motivational." In M.R. Jones (Ed.), *Nebraska symposium on motivation* (pp. 42–86). Lincoln, NE: University of Nebraska Press.

Krapp, A., Hidi, S., & Renninger, K.A. (1992). Interest, learning and development. In K.A. Renninger, S. Hidi, & A. Krapp (Eds.), *The role of interest in learning and development* (pp. 3–26). Hillsdale, NJ: Erlbaum.

Morrow, L.M. (1991). Promoting voluntary reading. In J. Flood, J.M. Jensen, D. Lapp, & J.R. Squire (Eds.), *Handbook of research on teaching the English language arts* (pp. 681–690). New York: Macmillan.

Nell, V. (1988). The psychology of reading for pleasure: Needs and gratifications. *Reading Research Quarterly, 23,* 6–50.

Nystrand, M. (1982). The structure of textual space. In M. Nystrand (Ed.), *What writers know: The language, process, and structure of written discourse* (pp. 75–86). New York: Academic.

Pearson, P.D., & Tierney, R.J. (1984). On becoming a thoughtful reader: Learning to read like a writer. In A. Purves & O. Niles (Eds.), *Becoming readers in a complex society* (p. 33). Chicago, IL: National Society for the Study of Education.

Person, E.S. (1988). *Dreams of love and fateful encounters: The power of romantic passion.* New York: Penguin.

Raphael, T.E., & McMahon, S.I. (1994). "Book Club": An alternative framework for reading instruction. *The Reading Teacher, 48,* 102–116.

Red, D. (1988). *Using college textbooks written in a foreign language: A study in Nepal.* Unpublished doctoral dissertation, University of Texas at Austin.

Reed, J.H., Hagen, A.S., Wicker, F.W., & Schallert, D.L. (1996). The temporal dynamics of involvement in academic tasks: Motivational and cognitive correlates. *Journal of Educational Psychology, 88,* 101–109.

Reed, J.H., & Schallert, D.L. (1993). The nature of involvement in academic discourse tasks. *Journal of Educational Psychology, 85,* 253–266.

Reed, J.H., Schallert, D.L., & Goetz, E.T. (1992). *Exploring the reciprocal relationships among comprehensibility, interestingness, and involvement in academic reading tasks.* Paper presented at the annual meeting of the American Educational Research Association, San Francisco, CA.

Rosenblatt, L. (1978). *The reader, the text, the poem: The transactional theory of the literary work.* Carbondale, IL: Southern Illinois University Press.

Sacks, O. (1995). *An anthropologist on Mars.* New York: Vintage.

Salomon, G. (Ed.). (1993). *Distributed cognitions: Psychological and educational considerations.* Cambridge, England: Cambridge University Press.

Schallert, D.L., Reed, J.H., & Goetz, E.T. (1994). *How are we measuring engagement, involvement, and interest in comprehension research?* Paper presented at the annual meeting of the American Educational Research Association, New Orleans, LA.

Wade, S.E. (1992). How interest affects learning from text. In K.A. Renninger, S. Hidi, & A. Krapp (Eds.), *The role of interest in learning and development* (pp. 255–278). Hillsdale, NJ: Erlbaum.

Teacher Perceptions of Student Motivation and Their Relation to Literacy Learning

Anne P. Sweet

As Guthrie and Wigfield noted in the introduction, teachers have long recognized the important role that motivation plays in their students' learning, and a 1992 National Reading Research Center poll showed that teachers consider motivation for reading to be the most important issue affecting education. This is illustrated by the fact that many teacher magazines and related professional publications contain articles related to this topic. Articles about motivational activities for use by teachers found in professional journals and other writings are written not only by theorists, social scientists, and researchers, but also to an increasing extent by teachers, for teachers. The need for knowledge about effective motivational programs and practices has spawn a network of paper media, electronic media, and other forums designed to help teachers meet the daily challenge of inspiring students to engage in reading and literacy-related activities. The International Reading Association publication *Fostering the Love of Reading: The Affective Domain in Reading Education* (Cramer & Castle, 1994) is one example of a book written to meet the demand for helping teachers enhance students' motivation and maximize literacy learning in their classrooms. It is not surprising that at professional conferences such as the IRA Annual Convention and in education discourse community exchanges on the Internet, sessions on students' motivation are prevalent.

Motivation has received much attention as a research topic for the past several decades (see, for example, Bandura, 1982; Corno & Rohrkemper, 1985; deCharms, 1976; Deci, 1975; Harter, 1982; Nolen, 1988; Pintrich & DeGroot, 1990; Wentzel, 1995). Students' motivation in particular has been studied extensively by social scientists and motivation theorists (although motivation for reading has been studied less, as mentioned in the introduction). Most prior research and theories of motivation were based largely on self-report data from students: researchers asked students about their views and feelings on their motivation and used this information to test their theories and modify them accordingly. Although researchers have learned a great deal about motivation by using students' self-report data, teacher perceptions also are likely to be important. However, relatively little is known about teachers' perceptions of students' motivation. When combined with student self-report data, information about teachers' perceptions can offer a more complete picture of what the engaged reader may look like. Understanding students' own motivation, combined with what teachers think about motivation and which students they see as motivated and unmotivated, can help educators foster students' literacy engagement. Information about teachers' perceptions also can be used to improve predictions of academic performance. Finally, data on teacher perceptions can be used to help describe teachers themselves.

In our article (Sweet & Guthrie, 1996) on motivation that appeared in *The Reading Teacher*, Guthrie and I examine the spectrum of motivations that children bring into the classroom and discuss how these motivations connect to instruction. This chapter is an extension of that discussion in which I provide more in-depth insights about teachers' perceptions of students' motivations and their relation to literacy learning. Before this discussion, I explain types of motivation, elaborating on the distinctions between intrinsic and extrinsic motivation. Further, I address self-determination theory and how teachers perceive students' relatedness (social needs), competency, and ability to handle freedom (autonomy) as they pertain to literacy development. In this portion of the chapter, I describe the way that teachers' perceptions of students converge with students' views of themselves during the course of schooling. Next, I depict recent findings of reciprocity between teacher and student perceptions. For example, students' motivations for learning are influenced by how they are perceived by the teacher; at the same time, the teacher's management of literacy instruction is influenced by how he or she views the students' motivations. Finally, I discuss the value of differentiation among types of motivations and types of supportive environments for the improvement of literacy instruction, with a focus on how teachers are able to create different contexts that support the needs of relatedness, competency, and autonomy.

Intrinsic and Extrinsic Motivation Theory

Several theories of motivation point to two types of motivation—intrinsic and extrinsic—as mentioned in earlier chapters. Theorists and researchers (Deci, 1975; Deci & Ryan, 1985; Lepper & Greene, 1978; Malone & Lepper, 1987) draw a distinction between these motivation types. Intrinsic motivation refers to a person's inner desire to engage in an activity, regardless of whether the activity has an external value. For example, an intrinsically motivated learner will choose books and read them during free time at school or at home. Such a student actively seeks opportunities to engage in book reading, often losing track of time while immersed in the task. In contrast, extrinsic motivation refers to a person's being prompted to engage in an activity by an incentive or anticipated outcome that is external to the activity. An extrinsically motivated student will complete an assigned reading primarily to meet course requirements. Such a student is motivated to work hard because he or she views doing so as a means to an end (for example, to receive a high report card grade) that is unrelated to the reading task.

Although both intrinsic and extrinsic motivation operate within U.S. schools and classrooms, the educational system is structured in such a way as to promote students' extrinsic motivation (Ryan, Connell, & Deci, 1985). This fact is apparent when one considers that many schools and school communities focus a great deal of attention, expend considerable workforce efforts, and spend inordinate amounts of monetary resources on extrinsic motivators of student achievement. For instance, much attention is directed at school incentive programs for reading in which students read books to accrue points toward a prize that is unrelated to book reading—such as the fun of watching the school principal jump into a huge vat of lime green jello! At the school event I witnessed, children pooled the number of pages they read to win this collective prize. It is questionable whether students would choose to read after achieving the prize without another enticing inducement being placed before them.

There are ways to design reading incentive programs that minimize the extrinsic nature of a reward, and there is good reason for doing so. In their meta-analytical review of research on the effects of reinforcement on intrinsic motivation, Cameron and Pierce (1994) found that there is a negative effect on intrinsic motivation when individuals perform a task for expected tangible rewards, regardless of their level of performance. Such tasks are akin to reading incentive programs that are predicated on students' receipt of a reward for reading the requisite number of pages or books. One way to protect students' intrinsic motivation in this situation is to ensure that students choose which books they read (Gambrell et al., 1995) and to require that they engage in follow-up activities that link their book reading to demonstrated success on a related task.

Despite the general reliance on extrinsic motivators in schools, some students are or do become intrinsically motivated to succeed on school-related tasks and specifically literacy-related tasks. These intrinsically motivated students also choose to engage in what they perceive to be enjoyable activities, such as book reading, outside of the classroom.

The instructional practices that teachers employ, along with the classroom management procedures they follow, affect students' motivation. Some of these practices and procedures promote students' intrinsic motivations, and others prompt students to become externally oriented in terms of their motivation to engage in school- and literacy-related tasks. One way to increase students' intrinsic motivation is to construct integrated instruction that unifies reading, writing, literature, science, and social studies (see Guthrie et al., 1997; Morrow, Pressley, & Smith, 1995; Sweet, 1997), a strategy that is discussed in detail in the second section of this volume. Successful integrated instruction is based on learners' curiosities and aesthetic involvement and permits students to connect ideas across many types of texts. Integrated instruction requires self-directed learning: students identify their own interests, choose appropriate books, and extend their literacy in ways that fulfill their own ideas. An emphasis on intrinsic motivations leads to collaborative activity among students because social motivations are prominent among elementary and middle school learners. Direct instruction in skills and strategies is not neglected, but it is situated in ways that serve content learning.

Teachers who integrate instruction confirm the importance of intrinsic motivation to literacy learning (Sweet, Guthrie, & Ng, 1996). These teachers describe highly motivated learners as intrinsically involved, engrossed in learning, and sharply focused on lesson content. They expect their students to use higher order strategies, to interact socially with peers, and to persist despite difficulties. In contrast, students who are less intrinsically motivated are not expected to exhibit this level of engagement.

Integrated instruction cannot be developed easily through the use of extrinsic motivational schemes. A system of points and external rewards will not sustain the long-term, self-directed, collaborative learning that is required in highly integrated instruction. It is important for teachers to become aware of the different effects their instructional and management actions have on students' motivation so that they can become more deliberate in planning which actions to use to promote children's *internal motivation*.

Self-Determination

The cognitions that accompany extrinsic motivation are fairly straightforward. When a person is motivated extrinsically by the desire to achieve a goal such as receiving a good grade, he or she determines what is necessary to achieve this goal and modifies his or her behavior accordingly to increase the likelihood of achieving this desired outcome. The cognitions that accompany intrinsic motivation are more complex. Why some individuals choose to read and find great pleasure in reading a mystery novel while others do not is less clear. Self-determination theory and research findings on this topic provide some insight.

Self-determination theory focuses on individuals' opportunities to make choices or decisions about how to behave or think as precursors to their perceived control (Deci, 1975, 1980; Deci & Ryan, 1985). Three psychological needs play an important role in self-determination theory: relatedness, competency, and autonomy. Relatedness is the notion that a sense of belonging in the classroom is derived from social relationships that are based on trust, caring, and mutual concern for one another's social and emotional well-being. Research has shown that children who choose to read and who read well come from homes with plenty of books, where everyone reads, and where parents encourage reading. The sense of relatedness that children acquire in homes where books and reading are common appears to play an important role in their interest in reading. In other words, people appear to be drawn toward activities that are meaningful to others in their social environment.

A sense of relatedness can be a critical motivator of engagement in academic pursuits and of socially appropriate behavior in the classroom (Baumeister & Leary, 1995; Connell & Wellborn, 1991). It has been shown that students in classrooms where teachers promote this sense of relatedness are motivated to engage in academic activities and positive social behaviors (Noddings, 1992; Wentzel, 1995). In her study of caring teachers, Wentzel (1995) found that teachers perceived to be caring by students are those who set rules and enforce them consistently, demand maturity and working to one's potential, engage in democratic interactions, provide nurturance, and model interest in learning.

Competency is another psychological component that is central to self-determination theory. Harter (1982) found that perceived competency and intrinsic motivation were positively correlated for students in upper elementary and junior high school. This finding supports the notion that feeling competent or effective when engaged in challenging activities is an important element of intrinsic motivation. Further, Harter (1992) and her colleagues found that children who perceived themselves to be competent felt better and showed less anxiety about their school performance, which led them to adopt or maintain an intrinsic motivational orientation. In contrast, she found that students with low levels of perceived competence felt bad about their performance, were more anxious, and adopted an extrinsic motivational orientation.

Self-determination theory asserts that intrinsic motivation is innate and that it becomes differentiated in ways that direct children's interest toward certain activities (Deci, 1975; Deci & Ryan, 1985, 1992). Moreover, environmental factors influence the activities that children's intrinsic interest is directed toward by affecting their experience of competency and self-determination. According to this view, activities must be optimally challenging to be interesting and to promote intrinsic motivation. This means that the activities must not be too difficult or too easy to sustain children's intrinsic motivation. Under these circumstances, children will choose to engage in activities that permit them to experience a sense of competency, such as reading a book at a comfortable level of difficulty.

Equally important is the element of autonomy or freedom, which is a final psychological component that is central to self-determination theory. For instance, the opportunity to make choices has been found to enhance intrinsic motivation to read (Gambrell & Morrow, 1996; Gambrell, Codling, & Palmer, 1996). After all, the ultimate goal of reading instruction is to develop students who choose to read. Students who choose to read are motivated to read for reading's own sake. Research suggests that allowing students to choose the material they read promotes their motivation to pick up a book and read. So, for example, if children are interested in dinosaurs, they will be motivated to read and choose books about this and related topics. In so doing, by interacting with the text and discussing what they have read with peers and adults, students will become better readers and will learn about or learn more about their interests and the world around them. Children develop their ability to comprehend by sharing books that are meaningful to them with peers and adults.

Relatedness, competency, and autonomy are the cornerstones for the process of internalization (Ryan, Connell, & Grolnick, 1992). This process leads individuals toward an intrinsic orientation, to self-regulation (Pintrich & DeGroot, 1990; Nolen, 1988) and self-regulated learning (Brown, 1980; Schunk, 1989). Teachers rate children who are advanced in this process as more motivated, independent, and in need of less outside pressure to do their work (Harter, 1982; deCharms, 1976). At the same time, these children view their teachers as autonomy oriented and supportive, rather than controlling. In elementary school, autonomous students have higher self-esteem, higher perceived cognitive competence, and are less projective in coping with perceived failure (Ryan, Connell, & Grolnick, 1992).

Support for the importance of autonomy in students' motivations comes from research studying the differential effects of autonomy- and control-oriented teachers on students' motivational orientation. Findings from these studies indicate that an autonomy orientation, when compared with a controlling one, promotes a greater degree of students' intrinsic motivation, stronger beliefs about their intellectual competence, and a higher level of self-esteem (Deci et al., 1981; Ryan & Grolnick, 1986). Teachers who provide support for children's solving their own problems in the context of a warm, structured atmosphere are autonomy oriented. Children in the classrooms of autonomy-oriented teachers increase their identification with the value and importance of achievement-related behaviors, relative to children in classrooms of control-oriented teachers (Ryan, Connell, & Grolnick, 1992). Teachers in this study reported that students who were allowed to take more responsibility and who were less externally pressured were likely to report more self-determined regulation. In sum, teachers' support for children's autonomy can enhance their self-regulatory capacities and can affect their adjustment in school. This means that when teachers afford children reasonable autonomy in learning, when the learning tasks are optimally challenging, and when the children are provided information about the relevance and meaningfulness of the required tasks, children's motivational development can progress toward autonomy and self-regulated learning.

Underlying self-determination theory is the notion that receiving extrinsic rewards for tasks makes people feel that the reason they participated in the task was because they were receiving a reward rather than because they wanted to participate. The result is that the self-perceived autonomy of the individuals who receive a reward is undermined, thereby weakening their intrinsic motivation to participate in the interesting task. Research based on self-determination theory has shown that extrinsic rewards such as reading books for money cause decreases in the extent to which students think they have control in a given situation and in their intrinsic interest in the task. Yet few reading teachers are aware of the relation between intrinsic and extrinsic motivation and the conditions of the classroom that are associated with them (Lepper, Greene, & Nisbett, 1973).

Students whose school-related activity is externally regulated depend on parents and teachers for their motivations. These students are rated by teachers as being less independent and motivated and are described as requiring more prodding to do their work (Ryan, Connell, & Grolnick, 1992). Children who tend to be externally regulated also are seen by teachers as having lower confidence and self-esteem (Harter, 1982). In turn, these students tend to see themselves as less autonomous, less motivated, and as having less control over events and outcomes. Teachers report that many children with a highly externally regulated style have learning difficulties and act out frequently. External regulatory style appears to be a dominant characteristic of children who become discouraged in school and are at risk for a variety of academic and social difficulties (Grolnick, Ryan, & Deci, 1991).

In sum, self-perceptions seem to be context dependent and appear to shape an individual's motivations. Thus, people tend to be intrinsically motivated in situations in which they feel both competent and self-determining (Deci, 1975; Deci & Ryan, 1985, 1992). If individuals perceive themselves as being adept at performing in a particular situation (Bandura & Schunk, 1981; Schunk, 1989, 1991) and they sense that they have significant control in that situation (Corno & Rohrkemper, 1985; Stipek & Weisz, 1981; Weisz & Cameron, 1985), they are likely to be intrinsically motivated. If either or both of these self-perceptions are absent under the same conditions, the likelihood of their being intrinsically motivated would be lessened.

Teacher Perceptions and Student Engagement

There is a complex web of relations between teacher perceptions and student engagement. Teachers' perceptions and students' perceptions have been found to influence each other. In recent studies, teacher perceptions of student engagement were found to have reciprocal effects with students' self-report of perceived control and academic performance (Skinner, Wellborn, & Connell, 1990). Specifically, students' perceived control influenced their academic performance by promoting learning engagement, as reported by teachers; and teachers positively influenced students' perceived control through their contingency and involvement, as reported by students. Moreover, when the effects of teacher behavior on student engagement over the course of a school year were examined (Skinner & Belmont, 1993), teacher perceptions of student engagement appeared to have reciprocal effects with teachers' own behavior and with students' self-reports of engagement.

Students' perceived control seems to influence their academic performance by promoting their learning engagement, and teachers positively influence students' perceived control by their involvement with students and by conveying a sense of choice to them. Moreover, teachers' perceptions of student engagement appear to affect teachers' own behavior toward students and their instruction as well as students' perceptions of their own engagement. Hence, a series of interactions seems to occur between teachers and students that affects changes in each other's self-perceptions and perceptions of each other. These changes appear to precipitate changes in teachers' and students' behavior in the classroom.

Although research on teachers' perceptions has just begun, findings on the reciprocity that exists between teachers' and students' perceptions have implications for teachers' management of literacy instruction. Teachers who are knowledgeable about these interactions can structure particular activities and contexts that are likely to increase students' intrinsic motivations and bolster students' feelings of competency and self-determination in the literacy learning environment.

Studying Teacher Perceptions of Student Motivation

Before we can help teachers bolster students' self-determination and competency, we need more information about how teachers actually perceive students' literacy motivations. Guthrie and I (Sweet & Guthrie, 1994) examined these perceptions in an exploratory study. Results show that teachers perceive students as possessing a rather general motivation for literacy that is either relatively high or relatively low. With another colleague, we (Sweet, Guthrie, and Ng, 1996) extended this work by developing a more elaborate questionnaire to assess teachers' perceptions of student motivation. The questionnaire is based largely on Deci's (1975, 1980) self-determination perspective but also includes six constructs related specifically to reading, listed as follows:

1. Activity: teachers' observations that students read in areas in which they have been actively participating—for example, a student reads about a theme related to a field-trip.

2. Autonomy: teachers' perceptions that students are motivated by choice.

3. Social: teachers' perceptions that students read to share or to exchange with peers or family.

4. Topic: attributes the source of reading motivation to the subject matter or genre—for example, a student is motivated when he or she reads about a topic such as dinosaurs or a genre such as mysteries in which he or she is interested.

5. Individual: teachers attribute motivation to the internal qualities of students—for instance, a student is motivated because he or she becomes engrossed in reading.

6. Writing: teachers' perceptions that some students like to write about books or texts.

Questionnaire items from these six motivational categories, as depicted in the table on page 94, correspond to teachers' perceptions of student competency, autonomy, and relatedness. Note that we added "writing" as a discrete category because it is an integral component of literacy competence.

My collaborators and I compared teachers' perceptions of student motivation at different report card grade levels. To conduct this comparison, we asked, "Do teachers consider high-achieving students as motivated by different factors than students who are lower achievers? Report card grade in reading was the indicator of achievement, with students receiving an "A" in reading designated as high achievers, and students receiving a "B," "C," or "D" designated as lower achievers. We conducted a multivariate analysis of variance with four levels of report card grades and six levels of motivation as a repeated measure. The finding was positive: teachers did, in fact, perceive differences in the motivational profiles of higher and lower achievers in the classroom.

The pattern, presented in the figure on page 95, is as follows. Teachers perceived higher achievers as possessing high individual or internal motivation. The students' *individual* motivation exceeded all other motivational factors. These high achievers also were motivated by the topics of the classroom lessons, especially science and literature. The motivational factors of *activity* and *autonomy* were significantly lower than the motivations of *individual* and *topic*. It can be inferred from this finding that teachers considered these students to be less influenced by practical activities and support for their choices than they

Conceptual Item Clusters: Teacher Questionnaire on Student Motivation to Read (Third Edition)

Construct	Item Clusters
Activity	Enjoys reading about a favorite activity
	Follows up reading by getting involved in a related activity
	Does better on reading and writing when they are related to activities in which he or she has participated
	Reads frequently about a specialized recreational or extracurricular interest
Autonomy	Content to read books that are preselected by the teacher
	Prefers finding his or her own books to read
	Knows how to choose a book he or she would want to read
	Does better work when allowed to choose books that interest him or her
Social	Talks about his or her feelings related to a book or story
	Avoids participating in reading group activities
	Discussion with teacher and peers is complex—including motivations, plot, and personal response
	Does better on reading and writing activities when working with peers
Topic	Has definite preferences for favorite topics or authors
	Has no specialized reading interest
	Spends a long time reading about topics he or she likes
	Chooses to read about favorite subjects
Individual	Easily distracted while reading
	Is a voracious reader
	Hides in books
	Easily discouraged when he or she encounters difficult text
	Is enthusiastic about reading
Writing	Writes personal responses in journal regularly and often
	Wants to write about what he or she reads
	Writes incompletely or superficially in journal

were by their own personal goals and topical interests. In other words, high achievers were intrinsically motivated to learn the content of instruction, and they seemed to have internalized the mastery goals that teachers held for all students.

Teachers perceived the lower achievers differently. They were perceived to be responsive to activities and autonomy support in their reading and literacy. Teachers thought these students were more likely to become invested in reading and writing if they engaged in a hands-on

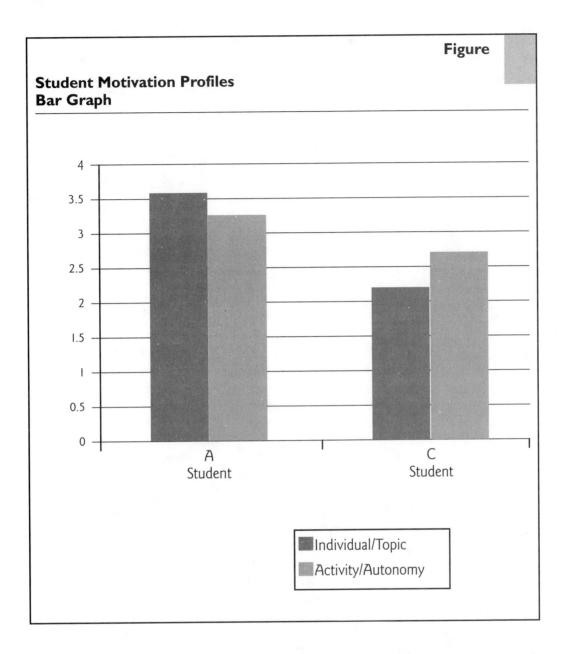

Figure

Student Motivation Profiles
Bar Graph

Legend:
- Individual/Topic
- Activity/Autonomy

activity and if they could choose what they read, who they worked with, and how they wrote. For lower achievers, the *individual* and *topic* motivations were significantly weaker than the *activity* and *autonomy* motivations. It should be noted that the lower achievers were lower than the higher achievers relative to teachers' perceptions of all the motivational constructs being assessed. However, it is the pattern among the constructs that distinguishes the motivational characteristics of students at different achievement levels most decisively.

This pattern of teacher perceptions from our study is consistent with Deci's view of the development of self-determination for literacy. Higher achievers, who possessed excellent strategies and competencies for reading, writing, and thinking about informational and literary text, were self-determining. These academically stronger students were intrinsically motivated and possessed internal goals and well-formed subject-matter interests. Students with less knowledge and use of literacy strategies were more dependent on external, environmental supports for literacy. Lower achievers needed more choices in reading and writing situations to initiate and sustain their effort and attention. Lower achievers also needed more relevant activities connected to reading and writing, which enabled them to see the usefulness of literacy, gain confidence in their abilities, and enhance their self-perceived competence.

This pattern is consistent with the perspective that when students become self-determining, they achieve more. By directing their own learning, self-determined students become involved in more literacy pursuits, use appropriate strategies more often, and experience success more frequently. Consequently, self-determined learners acquire a higher competence in literacy than less self-determined learners. Achievement in the form of strategic competence in literacy may lend students the confidence to pursue their interests, develop mastery goals, and become increasingly self-determined. My collaborators and I expect that self-determination and achievement are reciprocal and mutually facilitative.

The findings confirm that teachers appear to possess an implicit theory of the association of self-determination and achievement that is remarkably compatible with Deci's perspective. Teachers appear to believe that students who become the agents of their own literacy development grow more rapidly in literacy knowledge and skills. To attain these intrinsic motivational goals, students benefit from support for making their own choices, relative to their attained level of reading fluency. Students also gain from classroom activities in which literacy has a practical return for effort, thus enhancing their self-perceived competence as literacy users.

Interestingly, teachers did not appear to distinguish motivated literacy activity that may have been ignited by social interaction among students; teachers appeared to be neutral on this element. This finding was apparent across student profiles constructed from teachers' perceptions. It seemed that teachers had not internalized how social interaction within literacy instruction can move students toward self-determination.

This observation became more apparent when data from the qualitative phase of the study were analyzed. The qualitative phase involved videotaping students during literacy instruction and interviewing teachers about these students. Teachers' differentiated to a lesser extent on the social motivation category in the teacher interviews than on the teacher questionnaire. Had teachers reacted strongly to the social motivation category, my colleagues and I would have expected to see an enriched pattern of differentiation on the teacher interviews. Instead, when questioned about students' social interactions in a literacy event, most teachers indicated that the student being observed would have performed about equally as well, or in one case better, had he or she worked alone rather than in a group. Based on this finding, we concluded that teachers did not discern the motivational power of social interaction as an element that moves students toward self-determination in their learning.

Planning for Instruction: Creating Supportive Environments

Knowledge about the differentiation among types of motivation is valuable because it permits educators to construct environments that are supportive of instruction and that lead to improvements in literacy learning. Teachers are able to create different contexts that support students' need for autonomy, competency, and relatedness by careful instructional planning. We know that successful performances enhance students' self-perceptions of competence (Bandura, 1982). Therefore, it is important for students to begin reading instruction each day with a successful experience to bolster these perceptions of self-competence, which can positively affect their success at more difficult literacy tasks that they encounter during the day. Students also must be challenged so that they develop new reading competencies. Presenting students with challenging tasks is necessary for the development and sustenance of intrinsic motivation. For challenging tasks to be affirming, teachers must ensure that students succeed on these tasks. Although student self-direction is important, it must be accompanied by successful task completion. Hence, teachers must create a literacy-learning environment in which students operate at their zone of proximal development (Vygotsky, 1978)—a situation in which students will have ample opportunities to obtain assistance from the teacher or more skilled peers. The key here is that tasks need to be moderately challenging for students to be successful in gaining new knowledge and acquiring advanced skills.

An instructional environment that includes ability grouping warrants particular caution. For example, teachers can begin to perceive all members of a reading group as equal despite the considerable variation usually found within groups (Rosenbaum, 1980). Reading group placement, in particular, has been found to have a significant effect on students' long-term performance (Weinstein, 1976). In addition, reading lessons for high groups as compared with low groups are structured differently (Borko & Eisenhart, 1986; Hart, 1982; Hiebert, 1983). Specifically, teachers focus on lower level activities such as decoding skills with low reading groups that are firmly structured, whereas with high reading groups that are more loosely structured, teachers focus more on meaning-related activities that afford students opportunities to connect reading with personal experiences (Hiebert, 1983; McDermott, 1987).

An important point is that teachers' perceptions about students and the expectations they hold for them tend to persist over time. Moreover, these expectations can inhibit teachers from providing some students with appropriate instruction (Goldenberg, 1989). For example, if a child's teacher predicts that he will have no difficulty in learning to read because he has good reading readiness scores and seemingly well-developed language and listening skills, the teacher may not readily adjust her expectations about the likelihood of this child's learning to read without difficulty, even though he is not progressing as well as can be expected. Hence, the teacher may not adjust instruction for the student until he becomes one of the poorest readers in the class. A related point is that teachers partly interpret students' behaviors in light of their perceptions about students' abilities, and they base important instructional decisions on these interpretations. Teachers need to develop accurate perceptions and reexamine them continually so they can recognize and act on student behavior that is not consistent with their initial expectations.

Affective, cognitive, and social aspects of learning are all important factors that must be considered in planning for instruction within the broader context of literacy learning, discipline-based learning, and knowledge construction (Sweet, 1997). These factors, when considered together, shape a supportive environment that ensures students' success. The Concept-Oriented Reading Instruction (CORI) model, described in Chapter 7 in this book, was designed to provide for a supportive instructional environment. Other programs that provide supportive instructional environments are described in the chapters in the second section of this volume.

The example of integrated literacy and science instruction in the vignette presented in the introduction is illustrative of instruction in a CORI classroom. Recall that Robert and Kantu, two fifth-grade students, are teamed with each other while the class studies the life cycles of plants and animals within their environments. As this activity begins, Robert states, "I want to know whether crickets have a brain," and Kantu wants to know, "Why do crickets live here in the summer and where do they go in winter?" To ensure the students' success and to sustain their intrinsic motivation, the teacher first encourages Robert and Kantu to browse through classroom trade books to find answers to their questions. The teacher guides the boys in their selection of books on insects and gives them tips on search strategies. In addition, the teacher introduces Robert and Kantu and other members of the class to relevant literature, instructs them to compose a concept web of the cricket's adaptation, and later has the teams collaborate to construct a large poster of their findings.

Clearly, this teacher has created an instructional context for students in which they have ample opportunities to share and challenge one another's thinking while the teacher provides them with appropriate resources and guidance. Moreover, by participating fully in this set of instructional activities, Robert and Kantu demonstrate and further extend their competence by engaging in search strategies modeled by the teacher; they exercise their autonomy in numerous ways such as by choosing to pursue their particular curiosities; and they experience a sustained sense of relatedness through their continuous interaction with each other, members of other teams, and the teacher. In the final activity in this carefully orchestrated learning unit, teams demonstrate their understanding of adaptation to other students. After composing a narrative story using the information they garnered from multiple sources, Robert and Kantu choose to produce a video of themselves, as experts, explaining the life cycle of the monarch butterfly. The recognition they receive from their school peers on this team project indelibly seals these students' positive self-perceptions of self-determination, competence, autonomy, and relatedness, and it propels their interest in learning more about adaptation.

The same vignette, based on actual classroom events, dialogue, and interactions, serves to illustrate that teachers create instructional environments for literacy and related learning that are reflective of research findings (Sweet, Guthrie, & Ng, 1996). These findings point toward teachers' differentiating mostly on activity-based connections to literacy motivations within which students have autonomy and topical interests. Teachers know that students are motivated to read by engaging in activity-based tasks that pique their interest and that enable them to make choices within the boundaries set by the teacher in defining instructional tasks. At the same time, research has shown that although teachers are cognizant of these crucial factors, they do not always provide for them in practice. At the very least, this combination of motivation-related variables—activity-based connections to reading, student freedom to choose or autonomy, and interest in a topic—should be strategically woven into teachers' lesson plans for literacy instruction on a daily basis. Teachers can enhance the development of long-term literacy engagement by aligning their motivational support system with their instructional practices.

References

Bandura, A. (1982). The self and mechanisms of agency. In J. Sils (Ed.), *Psychological perspectives on the self* (Vol. 1, pp. 3–39). Hillsdale, NJ: Erlbaum.

Bandura, A., & Schunk, D. (1981). Cultivating competence, self-efficacy, and intrinsic interest through proximal self-motivation. *Journal of Personality and Social Psychology, 41*, 586–598.

Baumeister, R.F., & Leary, M.R. (1995). The need to belong: Desire for interpersonal attachments as a fundamental human motivation. *Psychological Bulletin, 117*, 497–529.

Borko, H., & Eisenhart, M. (1986). Students' conceptions of reading and their experiences in school. *The Elementary School Journal, 86*, 589–611.

Brown, A.L. (1980). Metacognitive development and reading. In R.J. Spiro, B.C. Bruce, & W.F. Brewer (Eds.), *Theoretical issues in reading comprehension* (pp. 453–482). Hillsdale, NJ: Erlbaum.

Cameron, J., & Pierce, W.D. (1994). Reinforcement, reward, and intrinsic motivation: A meta-analysis. *Review of Educational Research, 64*, 363–423.

Connell, J.P., & Wellborn, J.G. (1991). Competence, autonomy, and relatedness: A motivational analysis of self-system processes. In M.R. Gunnar & L.A. Stroufe (Eds.), *Self-processes and development: The Minnesota symposia on child development* (Vol. 23, pp. 43–78). Hillsdale, NJ: Erlbaum.

Corno, L., & Rohrkemper, M.M. (1985). The intrinsic motivation to learn in classrooms. In C. Ames & R.E. Ames (Eds.), *Research on motivation in education: Vol. 2. The classroom milieu* (pp. 53–90). San Diego, CA: Academic.

Cramer, E.H., & Castle, M. (Eds.). (1994). *Fostering the love of reading: The affective domain in reading education*. Newark, DE: International Reading Association.

deCharms, R. (1976). *Enhancing motivation: Change in the classroom*. New York: Irvington.

Deci, E.L. (1975). *Intrinsic motivation*. New York: Plenum.

Deci, E.L. (1980). *The psychology of self-determination*. Lexington, MA: D.C. Heath.

Deci, E.L., & Ryan, R.M. (1985). *Intrinsic motivation and self-determination in human behavior*. New York: Plenum.

Deci, E.L., & Ryan, R.M. (1992). The initiation and regulation of intrinsically motivated learning and achievement. In A.K. Boggiano & T.S. Pittman (Eds.), *Achievement and motivation: A social developmental perspective*. (pp. 3–36). New York: Cambridge University Press.

Deci, E.L., Schwartz, A.J., Sheinman, L., & Ryan, R.M. (1981). An instrument to assess adults' orientations toward control versus autonomy with children: Reflections on intrinsic motivation and perceived competence. *Journal of Educational Psychology, 73*, 642–650.

Gambrell, L.B., Almasi, J.F., Xie, Q., & Heland, V.J. (1995). Helping first graders get a running start in reading. In L.M. Morrow (Ed.), *Family literacy connections in schools and communities* (pp. 143–154). Newark, DE: International Reading Association.

Gambrell, L.B., & Morrow, L.M. (1996). Creating motivating contexts for literacy learning. In L. Baker, P. Afflerbach, & D. Reinking (Eds.), *Developing engaged readers in school and home communities* (pp. 115–136). Hillsdale, NJ: Erlbaum.

Gambrell, L.B., Codling, R.M., & Palmer, B.M. (1996). *Elementary students' motivation to read* (Reading Research Report No. 52). Athens, GA: National Reading Research Center.

Goldenberg, C. (1989). Making success a more common occurrence for children at-risk for failure: Lessons for Hispanic first-graders learning to read. In J. Allen & J. Mason (Eds.), *Risk makers, risk takers, risk breakers: Reducing the risk for young literacy learners* (pp. 48–78). Portsmouth, NH: Heinemann.

Grolnick, W.S., Ryan, R.M., & Deci, E.L. (1991). The inner resources for school achievement: Motivational mediators of children's perceptions of their parents. *Journal of Educational Psychology, 83*, 508–517.

Guthrie, J.T., McCann, A., Hynd, C., & Stahl, S. (1997). Classroom contexts promoting literacy engagement. In J. Flood, D. Lapp, & S.B. Heath (Eds.), *Handbook for literacy educators: Research on teaching the communicative and visual arts.* New York: Macmillan.

Hart, S. (1982). Analyzing the social organization for reading in one elementary school. In G. Spindler (Ed.), *Doing the ethnography of schooling* (pp. 410–438). New York: Holt, Rinehart, & Winston.

Harter, S. (1982). The perceived competence scale for children. *Child Development, 53*, 87–97.

Harter, S. (1992). The relationship between perceived competence, affect, and motivational orientation within the classroom: Processes and patterns of change. In A.K. Boggiano & T.S. Pittman (Eds.), *Achievement and motivation: A social developmental perspective* (pp. 77–114). New York: Cambridge University Press.

Hiebert, E. (1983). An examination of ability grouping in reading instruction. *Reading Research Quarterly, 18*, 231–255.

Lepper, M.R., & Greene, D. (Eds.). (1978). *The hidden costs of reward: New perspectives on the psychology of motivation.* Hillsdale, NJ: Erlbaum.

Lepper, M.R., Greene, D., & Nisbett, R.E. (1973). Understanding children's intrinsic interest with external rewards. *Journal of Personality and Social Psychology, 28*, 124–137.

Malone, T., & Lepper, M. (1987). Making learning fun: A taxonomy of intrinsic motivation for learning. In R.E. Snow & M.J. Farr (Eds.), *Aptitude, learning, and instruction: Vol. 3. Cognitive and affective process analyses* (pp. 223–253). Hillsdale, NJ: Erlbaum.

McDermott, R. (1987). The explanation of minority school failure, again. *Anthropology and Education Quarterly, 18*, 361–364.

Morrow, L.M., Pressley, M., & Smith, J.K. (1995). *The effect of a literature-based program integrated into literacy and science instruction on achievement, use, and attitudes toward literacy and science* (Reading Research Report No. 37). Athens, GA: National Reading Research Center.

Noddings, N. (1992). *The challenge to care in schools: An alternative approach to education.* New York: Teachers College Press.

Nolen, S.B. (1988). Reasons for studying: Motivational orientations and study strategies. *Cognition and Instruction, 5*, 269–287.

Pintrich, P.R., & DeGroot, E.V. (1990). Motivational and self-regulated learning components of classroom academic performance [Special Section: Motivation and efficacy in education: Research and new directions]. *Journal of Educational Psychology, 82*(1), 33–40.

Rosenbaum, J. (1980). Social implications of educational grouping. In D. Berliner (Ed.), *Review of research in education* (Vol. 8, pp. 361–401). Washington, DC: American Educational Research Association.

Ryan, R.M., Connell, J.P., & Deci, E.L. (1985). A motivational analysis of self-determination and self-regulation. In C. Ames & R.E. Ames (Eds.), *Research on motivation in education: Vol. 2. The classroom milieu.* Orlando, FL: Academic.

Ryan, R.M., Connell, J.P., & Grolnick, W.S. (1992). When achievement is not intrinsically motivated: A theory of internalization and self-regulation in school. In A.K. Boggiano & T.S. Pittman (Eds.), *Achievement and motivation: A social developmental perspective* (pp. 167–188). New York: Cambridge University Press.

Ryan, R.M., & Grolnick, W.S. (1986). Origins and pawns in the classroom: Self-report and projective assessments of individual differences in children's perceptions. *Journal of Personality and Social Psychology, 50,* 550–558.

Schunk, D.H. (1989). Self-efficacy and cognitive skill learning. In C. Ames & R.E. Ames (Eds.), *Research on motivation in education: Vol. 3. Goals and cognition.* San Diego, CA: Academic.

Schunk, D.H. (1991). Self-efficacy and academic motivation. *Educational Psychologist, 26,* 207–232.

Skinner, E.A., & Belmont, M.J. (1993). Motivation in the classroom: Reciprocal effects of teacher behavior and student engagement across the school year. *Journal of Educational Psychology, 85,* 571–581.

Skinner, E.A., Wellborn, J.G., & Connell, J.P. (1990). What it takes to do well in school and whether I've got it: A process model of perceived control and children's engagement and achievement in school. *Journal of Educational Psychology, 82,* 22–32.

Stipek, D.J., & Weisz, J. (1981). Perceived personal control and academic achievement. *Review of Educational Research, 51,* 101–137.

Sweet, A.P. (1997). A national policy perspective on research intersections between literacy and the visual/communicative arts. In J. Flood, D. Lapp, & S.B. Heath (Eds.), *Handbook for literacy educators: Research on teaching the communicative and visual arts.* New York: Macmillan.

Sweet, A.P., & Guthrie, J.T. (1994). *Teacher perceptions and students' motivation to read* (Reading Research Report No. 29). Athens, GA: National Reading Research Center.

Sweet, A.P., & Guthrie, J.T. (1996). How children's motivations relate to literacy development and instruction. *The Reading Teacher, 49,* 660–662.

Sweet, A.P., Guthrie, J.T., & Ng, M. (1996). *Teacher perceptions and students' motivation to read* (Reading Research Report No. 69). Athens, GA: National Reading Research Center.

Vygotsky, L.S. (1978). *Mind in society: The development of higher psychological processes.* Cambridge, MA: Harvard University Press.

Weinstein, R. (1976). Reading group membership in first grade: Teacher behaviors and pupil experience over time. *Journal of Educational Psychology, 68,* 103–116.

Weisz, J., & Cameron, A. (1985). Individual differences in the student's sense of control. In C. Ames & R.E. Ames (Eds.), *Research on motivation in education: Vol. 2. The classroom milieu* (pp. 93–140). Orlando, FL: Academic.

Wentzel, K.R. (1995). *Teachers who care: Implications for student motivation and classroom behavior* (OERI Final Report, Fellows Program). Washington, DC: U.S. Department of Education.

The Role of Responsive Teaching in Focusing Reader Intention and Developing Reader Motivation

6

Robert B. Ruddell and Norman J. Unrau

Because there can be no responsive, reflective teaching of literacy without a responsive, reflective teacher, we intend in this chapter to explore the characteristics that such teachers bring to teaching. From the study of influential teachers, their behavior in the classroom, and their impact on students (Ruddell, 1994, 1995; Ruddell, Draheim, & Barnes, 1990; Ruddell & Haggard, 1982), we can garner insights into responsive teachers and ways they promote literacy engagement. Influential teachers may be defined as teachers who have been identified by a former student as having had a significant influence on the student's academic or personal success in school. Influential teachers share characteristics in several areas that include the following:

- They show that they care about their students.
- They help their students to understand and solve their personal and academic problems.
- They manifest excitement and enthusiasm about what they teach.
- They adapt instruction to the individual needs, motives, interests, and aptitudes of their students and have high expectations for them.
- They use motivating and effective strategies when they teach, including clarity in stating problems, use of concrete examples, analysis of abstract concepts, and application of concepts to new contexts.
- They engage students in a process of intellectual discovery.

We also have learned that high-achieving students, those we could suspect are more motivated for learning, can identify at least twice as many influential teachers as lower achieving students. Whether high or low achieving, these students see their influential teachers as having clear instructional goals, plans, and strategies that contribute to a classroom learning environment that the teacher closely monitors. Further, by emphasizing intrinsic over extrinsic motivation, these influential teachers elicit students' internal motivation by stimulating intellectual curiosity, exploring students' self-understanding, using aesthetic imagery and expression, and focusing on problem solving.

These findings about influencial teachers inform our purposes for this chapter. In it, we tell the story of Ms. Hawthorne, an influential teacher who is striving to redesign her instructional program to promote her students' literacy and learning through an integrated language arts and history curriculum. To better understand Ms. Hawthorne's dilemma and its resolution, we investigate and describe psychological and instructional factors that are critical to the development of both reader and teacher intention and motivation. These psychological and instructional factors form three major categories for both readers and teachers: the developing self, instructional orientation, and task engagement resources. After presenting a model that represents these features and their influence on the focus of intention, we describe a classroom learning environment that emphasizes meaning negotiation, nourishes the developing self, activates students' instructional orientation, and provides potential for readers to sharpen their focus of intention on reading and meaning construction. We then identify key guidelines for designing literacy-enhancing instruction to develop reader intention and motivation and apply these to Ms. Hawthorne's classroom. We conclude with implications for research.

Ms. Hawthorne's Dilemma

Ms. Hawthorne was discontented with the language arts and history program she had inherited when she began teaching at Taft Junior High School in central Los Angeles two years ago. Some of her seventh-grade students read books and completed tasks she assigned, but too many did so halfheartedly, infrequently, or not at all. The program seemed unresponsive, impersonal, and unengaging. She knew that she and her students could do better. With the encouragement of colleagues, a new principal, and faculty at a local university, she decided to investigate what she might do to redesign her program so that more students would become engaged.

She began her action research by collecting as much information as she could about her students to discover who they were—not only as readers but also as people. To get to know individual students better, to understand their motivations and their reading strategies, Ms. Hawthorne decided to conduct a few tutorial sessions once a week after school. Several students responded to this idea; one student, Cynthia, jumped at the opportunity.

At the beginning of the school year, Ms. Hawthorne got the impression that Cynthia was slightly hyperactive and quite social. But, as she got to know Cynthia during the tutorial meetings, she discovered she was far more complex. The enthusiasm that Cynthia expressed when Ms. Hawthorne offered tutorial help demonstrated some aspects of Cynthia's sense of self and her motivation to learn. At her initial tutoring session, Cynthia told Ms. Hawthorne that she had good memories about school. She said she liked it because she had lots of opportunities to socialize with her friends. Both her parents helped her with schoolwork, her mother in reading and writing and her father in math. In earlier elementary grades, Cynthia often was on the honor role. Like her mother, Cynthia was thinking about becoming a nurse, but she also imagined herself being a story writer, a travel agent, a model, and a fashion designer. She obviously was exploring possibilities for herself.

Cynthia said her favorite subject was history, and she had a passion for books about "old-fashioned" family life and orphans. She told Ms. Hawthorne that she had many of these stories in her head and would much rather write them than complete assigned compositions. During their first meeting, Cynthia told Ms. Hawthorne that two of her goals for the year were to improve her reading and to reduce the number of mistakes she made in her writing.

To get an idea of Cynthia's reading level, Ms. Hawthorne administered an individual reading inventory. She found that Cynthia had an independent reading level of fourth grade, an instructional level of fifth grade, and a frustration level of sixth grade. She also discovered that Cynthia, who said that she understood text that she had read, was unable to answer many literal and interpretive questions about that text. After the assessment, Cynthia complained to Ms. Hawthorne that the last paragraph on the test, one at the seventh-grade level, was unfair because there were words in it that she did not recognize. During the assessment and later in the tutorial, Ms. Hawthorne found that Cynthia had difficulty comprehending what she read and connecting concepts to make meaning. Ms. Hawthorne also observed that Cynthia gave up easily with text she had difficulty understanding and expressed boredom or self-defeat rather than increased effort.

Ms. Hawthorne was impressed with Cynthia's "zest" for writing. Cynthia could construct concept maps or outlines and finish a five-paragraph essay in one period. However, Ms. Hawthorne discovered that Cynthia often misplaced her essays before turning them in. Further, Ms. Hawthorne thought that Cynthia's writing was rudimentary in content and structure. In an essay containing paragraphs with four or five simple sentences, she simply restated the assignment and discussed only the most obvious points, which Ms. Hawthorne described as "conceptually dull" writing. Also, Cynthia's essays contained many grammar and spelling errors, which Cynthia wanted to improve.

As the special tutoring progressed, Ms. Hawthorne discovered that Cynthia's self-projected image of an enthusiastic learner was not always consistent with Cynthia's behavior. Although Cynthia first appeared earnest in seeking help for her literacy needs, Ms. Hawthorne began to think that she was seeking attention and trying to evade standard class work. Ms. Hawthorne also noticed that, although Cynthia wrote enthusiastically, she often did not complete reading assignments, and her written work rarely was turned in when it was due. Inconsistency and irresponsibility marked her performance. In short, while Cynthia showed enthusiasm for improvement, she appeared to have problems with self-regulation in addressing schoolwork.

Cynthia's portrait is similar to that of many middle school students who reveal several selves, including images of the enthusiastic learner, the engaged reader, the fast problem solver, the school socialite, the irresponsible kid, and the budding historian. Cynthia has had opportunities that others in her school have not had available, such as a mother and father she views as supportive, but she is beset with motivational problems that keep her from making the kinds of effort that would result in more success. What moves students, like Cynthia, to read? How might her skills as a reader grow? What kinds of activities might her teachers use in classroom environments to promote literacy engagement?

Factors Critical to Reader and Teacher Motivation

The outcomes of a reader's reading and a teacher's instructional design are quite different. However, the two processes have many features in common. Both reader and teacher have a *developing self* (an identity and self-schema, a sense of self-efficacy and self-worth, expectations, an experiential self, and self-knowledge), an *instructional orientation* (achievement goals, task values, sociocultural values and beliefs, and stances), and *task engagement resources* (reader text-processing resources or teacher instructional design resources). In the following sections, we describe these features, which are depicted in Figure 1, and show how they are of particular importance to the motivational state of both readers and teachers.

Using an image to help us render and understand reading and instructional design processes, we envision the eye as a metaphor for focusing motivation and intention. In Figure 1, the central, inner circle, the focus of intention, may be seen as the pupil. Factors that influence the focus of intention radiate from the pupil and form a larger concentric circle around it, somewhat like the eye's iris. Perhaps this metaphor will help us understand the complex array of features and processes that affect intentionality.

The Focus of Intention

At the center of Figure 1 is the *focus of intention*. It may be compared to the eye's pupil focusing intention not in response to light but in response to the confluence of many motivational factors that influence readers and teachers. This focus is the central point of the mind's intent—of its direction, purpose, and intensity when interacting with a learning environment. We have modified and integrated into our perspective a view of intention that Mathewson (1994) developed and built into his model of attitude's influence on reading and learning to read. In that model, intention functions as a mediator between attitude toward reading and reading itself and is defined as a "commitment to a plan for achieving one or more reading purposes at a more or less specified time in the future" (p. 1135). In the reader/teacher self-system presented in Figure 1, we have extended intention to both reader and teacher. The term intention implies not only purpose and goal, but also a self becoming and emerging from a cognitive-affective background. Mathewson refers to these background factors as cornerstone concepts, including values, goals, and self-concepts that are influenced by home and school environments. In light of psychological research on motivation, we have extended these cornerstone concepts to various features that control the focus of intention.

In describing the factors that influence motivation or the focus of intention, we aspire to the ideal of the optimally self-regulated reader or teacher. Self-regulation is essential for self-actualization, the pinnacle of Maslow's (1954) hierarchy of needs that drive motivation.

Figure 1

Factors Critical to Developing Reader/Teacher Focus of Intention and Motivation

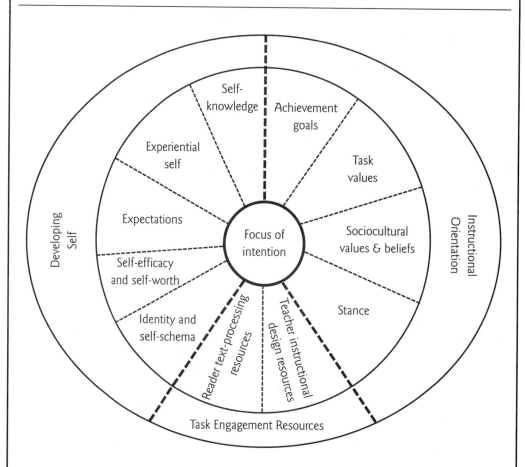

Reader text-processing resources:
Knowledge of language
Word analysis
Text-processing strategies
Metacognitive strategies
Knowledge of classroom and social
   interaction
World knowledge

Teacher instructional design resources:
Knowledge of students and their meaning-
   construction process
Knowledge of literature and content areas
Teaching strategies
World knowledge
Metacognitive knowledge

Developing Self

The developing self comprises those aspects of the reader's or teacher's self-system that shape life's meaning and purpose. As structures in the self-system, they contribute to our focus of intention as readers and learners (Mathewson, 1994). The components of the developing self that govern the focus of intention are arrayed clockwise from the lower left in Figure 1. We will explore each of these constructs and illustrate them with references to Ms. Hawthorne and Cynthia.

Identity and self-schema. Both Ms. Hawthorne and Cynthia, as teacher and student, have a sense of who they are—that is, they have an identity. Ms. Hawthorne's identity is far more consolidated in her role as a developing teacher; Cynthia is still exploring what she might become in a stage Erikson (1968) labels identity versus identity confusion. According to Erikson, core identity includes two aspects of self: a sense of self garnered from the integration of many selves or aspects of those selves that have been assumed, played out, rejected, or embraced and a sense of self as an organizing agency that enables self-representation.

The first sense of self in past, present, and future arises from self-schema. Teachers, like their students, access past, present, and future self-schemata (Markus & Nurius, 1986) as facets of their self-system. Those lived, remembered, and possible selves influence each student's and teacher's behavior and motivation. Images of the self shape the choices made, the actions carried out, and the possibilities pursued or resisted.

Cynthia has many images of herself as a young woman in the future. She imagines she could be a nurse, a fashion designer, or a writer. Like students, teachers have self-schemata in the form of possible or potential selves. Ms. Hawthorne often sees herself as a dynamic teacher promoting more engagement with reading than she now witnesses in her classroom. A teacher's activated self-schema provides not only a foundation for the interpretation of students in a learning context, such as the way Ms. Hawthorne interprets Cynthia's behavior, but also an internal context for the interpretation of a specific text, such as a poem.

Garcia and Pintrich (1994) demonstrate how self-schemata contribute to an individual's desire to develop literacy skills or to avoid their development. Cynthia shows both these trends. An individual's schema can generate an identity perceived by ourselves and others that ranges from loathed to loved, failed to fulfilled, incompetent to incomparable.

An example from Moyer (1995) illustrates the self-schema's motivational strength. A poet and teacher who discovered the power of literacy in prison, Jimmy Santiago Baca, eventually won an American Book Award and founded Black Mesa Enterprises, an organization that provides young people with alternatives to violence through a language-centered community. Before becoming a writer, he struggled with a self-schema that profoundly rejected literacy. While in jail, Baca proclaimed,

> Sissies read books. You couldn't do *anything* with a book. You couldn't fix a '57 Chevy with a book. You couldn't take money from some hustler with a book. You couldn't convince

or persuade anybody with a book. Books were in the way. And not only that, they were the great enemy. Books were where you found the pain.... So why should I go open a book and give myself all this pain? I didn't *need* that. (pp. 35–36)

However, language and literacy and another possible self caught Baca in what he calls "the fiercest typhoon I have ever been in and from which I have never escaped. I have continually swirled like a leaf" (p. 36).

The second organizing agency of our identity Erikson (1968) refers to as ego-identity, the "actually attained but forever-to-be-revised sense of reality of the self within social reality" (p. 211). Erikson's conception of identity is tied to his theory of identity formation through the life cycle. Students' and teachers' lives can be viewed as psychohistories that, if examined closely, reveal the outcome of the various crises through which they have passed in home, community, and school on their way to manifesting their current role and identity as a student or a teacher.

Seeing a student like Cynthia or a teacher like Ms. Hawthorne as an individual passing through a "forever-to-be-revised sense of reality of the self" provides a perspective that is both practical and theoretically powerful. With the concept of identity as both a capacity to organize selves in a social environment and as a composite of sustainable self-impressions that provides an internal, personal core of reference, we can more clearly appreciate the role of influential teachers in the shaping of both a student's and a teacher's identity. If, as Ruddell and his associates (Ruddell & Greybeck, 1992; Ruddell & Kern, 1986) have demonstrated, influential teachers provide students with models with whom they identify and attempt to emulate, then such influential teachers also may serve as focal images that students and teachers-to-be might use to help themselves organize their ego identities.

The concepts of identity and identification also enable us to understand a teacher's and his or her students' motivation to read at a deeper level. Students may not only decide to enter the field of education because of identification with an influential teacher; they also may be moved to emulate the teaching style of an influential teacher. Responsive teachers, like Ms. Hawthorne, are likely to recognize that their students' identities, and thus their students' motives for learning, are shaped by crises of identity before and during schooling and by identifications with family, community, and cultural figures.

Responsive teachers also recognize that many young people, especially those attending innercity schools, may see themselves excluded from the school's culture and seek affirmation of an identity and affiliation on the streets (Heath & McLaughlin, 1993). These are often the at-risk students who, by the time they enter middle school, have begun to disidentify with school and become socialized through gang life (Vigil, 1993). Some of these at-risk students may find alternative groups and organizations, such as boys and girls clubs, community organizations, or church groups, in which identities can be found or formed. Some innercity schools have developed programs, such as crossaged tutoring programs for pregnant teenage girls, to encourage students to find affirmation of their emerging identities in the schools.

Self-efficacy and self-worth. What we believe ourselves capable of doing or learning constitutes our self-efficacy. Cynthia, for example, believes that she knows quite a lot about what she calls "old-fashioned times" in the United States and that she can read stories about people living in those times very well. When Ms. Hawthorne lets her read such stories, Cynthia feels a high sense of self-efficacy and a sharpened focus of intention. As Schunk and Zimmerman in Chapter 2 point out, the self-efficacy of a student will predict his or her motivation for engaging in reading. A student with high self-efficacy will work harder, longer, and more willingly than one with low self-efficacy. Even though Cynthia may encounter challenging vocabulary and difficult narrative, she is likely to be effortful and to work hard to understand.

Schunk (1991, 1994) has shown that teaching students to be more efficacious and persuading them that they are efficacious improves their performance. During her tutorial with Cynthia, Ms. Hawthorne models strategies that she believes will help Cynthia increase her sense of self-efficacy. She shows her how to summarize as she reads, to make predictions, to seek clarification, and to ask questions—strategies that build comprehension and self-regulation (Palincsar & Brown, 1986).

Self-worth may be viewed as a reflection of self-efficacy. According to self-worth theorists, students' highest concern is to protect a sense of ability (Covington, 1992). Accordingly, learners' motivation to engage in school settings frequently depends on their perception of the impact of a learning event on self-esteem. The protection of self-worth may be achieved at the expense of earning low grades if students believe that not studying will preserve esteem more effectively than studying. If students do not engage in reading tasks for school, they may be avoiding them not because they lack motivation but because they are motivated by a paramount concern: the preservation of esteem. By not reading, a student can say to himself (and to his classmates) that he did not expect to perform well because he made no effort to do so. Such a statement would not reflect on the student's ability to compete, which is frequently valued above effort in school cultures.

The concept of self-worth applies to teachers also. Teachers who have low self-esteem are less likely to rise to teaching challenges such as those Ms. Hawthorne is confronting. They may find it more assuring to continue past practices without making efforts and risking failure in planning for future changes in their teaching. What teachers like Ms. Hawthorne judge themselves capable of accomplishing in their classrooms has a determining effect on their motivation and the learning environments they construct.

Expectations. As mentioned in Chapter 2, expectation, a motivational construct related to self-efficacy (Schunk, 1994), often influences focus of intention. Covington (1992) has explored the relations between ability attributions and expectations. He notes that students' personal expectations influence their level of aspiration. That level of aspiration, in turn, may be shaped or limited by the expectations of others, especially teachers.

We know that children like Cynthia achieve at a higher level in classrooms where teachers expect all children to learn (Stipek, 1993). We also know that teachers communicate different expectation messages to students whom the teacher considers to have high or low expectations (Good, 1987). For example, teachers call on high-expectation students more often and wait longer for answers from them but criticize low-expectation students more often for incorrect answers.

It is critical that teachers communicate positive beliefs and attributions to young learners. Ms. Hawthorne knows and does this with Cynthia whenever she can during their work together. Studies of teachers and their students indicate that there is a strong relation between teachers' beliefs about their own efficacy to motivate and to teach students and students' beliefs about their own abilities and chances for success. For example, Midgley, Feldlaufer, & Eccles (1989) found that students who had high-efficacy teachers became significantly more positive (or demonstrated less negative change) compared with students who had low-efficacy teachers and who developed more negative beliefs during the school year. Perhaps responsive teachers like Ms. Hawthorne need to develop and maintain a flexible view of both their self-expectations and their expectations of students; this requires that teachers constantly monitor their own patterns of self-expectation and the patterns of expectation they hold for each student.

Experiential self. The experiential self is another feature of the developing self-system that controls the focus of intention (Epstein, 1994). The experiential self works parallel to and simultaneously with the other features described but less consciously and less rationally. The features previously described tend to be more verbally coded, such as occurs when Cynthia thinks of herself as "a student who likes history." In contrast, the experiential self processes imagery, narratives, and metaphors to give us a sense of our experience's meaning. In the other structures, reasoning may enable us to make connections between concepts, but in the experiential self there are looser associations among images, stories, and analogies. Truth may not be approached through reason but appears as self-evident; "thinking" tends to lack rational rigor and to leap to stereotypes. While the cognitive structures that we have explored are usually integrated, the experiential self is more likely to reveal dissociation or illogical complexes when, on rare occassions, it appears in consciousness. The experiential self is where seasoned teachers, like Ms. Hawthorne, have stored their teaching stories that contribute to their history and identity as teachers. They refer, almost unconsciously, to these stories to help them make instructional decisions. In their experiential self students also store their school stories that contribute to their focus of intention.

It is important to emphasize that the nonrational experiential self continually interacts with and influences the more rational structures that compose the developing self-system. Interaction that may occur on unconscious levels can influence the more rational structures, such as identity and self-schema, self-efficacy, self-worth, expectations, goals, and task values. The extent of the influence depends on the power of narratives, imagery, and metaphors contained in the experiential self.

The parallel and interactive aspects of the self-system enable us to understand more comprehensively both the reader's and the teacher's experience of texts that may be represented in long-term memory through words and images. Reading can be explained with the help of schema theory (Rumelhart, 1980), which is more verbally founded, and dual coding theory (Paivio, 1986; Sadoski & Paivio, 1994), which hypothesizes the existence of two means of encoding experience, namely through words and images. Further, the self-system we have postulated enables us to understand not only readers' motivations to seek and engage in literacy events but also their emotional or aesthetic experiences with stories or poetry.

Self-knowledge. A teacher's or a student's self-knowledge includes all that a teacher or student knows of his or her own self-system, instructional orientation, and task engagement resources. The assumptions that self-knowledge enables improvements in a teacher's performance and that the inclination to gain self-knowledge should extend throughout a teacher's professional life form the foundation for reflective teaching and the development of more reflective teachers (Schon, 1987; Valli, 1992). We suspect that the more teachers have looked at their own behavior in various settings, especially in classroom interactions, and the more they know about themselves as teachers and how they function, the more they will be able to construct productive learning relationships with their students and learning environments for them.

Students who have begun to gain some degree of self-knowledge often are able to use that knowledge in their reading and discussion of texts to gain more self-understanding. This is especially true if teachers encourage the use of literature to promote self-understanding, as Rosenblatt (1938/1995) has long advocated in works such as *Literature as Exploration*. Through classroom dialogue and reflective writing that allows students to make connections between their own emerging identities and the lives of fictional characters, students may gain deeper personal knowledge.

Both teachers and students can affect their focus of intention through self-knowledge of their own motivational system. Ms. Hawthorne, for example, knows that she is unhappy with her students' level of engagement and that she will continue to be discontent until she modifies her instructional program. She knows that she usually thinks of herself as a confident, capable, and caring teacher, and she tries to envision herself working productively with her students. In addition, she recognizes that what she wants to do involves some risks but is willing to take them in order to evolve in her own development as a teacher. All this self-knowledge will help Ms. Hawthorne understand and sustain herself as she moves through periods of challenge and change.

Summary. The constructs of the developing self-system, including identity and self-schema, self-efficacy and self-worth, expectations, the experiential self, and self-knowledge, are not isolated—they interact as they contribute to teacher or student focus of intention. Although a teacher like Ms. Hawthorne may be conscious of her sense of self as a teacher, of her abilities, and of her expectations, she may be less conscious but nonetheless motivationally influenced by her experiential self, which contains the classroom stories that quietly contribute to the intensity and direction of her focus of intention. Further, the constructs of the developing self interact with features that make up reader or teacher instructional orientation, which is discussed next.

Instructional Orientation

Instructional orientation, or the alignment of teacher or student with a teaching or learning task, affects intention and motivation. The following critical factors make up instructional orientation and regulate the focus of intention.

Achievement goals. If Ms. Hawthorne asks herself whether an instructional episode is leading toward her becoming a more competent teacher or merely toward the demonstration of her superior skills in classroom instruction, she is, according to Nicholls (1984), questioning achievement goals. Achievement-goal theory stresses the engagement of the learner in selecting, structuring, and making sense of achievement experience. Meece (1994) points out that research has focused on two kinds of achievement goals: mastery or task-oriented goals and performance or ego-oriented goals. Those seeking mastery goals are intrinsically motivated to acquire knowledge and skills that lead to their becoming more competent. The word "mastery" to describe these goals does not mean "mastery learning," "mastery teaching," or a behaviorist perspective of instruction. Ms. Hawthorne, for example, constructs mastery or task-oriented goals for herself as she investigates her students and contemplates redesigning her language arts program. Individuals who are pursuing performance goals are eager to seek opportunities to demonstrate their skills or knowledge in a competitive, public arena. Cynthia would be manifesting performance or ego-oriented goals if she were motivated to read her stories to her classmates primarily to show others her skills as a writer and storyteller.

What might move a teacher, or a reader, toward one or the other goal orientation? Perceptions of personal ability have been shown to be one critical factor that influences patterns of achievement (Meece, 1994). If individuals believe they can become better teachers, or readers, by making an effort, they are more likely to embrace a mastery-goal orientation. They see themselves as able to improve over time by making an effort to master challenging tasks. A teacher like Ms. Hawthorne or a student like Cynthia, who acquires knowledge and skills that lead to perceptions of incremental growth in competency, exemplifies a mastery orientation. By making the effort to acquire knowledge and skills, the teacher's or student's feelings of self-worth and competence are likely to increase.

Learners who adopt an ego or performance orientation view their abilities as unchangeable and judge them in comparison to the abilities of others, such as their colleagues, peers, or classmates. If a student must exert more effort to learn a concept, a performance-oriented learner would judge that classmate as having less ability even if both students eventually learn the concept. Performance-oriented learners become preoccupied with ability and see it as basic to success in school performance.

Children's goal orientations appear to result in part from their internalizing parental perspectives, especially the mother's view, of effort and ability in learning (Ames & Archer,

1987). School learning environments also have been found to shape students' goal orientations. Students can be influenced to adopt mastery goals if teachers create environments that accentuate self-improvement, discovery, engagement in meaningful tasks, and practicality while diminishing the importance of competition, demonstration of intellectual skills, and public comparisons of schoolwork (Ames, 1992; Hagen & Weinstein, 1995). We suspect that influential teachers who embrace a mastery or task orientation toward learning will not only create such environments in their classrooms but also will serve as models of learning with whom students can identify as they form their identity as students.

A teacher's expectations influence students, especially in relation to the teacher's degree of emphasis on mastery goals. When examining the differences in students' strategy-use patterns in high- and low-mastery classes, Meece (1994) found significant differences among teachers' expectations for students. In the high-mastery classes, teachers expected students to understand, apply, and make sense of their learning, whereas in low-mastery classes students spent more time memorizing information and had few opportunities to construct meaning or apply their learning in new situations. Such examples illustrate how teachers' expectations can shape students' literacy performance. Teachers can promote literacy engagement by emphasizing a mastery orientation that stresses conceptual understanding, provides for collaborative learning, minimizes social competition, and allows students to participate in curricular decision making.

Task values. Wigfield (1994; see also Chapter 1 in this volume) has identified and investigated several interacting components that make up an individual's perception of task values. These components include attainment value (the importance an individual attributes to a task), intrinsic-interest value (the task's subjective interest to an individual), utility value (the usefulness of a task in light of a person's future goals), and the cost of success (the "disadvantages" of accomplishing a task, such as experiencing anxiety). Both students like Cynthia and teachers like Ms. Hawthorne consider a task's values before undertaking it. For instance, Ms. Hawthorne, who is thinking about redesigning her language arts and history curriculum, needs to consider how important the redesign is to her, how interested she is in that redesign, how useful the revised program would be to her goals, and the time and effort necessary to redesign the program.

An additional incentive or purpose that teachers might have for engaging in a teaching task is its intrinsic enjoyment. According to Csikszentmihalyi (1990a, 1990b), motivation is closely related to autotelic experiences that are self-contained and self-rewarding. Autotelic experiences are not pursued for any future purpose or goal but for their intrinsic worth, their enjoyment. Csikszentmihalyi has referred to the autotelic experience as "flow," an optimal psychological experience that puts consciousness on a special level, as mentioned by other authors in this volume. When teachers experience a sense of flow in their teaching, they are enjoying the process as a self-justifying event. To experience flow, teachers must attain a balance between teaching challenge and teaching ability. Ms. Hawthorne has been frustrated because of her students' lack of engagement in reading and learning. She is seeking a more optimum psychological and instructional experience. However, if teaching a particular group of students to engage in a cooperative learning strategy to develop their reading or writing skills becomes too challenging, Ms. Hawthorne will experience anxiety and frustration; if teaching this strategy presents no challenge to her, she may become bored. If she can discover an optimal balance between challenge and ability and engage her students during their literacy activities (Csikszentmihalyi, 1990b), Ms. Hawthorne is likely to enjoy the flow of teaching, and if Cynthia can find books that provide a balance between challenge and boredom, she is more likely to relish the flow of reading.

Sociocultural values and beliefs. A teacher's sociocultural values and beliefs have a profound effect on the interpretation of texts, relationships with students, and instructional decision making. Research has shown that students are vulnerable to breakdowns in communication if their sociocultural values and beliefs do not match those of the teacher or if the teacher is not responsive to cultural differences (Erickson, 1979; Hull & Rose, 1994; Labov, 1972). For example, culturally diverse readers may enter a learning environment in a monocultural school where specific values and beliefs are essential for success, where achievement depends on the reader's valuing literacy and standard English, and where instructional routines, like turn taking, are traditional (Mehan, 1979; Phillips, 1970). If teachers hold such values and beliefs that differ vastly from those of their students, students' learning and motivation may be adversely affected.

As Heath (1983) discovered, teachers also can positively affect students who enter school cultures that are divergent from those in which they have grown up. Innovative work by Au and Mason (1981) and by Moll (1994) in understanding the social networks of Hispanic children illustrates how a teacher's awareness of varied sociocultural values and beliefs can enhance students' acquisition of literacy and motivation for learning. Teachers must be prepared to reflect on and examine the sociocultural values and beliefs that they and their students hold. Through reflection and self-exploration, teachers may become more responsive to students' values and beliefs in designing classroom instruction, which will affirm significant aspects of students' cultural and personal identities. (See also Chapter 9 in this volume, in which Au discusses culturally diverse students' literacy achievement.)

Stance. In literacy studies, stance pertains to the perspective and orientation that a reader adopts toward the reading of a particular text. By guiding the reader's focus of intention, reader's stance influences motivation. While reader's stance refers to the reader's perspective and orientation toward a given text, instructional stance refers to the teacher's perspective and orientation toward the teaching of a text. By guiding the reader's focus of attention and purpose, the teacher's instructional stance also influences a reader's intention to read.

Theorists and researchers (Beach & Hynes, 1990; Langer, 1990; Smith, 1984) have described several different stances that readers and teachers may adopt. Rosenblatt (1978) has strongly influenced the field with her identification and elaboration of two stances—efferent and aesthetic—which were mentioned in the introduction. When adopting an efferent stance, the reader concentrates on taking away information from the text. When taking an aesthetic stance, the reader experiences the text through imagination and feeling. When reading historical stories, Cynthia adopts an aesthetic stance and enters the "old-fashioned" world created in her imagination. We suspect that the experiential self is more deeply engaged during aesthetic readings that draw readers into the flow of narrative and imagery.

These are not either-or stances; rather, they are on a continuum along which the degree of emphasis may change. To varying degrees, the teacher and the reader can control stance. While progressing through a text, the teacher may encourage an instructional stance that guides readers toward the integration of both efferent and aesthetic stances in varied proportions. For example, when reading about Dimmesdale's struggle with Chillingworth in Nathanial Hawthorne's *The Scarlet Letter*, the reader may be encouraged to focus more attention on the aesthetic stance, but may be instructed to shift to a greater concentration on the efferent stance when trying to analyze Hester Prynne's relationship with her daughter Pearl. According to Rosenblatt (1985), teachers sometimes tend to emphasize an efferent stance at the expense of aesthetic readings; teachers expect students to analyze texts more than they encourage students to live through the experiences depicted in the literature they read. An overemphasis on efferent readings may, in some instances, reduce the value and enjoyment of students' transactions with literature. However, an emphasis on efferent responses may help students develop analytical skills important for critical thinking. Nevertheless, influential teachers tend to emphasize aesthetic responses over efferent ones (Ruddell, 1994).

Summary. Instructional-orientation constructs combined with those of the developing self contribute to creating and sustaining a focus of intention. This focus also may be affected by task engagement resources.

Task Engagement Resources

Task engagement resources refer to information structures that enable a teacher or a reader to undertake a learning task. While most of the features previously discussed contribute directly to motivational states, task engagement resources provide cognitive tools to accomplish the tasks for which readers or teachers are motivated (see Ruddell & Unrau, 1994, for a complete review). The reader's text processing resources include knowledge of language, word analysis, text processing strategies, metacognitive strategies, knowledge of classroom and social interaction, and world knowledge. Each of these resources helps readers not only focus their intention to read but also interact with texts to construct meanings that can be negotiated through classroom discussion. The teacher's instructional design resources include knowledge of students and their meaning-construction process, knowledge of literature and content areas, teaching strategies, world knowledge, and metacognitive knowledge. With these resources, teachers can create learning environments that nourish the developing self and activate students' instructional orientation. With these task engagement resources in mind, we present in the following section a model of text interpretation in a classroom context, which provides opportunity for readers to sharpen their focus of intention, heighten their motivation to read, and construct meaning in response to their reading.

Role of Meaning Negotiation in Developing Reader Intention and Motivation

The structures we have explored provide the foundation not only for the meanings that individual readers and teachers construct, but also for meanings negotiated among students during reader-based instruction. In addition, the design and function of the classroom learning environment further affects motivation to engage in literacy events and learning (Marshall, 1992; Unrau & Ruddell, 1995). We can expect readers to engage with reading, interact in the classroom community, and participate in the meaning-negotiation process if they are motivated to read and to learn, if prior knowledge is activated, if tasks are personally relevant, and if they are encouraged to actively construct meanings. As mentioned, the teacher who incorporates features like these is considered to be mastery-goal oriented and is more likely to witness productive learning among students (Ames, 1992; Covington, 1992).

The classroom meaning-negotiation process is represented in Figure 2. The three overlapping circles in the figure symbolize the interactive nature of the meaning-negotiation process for teachers, readers, and the classroom community. Note, however, that the process overlaps a text (shown by the representation of an open book) on which the dialogue is based. Thus, the text itself is not the sole object carrying meaning; instead, meanings arise from transactions with the text (Rosenblatt, 1978, 1985). During negotiation for meanings related to texts, readers bring their own interpretations to the interaction, teachers bring their understanding of the story and of the reading process, and members of the class interact with the text to shape—and reshape—meanings.

Through this model, we acknowledge that readers like Cynthia and teachers like Ms. Hawthorne read much more than a printed text. In effect, they read several texts—if texts are understood to mean events, situations, behavioral scripts, and other symbolic processes that require interpretation (Bloome & Bailey, 1992). Of course, students and teacher read the text on the page. But students in particular also need to read the task, the authority structure (whose interpretations will count?), the teacher (what are her expectations?), and the sociocultural setting. In addition, they must read the social dynamics of the class, including sociolinguistic rules, such as turn taking and question-answer response patterns. Responsive teaching entails not only an awareness of this process but also an intention and resources to foster its growth.

If the reader's focus of intention and motivation is to be developed, classroom community negotiation of meaning is imperative. The teacher provides activities that enable readers to shape and share meanings. The sharing of those meanings enables the evolution of an interpretive community that can develop criteria for the validation of interpretations.

Ruddell & Unrau

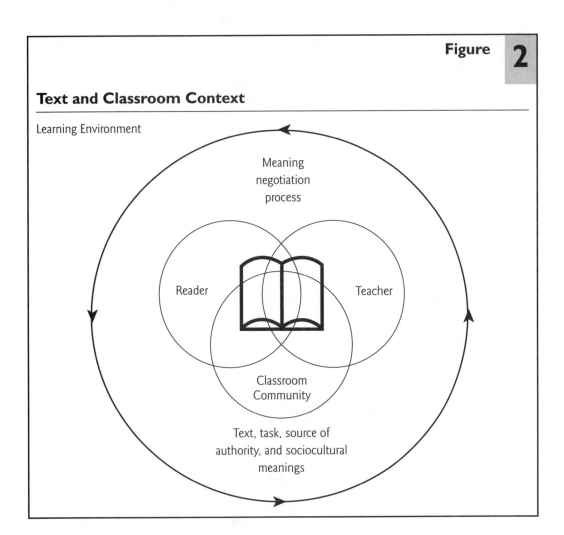

Figure 2

Text and Classroom Context

Learning Environment

Meaning negotiation process

Reader

Teacher

Classroom Community

Text, task, source of authority, and sociocultural meanings

Meanings are open—not closed or fixed—though they need to be grounded in the text. Readers and teacher may share common understandings in the interpretive community; however, those understandings or interpretations are not forever fixed. Meanings are shaped and reshaped in the hermeneutic circle (Dilthey, 1900/1976), which is represented by the circle with arrowheads surrounding the meaning negotiation process in Figure 2. Meaning construction is viewed as a circular and changing process of forming hypotheses and then testing, negotiating, and validating interpretations. As the reader's knowledge changes, as the reader interacts with other readers and with the teacher in a social context, constructed meanings can be expected to change. In a sense, while a text may be fixed, its meanings for the reader are always evolving. The understanding of this process of meaning negotiation is a hallmark of the responsive teacher and enables readers like Cynthia to focus intention and increase motivation.

Guidelines for Designing Literacy Enhancing Instructional Environments

Given the spectrum of motivational factors that influence the focus of intention, teachers can follow several guidelines that facilitate the creation of an optimal learning environment to promote engagement with literacy. Many of these guidelines operate in the model of text interpretation in classroom contexts that we have explored. However, we can present only in a summary fashion 12 guidelines that teachers might apply in their design of an ideal learning environment to promote both readers' intention and motivation and to cultivate literacy over time.

1. Provide for the exploration of student identity, its roots, and its possibilities; acknowledge that each student has self-schemata that shape behavior and warrant understanding; devise activities and interactions that bolster reflection and self-discovery.

2. Design an environment that intentionally builds student self-worth rather than one that unintentionally threatens it.

3. Promote a climate in which students work toward task-oriented goals that foster a sense of mastery and competency.

4. Develop an atmosphere in which students see that the acquisition of knowledge, skills, and strategies is incremental and proceeds through efforts that become increasingly self-regulated.

5. Activate and extend students' background knowledge to facilitate meaning construction.

6. Model reflectivity and metacognitive processes for students.

7. Design tasks that are perceived as important to students, that involve real-life issues, that have subjective and community-related interest, that are seen as useful in relation to students' future goals, and that provide the chance for the experience of flow.

8. Establish literacy expectations that are appropriate to each student's capacities and provide support for the attainment of those expectations.

9. Encourage the flexibility to view experience from multiple perspectives and to adopt instructional stances that promote literacy engagement; encourage, when appropriate, an aesthetic stance in response to reading in order to engage more of the experiential self and its narrative and imagery.

10. Discover and use students' sociocultural values and beliefs as resources for constructing an environment that reflects students' orientations while developing understanding of and tolerance for alternative value and belief systems.

11. Allow students to gain a sense of ownership and share authority in the interpretation of texts and criteria for validation of those interpretations.

12. Formulate or select tasks that are suitable to students' task engagement resources and that allow students to internalize knowledge and skills to become increasingly independent, self-regulating, and self-reliant learners.

These guidelines may be applied in the design of strategies used to construct a learning environment and to maintain that environment. Ms. Hawthorne applied many of these guidelines in redesigning her instructional program in language arts and history.

Ms. Hawthorne's Application of the Guidelines

To improve her instructional program, Ms. Hawthorne decided to take several steps, many of which actualize suggestions provided in the guidelines presented. Her goal was to deepen her students' engagement with literacy tasks including reading assignments in history, to sharpen their focus of intention, and to promote their long-term motivation to read and learn. She decided to shift emphasis from a teacher-centered and controlled curriculum, designed to develop a learning environment driven by extrinsic rewards and reinforcements, to a student-centered curriculum that would enhance intrinsic motivation. To build intrinsic motives in her students, she used guidelines to move her classroom more toward a community in which students could focus on mastery and competency. She wanted her students to acquire motives and strategies that would lead them toward a higher degree of self-regulation in their reading and learning than she had witnessed.

Ms. Hawthorne used principles of cooperative learning (Slavin, 1995; Slavin et al., 1994) to design her reader response groups. She delegated authority to each group that in turn had to share authority with each of its group members. In mixed-ability groups, members shared responsibilities for learning and were individually accountable for their learning and contributions. She structured the reading response groups so that each team read a different book that Ms. Hawthorne selected on the basis of the team's interests. Cynthia's team, for example, read several historical novels that were set in the time period covered in her history text and that ranged from the fifth- through seventh-grade reading levels. To develop her students' self-understanding and self-knowledge, Ms. Hawthorne used their responses to texts, such as those they wrote in journals, to help them explore their emerging identities (Rosenblatt, 1938/1995). To build vocabulary, she asked each member of a team to keep a journal that included a list of unfamiliar words that students selected.

Ms. Hawthorne also adapted reciprocal reading (Palincsar & Brown, 1986) for use in her reading groups. The modification allowed students to play the role of teacher, to summarize portions of text read, to ask teacher-like questions, and to make predictions. The procedure helped students internalize metacognitive strategies that improved their comprehension during independent reading.

To integrate her history and language arts curriculum while teaching about the Great Depression in America during the 1930s, Ms. Hawthorne had her class read Mildred Taylor's *Roll of Thunder, Hear My Cry*, a novel about a young black girl, Cassie Logan, and her family who struggle to survive and maintain their independence in rural Mississippi. Cynthia, who was striving for independence herself, easily identified with Cassie and her struggles. Ms. Hawthorne encouraged teams to develop interpretations of the novel that could be shared and discussed with the whole class. Extending the principle of shared authority over the negotiation of meaning, she talked with her students about what standards should govern the correctness of an interpretation. She also used strategies, such as Directed Reading-Thinking Activities (Stauffer, 1976) to engage her students' background knowledge in the construction of meanings. Before students began reading the novel, she asked them what they thought a book entitled *Roll of Thunder, Hear My Cry* would be about. The discussion moved many students to activate background knowledge, formulate hypotheses, and sharpen their focus of intention to read. When the class negotiated interpretations of events in the novel, meanings that teams and individuals constructed were shared in the classroom. While she supported questioning and interaction, Ms. Hawthorne asked teams and individuals to provide evidence from the text to support their interpretations, and she pointed out that historians also must substantiate their interpretations of history with reference to events. Ms. Hawthorne's approach focused the intention and motivation of Cynthia and her peers.

Summary with Implications for Research

If teachers are to become more effective in developing reader intention and motivation, they must carefully reflect on the nature of their teaching. Our discussion of factors critical to responsive teaching highlights the importance of three areas. First, the *developing self* accounts for teacher and student identity and self-schema, self-efficacy and self-worth, expectations, the experiential self, and self-knowledge—all of which underlie and influence a reader's intention to read or a teacher's intention to teach. Second, *instructional orientation* serves to identify and define an individual's goals, task values, sociocultural values and beliefs, and stance. These factors direct teachers' instructional purposes and students' reading purposes. Third, *task engagement resources* consist of text processing understandings that enable readers to comprehend various texts, and instructional design knowledge that enables teachers to skillfully direct instruction. These three areas, when combined, yield an interactive system of affective and cognitive factors that show how responsive teachers can help readers develop their focus of intention and motivation.

Critical to highly effective and responsive teaching is a clear understanding of the *meaning-negotiation process* that is essential to focusing readers' intention and motivation and engaging students in active learning. Of paramount importance, as we negotiate meanings, is our understanding of text appropriateness and task difficulty for the reader and our willingness to share our interpretive authority with students. We need to incorporate through active discussion the sociocultural meanings and interpretations of our students. This understanding and willingness serve to shift the responsibility for inquiry and learning to the reader, and it focuses the reader's intention, commitment, and motivation—as illustrated in Ms. Hawthorne's classroom and in her interaction with Cynthia.

We outlined 12 important instructional guidelines based on our exploration of the factors critical to responsive teaching and the meaning-negotiation process. These guidelines range from exploration and understanding of student identity and self-schema to establishing appropriate literacy expectations for students and adopting an instructional stance that promotes literacy engagement. We encourage teachers to examine carefully these guidelines and use them to reflect on their own teaching.

Although educators have progressed over the last decade in understanding the reader intention and motivation process, many areas still require further exploration for us to comprehend more fully this complex and critically important phenomenon. The following areas of inquiry warrant inclusion in further research.

- How are influential teachers formed? Could teacher preparation programs emphasize the growth of qualities of influential teachers, including their exceptional interpersonal and intrapersonal awareness, so that more students feel that they are understood and that their schooling contributes to the growth of their developing self, their identity, and their self-understanding?

- Which of the factors critical to developing reader and teacher focus of intention are the most effective and enduring motivators, and how do they interact? Further, are there additional factors that explain motivation to read and that would make the focus of intention even more inclusive?

- How can literacy teachers effectively model, transfer to students, and sustain belief in a mastery-goal orientation and the incremental benefits of effortful learning?

- How could we promote literacy engagement through an emphasis on self-regulated learning from the earliest school years? What forms of early school instruction foster metacognition and comprehension? Does student reflection on learning, problem solving, and study strategies promote self-regulation and engagement during reading?

- Knowing that motivation to read, especially to engage in pleasure reading, declines as children progress through school, what kinds of classroom and student-teacher interactions sustain or increase motivation? If responsive teachers in the early school years develop learning environments that encourage the growth of individual competency, mastery, self-regulation, and self-understanding within the classroom community, are students more likely to continue or expand their enjoyment of independent pleasure reading?

- What reader goals, values, and beliefs toward meaning negotiation promote highly productive engagement in the process? What kinds of texts and tasks support a reader's involvement or openness during meaning negotiation?

- We know little about the effects of the teacher's self-system or instructional orientation on motivation. How do narratives from past teaching episodes, which are stored in the experiential self, affect the design of lessons and classroom environments in the present? What contributes to the formation of reflective and responsive teachers, and how could the development of more reflective and responsive teachers be realized?

- How does a teacher's instructional stance affect lesson planning, reader intent, and especially students' motivation to engage in reading?

- What effects does a teacher's orientation toward authority and its role in classroom meaning negotiation have on a reader's comprehension and motivation? For example, do teachers who practice a teacher-directed style have a different impact on meaning negotiation and level of reader engagement from those teachers who consider the classroom community as the center of authority?

By enhancing our knowledge of the critical factors that influence the reader's developing self and the teacher's instructional orientation, we gain important insight into teaching that can lead to gains in the reader's focus of intention. Our understanding of the meaning-negotiation process enables us to create the instructional environment that encourages readers to participate in active learning, share learning responsibility, and experience an increase in reading motivation. The responsive, reflective teacher contributes to the development of focused reader intention and heightened motivation through active literacy engagement.

Authors' Note

Both Cynthia and Ms. Hawthorne are composites. We wish to thank teachers and graduate students at California State University, Los Angeles, for fieldwork contributing to these portraits.

References

Ames, C. (1992). Classrooms: Goals, structures, and student motivation. *Journal of Educational Psychology, 84,* 261–271.

Ames, C., & Archer, J. (1987). Mothers' beliefs about the role of ability and effort in school learning. *Journal of Educational Psychology, 79,* 409–414.

Au, K.H., & Mason, J.M. (1981). Social organizational factors in learning to read: The balance of rights hypothesis. *Reading Research Quarterly, 17,* 115–152.

Beach, R., & Hynes, S. (1990). *Developing discourse practices in adolescence and adulthood.* Norwood, NJ: Ablex.

Bloome, D., & Bailey, F. (1992). Studying language and literacy through events, particularities, and intertextuality. In R. Beach, J. Green, M. Kamil, & T. Shanahan (Eds.), *Multidisciplinary perspectives on literacy research* (pp. 181–210). Urbana, IL: National Council of Teachers of English.

Covington, M. (1992). *Making the grade: A self-worth perspective on motivation and school reform.* Cambridge, England: Cambridge University Press.

Csikszentmihalyi, M. (1990a). *Flow: The psychology of optimal experience.* New York: HarperCollins.

Csikszentmihalyi, M. (1990b). Literacy and intrinsic motivation. *Daedalus, 119*(2), 115–140.

Dilthey, W. (1976). The development of hermeneutics. In H. Rickman (Ed. & Trans.), *Selected writings* (pp. 246–263). Cambridge, England: Cambridge University Press. (Original work published 1900)

Epstein, S. (1994). Integration of cognitive and psychodynamic unconscious. *American Psychologist, 49,* 709–724.

Ruddell & Unrau

Erickson, F. (1979). Talking down: Some cultural sources of miscommunication in interracial interviews. In A. Wolfgang (Ed.), *Nonverbal behavior: Applications and cross-cultural implications* (pp. 99–126). New York: Academic.

Erikson, E. (1968). *Identity: Youth and crisis.* New York: Norton.

Garcia, T., & Pintrich, P.R. (1994). Regulating motivation and cognition in the classroom: The role of self-schemas and self-regulatory strategies. In D.H. Schunk & B.J. Zimmerman (Eds.), *Self-regulation of learning and performance: Issues and educational applications* (pp. 127–153). Hillsdale, NJ: Erlbaum.

Good, T. (1987). Teacher expectations. In D. Berliner & B. Rosenshine (Eds.), *Talks to teachers* (pp. 159–200). New York: Random House.

Hagen, A.S., & Weinstein, C.E. (1995). Achievement goals, self-regulated learning, and the role of classroom context. In P.R. Pintrich (Ed.), *Understanding self-regulated learning* (pp. 43–55). San Francisco, CA: Jossey-Bass.

Heath, S.B. (1983). *Ways with words: Language, life and work in communities and classrooms.* Cambridge, England: Cambridge University Press.

Heath, S.B., & McLaughlin, M.W. (1993). Building identities for inner-city youth. In S.B. Heath & M.W. McLaughlin (Eds.), *Identity and inner-city youth* (pp. 1–12). New York: Teachers College Press.

Hull, G., & Rose, M. (1994). "This wooden shack place": The logic of an unconventional reading. In R.B. Ruddell, M.R. Ruddell, & H. Singer (Eds.), *Theoretical models and processes of reading* (4th ed., pp. 231–243). Newark, DE: International Reading Association.

Labov, W. (1972). *Language in the inner city.* Philadelphia, PA: University of Pennsylvania Press.

Langer, J.A. (1990). The process of understanding: Reading for literary and informative purposes. *Research in the Teaching of English, 24,* 229–260.

Markus, H., & Nurius, P. (1986). Possible selves. *American Psychologist, 41,* 954–969.

Marshall, H. (1992). Associate editor's introduction to centennial articles on classroom learning and motivation. *Journal of Educational Psychology, 84,* 259–260.

Maslow, A.H. (1954). *Motivation and personality.* New York: Harper & Row.

Mathewson, G.C. (1994). Model of attitude influence upon reading and learning to read. In R.B. Ruddell, M.R. Ruddell, & H. Singer (Eds.), *Theoretical models and processes of reading* (4th ed., pp. 1131–1161). Newark, DE: International Reading Association.

Meece, J.L. (1994). The role of motivation in self-regulated learning. In D.H. Schunk & B.J. Zimmerman (Eds.), *Self-regulation of learning and performance: Issues and educational applications* (pp. 25–44). Hillsdale, NJ: Erlbaum.

Mehan, H. (1979). *Learning lessons.* Cambridge, MA: Harvard University Press.

Midgley, C., Feldlaufer, H., & Eccles, J. (1989). Change in teacher efficacy and student self- and task-related beliefs in mathematics during the transition to junior high school. *Journal of Educational Psychology, 49,* 529–538.

Moll, L.C. (1994). Literacy research in community and classrooms: A sociocultural approach. In R.B. Ruddell, M.R. Ruddell, & H. Singer (Eds.), *Theoretical models and processes of reading* (4th ed., pp. 179–207). Newark, DE: International Reading Association.

Moyer, B. (1995). *The language of life.* New York: Doubleday.

Nicholls, J.G. (1984). Achievement motivation: Conception of ability, subjective experience, task choice, and performance. *Psychological Review, 91,* 328–346.

Paivio, A. (1986). *Mental representations: A dual coding approach.* New York: Oxford University Press.

Palincsar, A.S., & Brown, A.L. (1986). Interactive teaching to promote independent learning from text. *The Reading Teacher, 39,* 771–777.

Phillips, S. (1970). Acquisition of rules for appropriate speech use. In J.E. Alatis (Ed.), *Bilingualism and language contact: Anthropological, linguistic, psychological, and sociological aspects* (Monograph Series on Languages and Linguistics No. 23). Washington, DC: Georgetown University Press.

Rosenblatt, L.M. (1978). *The reader, the text, the poem: The transactional theory of the literary work*. Carbondale, IL: Southern Illinois University Press.

Rosenblatt, L.M. (1985). The transactional theory of the literary work: Implications for research. In C.R. Cooper (Ed.), *Researching response to literature and the teaching of literature* (pp. 33–53). Norwood, NJ: Ablex.

Rosenblatt, L.M. (1995). *Literature as exploration* (5th ed.). New York: Modern Language Association. (Original work published 1938)

Ruddell, R.B. (1994). The development of children's comprehension and motivation during storybook discussion. In R.B. Ruddell, M.R. Ruddell, & H. Singer (Eds.), *Theoretical models and processes of reading* (4th ed., pp. 281–296). Newark, DE: International Reading Association.

Ruddell, R.B. (1995). Those influential literacy teachers: Meaning negotiators and motivation builders. *The Reading Teacher, 48*, 454–463.

Ruddell, R.B., Draheim, M., & Barnes, J. (1990). A comparative study of the teaching effectiveness of influential and non-influential teachers and reading comprehension development. In J. Zutell & S. McCormick (Eds.), *Literacy theory and research: Analyses from multiple paradigms* (pp. 153–162). Chicago, IL: National Reading Conference.

Ruddell, R.B., & Greybeck, B. (1992, December). *A study of teaching effectiveness of experienced literacy teachers: Connections between self-perceptions, former influential teachers, and observed teaching performance*. Paper presented at the 42nd Annual Meeting of the National Reading Conference, San Antonio, TX.

Ruddell, R.B., & Haggard, M.R. (1982). Influential teachers: Characteristics and classroom performance. In J.A. Niles & L.A. Harris (Eds.), *New inquiries in reading research and instruction* (Thirty-first Yearbook of the National Reading Conference, pp. 227–231). Rochester, NY: National Reading Conference.

Ruddell, R.B., & Kern, R.G. (1986). The development of belief systems and teaching effectiveness of influential teachers. In M.P. Douglass (Ed.), *Reading: The quest for meaning* (pp. 133–150). Claremont, CA: Claremont Reading Conference.

Ruddell, R.B., & Unrau, N.J. (1994). Reading as a meaning-construction process: The reader, the text, and the teacher. In R.B. Ruddell, M.R. Ruddell, & H. Singer (Eds.), *Theoretical models and processes of reading* (4th ed., pp. 996–1056). Newark, DE: International Reading Association.

Rumelhart, D.E. (1980). Schemata: The building blocks of cognition. In R.J. Spiro, B.C. Bruce, & W.F. Brewer (Eds.), *Theoretical issues in reading comprehension* (pp. 33–58). Hillsdale, NJ: Erlbaum.

Sadoski, M., & Paivio, A. (1994). A dual coding view of imagery and verbal processes in reading comprehension. In R.B. Ruddell, M.R. Ruddell, & H. Singer (Eds.), *Theoretical models and processes of reading* (4th ed., pp. 582–601). Newark, DE: International Reading Association.

Schon, D.A. (1987). *Educating the reflective practitioner*. San Francisco, CA: Jossey-Bass.

Schunk, D.H. (1991). Self-efficacy and academic motivation. *Educational Psychologist, 26*, 207–231.

Schunk, D.H. (1994). Self-regulation of self-efficacy and attributions in academic settings. In D.H. Schunk & B.J. Zimmerman (Eds.), *Self-regulation of learning and performance: Issues and educational applications* (pp. 75–99). Hillsdale, NJ: Erlbaum.

Slavin, R.E. (1995). *Cooperative learning* (2nd ed.). Boston, MA: Allyn & Bacon.

Slavin, R.E., Madden, N.A., Karweit, N.L., Dolan, L.J., & Wasik, B.A. (1994). Success for all: Getting reading right the first time. In E.H. Hiebert & B.M. Taylor (Eds.), *Getting reading right from the start* (pp. 125–147). Boston, MA: Allyn & Bacon.

Smith, F. (1984). Reading like a writer. In J.M. Jensen (Ed.), *Composing and comprehending* (pp. 47–56). Urbana, IL: National Council of Teachers of English.

Stauffer, R.B. (1976). *Teaching reading as a thinking process*. New York: Harper.

Stipek, D.J. (1993). *Motivation to learn: From theory to practice* (2nd ed.). Boston, MA: Allyn & Bacon.

Unrau, N.J., & Ruddell, R.B. (1995). Interpreting texts in classroom contexts. *Journal of Adolescent & Adult Literacy, 39*, 16–27.

Valli, L. (Ed.). (1992). *Reflective teacher education: Cases and critiques*. Albany, NY: State University of New York Press.

Vigil, J.D. (1993). Gangs, social control, and ethnicity: Ways to redirect. In S.B. Heath & M.W. McLaughlin (Eds.), *Identity and inner-city youth* (pp. 94–119). New York: Teachers College Press.

Wigfield, A. (1994). The role of children's achievement values in the self-regulation of their learning outcomes. In D.H. Schunk & B.J. Zimmerman (Eds.), *Self-regulation of learning and performance: Issues and educational applications* (101–124). Hillsdale, NJ: Erlbaum.

Section II   Classroom Contexts That Promote
Literacy Engagement

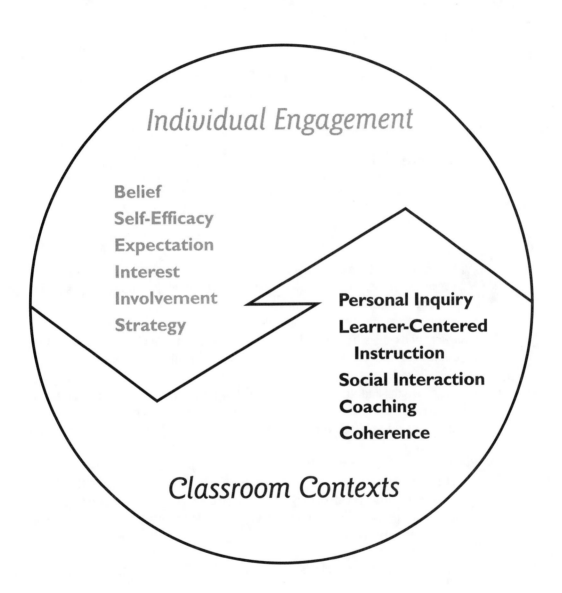

Individual Engagement

Belief
Self-Efficacy
Expectation
Interest
Involvement
Strategy

Personal Inquiry
Learner-Centered
Instruction
Social Interaction
Coaching
Coherence

Classroom Contexts

Characteristics of Classrooms That Promote Motivations and Strategies for Learning

John T. Guthrie and Ann Dacey McCann

What, then, does it mean to be an educated person? It means respecting the miracle of life, being empowered in the use of language, and responding sensitively to the aesthetic. Being truly educated means putting learning in historical perspective, understanding groups and institutions, having reverence for the natural world, and affirming the dignity of work. And, above all, being an educated person means being guided by values and beliefs and connecting the lessons of the classroom to the realities of life. (Boyer, 1995, p. 24)

We embrace Boyer's aspirations for all students, and we believe that literacy engagement moves students toward achieving this goal. Previous chapters in this book have discussed literacy engagement in terms of motivations for literacy such as curiosity, involvement, affective experience, self-efficacy, compliance, recognition, and the desire for good grades. These motivational goals determine whether the learner will be strategic in reading and writing activities. Students who are highly motivated with intrinsic goals will be more thoughtful, deliberate, and persistent in their literacy learning. Besides being motivated and strategic, the engaged learner participates in various social patterns in the classroom. Collaborating in partnerships and teams, the engaged learner shares his or her delights of aesthetic experience in literary genre and exchanges strategies for learning with peers.

What kinds of instructional contexts will support the development of literacy engagement? Because the engaged learner is continuously integrating diverse cognitive, motivational, and social attributes, designing an integrated context that will support these multiple aspects of the learner seems sensible. Our principles for integrated instruction contain three vital connections:

1. connections between disciplines, such as science and language arts, taught through conceptual themes;
2. connections between strategies for learning, such as searching, comprehending, interpreting, composing, and the teaching of content knowledge; and

128

3. connections among classroom activities that support motivations and social and cognitive development.

Although our rationale for integrated instruction is shared by others (Lipson et al., 1993), we have found very little empirical research to address the efficacy of this instructional approach. This chapter provides a review of the professional perspectives and the available empirical findings bearing on the effectiveness of integrated instruction.

This chapter also reports results of our collaborative research into integrated curricula. Our team of teachers and reading specialists has implemented an integrated language arts and science program for elementary children from multicultural populations. We have evolved seven principles that characterize this form of integrated teaching. Our principles refer to classroom contexts as conceptual, observational, self-directed, strategy supportive, collaborative, self-expressive, and coherent. We present these principles and briefly describe their reliance on one another.

In addition, this chapter reports our initial appraisals of the impact of integrated instruction on literacy engagement. We have examined whether motivations and strategies for learning in language arts and science are initiated, sustained, and enhanced by Concept-Oriented Reading Instruction (CORI). Our investigations have been descriptive, correlational, and experimental with an emphasis on using classroom-based measures and theoretical grounding of the basic motivational and cognitive constructs.

Points of Departure for Integrated Curricula

In professional educational literature, integration takes many forms. One basic distinction among integrated curricula is whether they are intradisciplinary or interdisciplinary. Common intradisciplinary integrations include the connection of reading and writing in language arts, a practice that is embraced by most language arts teachers (National Assessment of Educational Progress, 1992). Intradisciplinary integration occurs, for example, when science processes of observing, predicting, inferring, and drawing conclusions are taught explicitly with the content of science.

Interdisciplinary curricula represent combinations of knowledge domains that are traditionally separated. For instance, the language arts have been fused with the content of history in some progressive classrooms (Stephenson & Carr, 1993). In these integrations, students read the literary works of an era and learn the historical themes of the period simultaneously. More recently, the areas of science and language arts are being connected, in which students conduct observational science explorations and learn language arts through activities with science trade books.

Well-formed interdisciplinary teaching often is tied to the presence of a rich conceptual theme that links the disciplines. A question usually focuses the learning of students who are pursuing knowledge and understanding of an interdisciplinary topic (Blumenfeld et al., 1991). To be effective, a theme must have enough breadth to embrace the disciplines that are being combined, and it must have the depth to support increasing growth in students' cognitive skills. An encompassing theme provides a place for skill instruction within the framework of interesting content (Lipson et al., 1993). When a theme is launched successfully with an abundance of time and supportive materials, ideas from the original theme can lead to new discoveries in related fields. Themes that enable students to make new discoveries have been described by Bruner (1969) as "lithe, beautiful, and immensely generative" (cited in Brown, 1992, p. 171).

One comprehensive proposal for integration is the "coherent curriculum" (Pate, McGinnis, & Homstead, 1995), which contains the following factors:

- goals of learning how to learn, problem solving, student responsibility, collaboration, deep content understanding, and risk taking;
- content integrations of science, social studies, math, language arts, and fine arts;
- multiple forms of assessment that exhibit student achievement;
- personalized learning in which student interests and skills determine learning activities;
- school scheduling to allow blocks of time for projects;
- communication to parents; and
- teacher reflection on instruction.

The reasons for introducing a coherent instructional agenda in the classroom are compelling and intuitively sensible. Connections in the curriculum have been promoted as an improvement for students and teachers over traditional, separate-subject instructional techniques. Proposed rationales for integrating instruction include the idea that students will understand "why they are doing what they are doing—coherence across areas will keep students from thinking...that the work on grammar in English has nothing to do with what is done in writing or spelling" (Lipson et al., 1993, p. 253). The implication is that if students perceive these connections, they will transfer problem-solving tactics and metacognitive skills across subject areas. Other proponents claim that if students learn abstract ideas in the context of a conceptual theme, they will apply their learning outside of school more readily (Beane, 1995).

It is widely assumed that students will be motivated to learn new strategies if the strategies fit into a framework that children understand. Researchers surmise that learners will feel more of an investment in their studies if they pursue meaningful content through student-directed inquiry in small groups or individually (Lapp & Flood, 1994). Developing autonomy in students also is cited as a reason to integrate the school day. In an integrated unit, students can research questions of personal interest, acquiring transferable skills in the process. Students' assuming greater responsibility for their own learning is thought to be a valuable aspect of integrated curriculum programs because students have more opportunities to construct connections across content areas.

The benefits of an integrated curriculum are believed to permeate the organizational structure of schools. If teachers of different grade levels share their ideas with one another in a comprehensive plan for integrating the instruction, the coherence of the schoolwide curriculum can be enhanced. A school-level infrastructure for integration maximizes the strengths of the faculty, promotes investment in the necessary materials, and preserves instructional time efficiently. From a teacher's perspective, integrating across disciplines allows for more coverage of material in less time and for investigations of topics that do not fall clearly into a single subject area (Brandt, 1991).

There are several potential hazards to instructional integration. An inherent danger is loss of integrity in one of the disciplines. For example, we observed one integrated math and language arts lesson in which students calculated the proportion of vowels to consonants in English as a math activity, without reference to the possible significance of this relation for the English language. Equally questionable in concept-building value was an art and history lesson in which children carved pumpkins to look like famous U.S. presidents (Brophy & Alleman, 1991). Such activities may lead to serious misconceptions about the discipline (such as language arts or history) in which they are used. The potential of the conceptual theme-driven model depends on the selection of a generative topic that is educationally valuable for advanced learning of content and skills (Lipson et al., 1993).

Another potential hazard to integrated instruction is the loss of breadth in knowledge. Conceptual themes are likely to provide in-depth learning in one area at the expense of broader knowledge. If this in-depth knowledge provides the conditions for increased strategy development, the sacrifice of broader knowledge may be justified. However, if integrated instruction on a conceptual theme does not succeed in increasing high-level strategies, the loss of breadth is not acceptable. A similar problem arises for collaboration among students. If much time is devoted to cooperative learning, but it is not sufficiently oriented to content knowledge, this social emphasis may lead to a decrease in long-term knowledge acquisition.

Integrated instruction, if poorly implemented, can lead to decline in skill. In the 1960s the popular language experience approach integrated the language arts, but students failed to learn basic word recognition and vocabulary (Bond & Dykstra, 1967). More recently, there is doubt that whole language can support the development of word reading fluency (Adams, 1990), and project-based science approaches may not assure fluency in basic skills of coordinating data with theory (Meece, Blumenfeld, & Hoyle, 1988).

Finally, another potential hazard is the temptation to "add-on" an integrated unit to an existing curriculum plan. An integration of disciplines cannot be properly launched or sustained as a mere supplement to a mainstream curriculum. Teacher planning, collecting books and resources, scheduling activities, and designing authentic assessments demand the time and talents associated with a full program. The potential benefits of interdisciplinary contexts need to be established and weighed against potential costs to learners, teachers, and administrators.

What Evidence Supports Integrated Instruction?

The rhetoric behind the movement to integrate the curriculum in schools is powerful. Teachers, both new and experienced, are pushed to integrate their instruction by progressive administrators, consultants, and enthusiastic entries in professional journals

(Lipson et al., 1993). Integrating seems logical, and the promised improvements in student motivation and interest, strategy use, problem solving, conceptual knowledge, and instructional efficiency are enticing. It is pertinent to ask, however, if these compelling rationales have been supported by any evidence in the research literature. Roth (1994) shares this concern, wondering as both a researcher and a teacher, if we should be "jumping on the bandwagon" of thematic teaching before we collect and examine any data.

A review of the research literature reveals a scant amount of empirical evidence supporting integrated instruction. Most rationales for integration are based on anecdotal reports of student interest and increased motivation for learning while participating in a thematic unit (for example, Peters, Schubeck, & Hopkins, 1995). Proponents of integration suggest that teachers should step back from the arbitrary boundaries that define separate subject areas in school. For example, Beane (1995) contends that if children were schooled in fewer, broader, disciplines, a merger of abstract and concrete thinking would be characteristic of the learning environment. The benefits of this merger are presumed to be self-evident. Although thoughtful treatments of what integrated curriculum could be are valuable, the education community should demand more empirical evidence to validate this notion.

Many of the studies purporting to support integration are extremely weak. Vars (1991) cites 62 studies that claim to show positive effects of curriculum integration. He reports that students who were enrolled in interdisciplinary programs performed as well as or better than students in traditional curricula on standardized tests. However, the original studies were unpublished dissertations or reports in nonempirical journals, leaving doubts as to the quality of the evidence. Support for interdisciplinary integration also emerged from evaluations of the Mid-California Science Improvement Program after it had been operating in elementary schools for two years. However, although science achievement tests were administered to students in an integrated program and 78 percent of the participants improved in their scores (Greene, 1991), suitable control groups were not included. Thus, the hopes and claims of the author were not supported by the data.

Positive evidence for integration does appear in two studies. In an investigation of student engagement, the coherence of a language art curriculum was measured by recording the ratings for connectedness teachers gave their English lessons every week. Higher levels of achievement were found on a specially tailored literature exam for the students who were members of classes with higher levels of coherence in their studies (Gamoran & Nystrand, 1992). In a separate investigation, students involved in Brown's (1992) "community of learners" appeared to improve in knowledge acquisition. Students learning environmental science within a rich conceptual theme outperformed students in less integrated classroom settings. Learning about principles of animal adaptation in a guided discovery context yielded accurate information as well as more innovative, appropriate ideas.

Many educators write about the benefits of a coherent curriculum based on their synthesis of practical resources and on years of experience working with classroom teachers. Lipson et al. (1993) reviewed an extensive collection of materials that are meant to guide teachers to the implementation of an integrated curriculum. However, nearly half of these instructional resources do not discuss the issues of connecting content and learning processes across disciplines in any way. Books and materials that do provide information on teaching with a conceptual theme are vague on details of how to choose a viable theme for study. Very little evidence is cited showing the superiority of an integrated curriculum over an ordinary instructional framework.

Perkins (1991) believes that higher levels of understanding and intellectual passion are fostered by a curriculum in which broad themes are addressed. However, he provides no data to justify this claim. Lapp and Flood (1994) encourage integration because of the successful thematic units they have witnessed in classrooms. Jacobs (1991) confirms the positive reports of teachers who have switched to integrated instruction. Yet again, reasons and rationales for teaching in a way that fosters connections are plentiful, but they exist without an empirical base.

Perhaps the most compelling appeal for coherence in learning environments comes from a literary figure. A world brimming with curiosities was portrayed by Emerson, who wrote:

> To the young mind everything is individual, stands by itself. By and by, it finds how to join two things and see in them one nature; then three, then three thousand...discovering roots running underground whereby contrary and remote things cohere and flower out from one stem. (Cited in Fogarty, 1991, p. 61)

Our challenge is to explore the essence of these ideas through theoretical and empirical inquiry into the complexities of curriculum integration. Our first step is to portray our perspective on the integration of science and language arts through Concept-Oriented Reading Instruction (CORI).

Concept-Oriented Reading Instruction

CORI was initially implemented in one fifth-grade classroom in which language arts and science were integrated in a year-long curriculum. In the following year the project was expanded to include third- and fifth-grade classrooms from two schools in which language arts and science were integrated. All schools were located in metropolitan Washington, DC, and the student population included children of African American, Hispanic, Asian, and Caucasian backgrounds. The teachers were experienced professionals who volunteered to work with us to design, implement, and sustain the instruction through the year. Figure 1 depicts the instructional characteristics of CORI encircling the qualities of engaged learners that are shown as a diamond.

Conceptual Theme

CORI was organized around broad, interdisciplinary, conceptual themes. The primary goal of teaching was to enable students to gain a conceptual understanding that was flexible, transferable, and informed by multiple genres. The scientific themes were the orga-

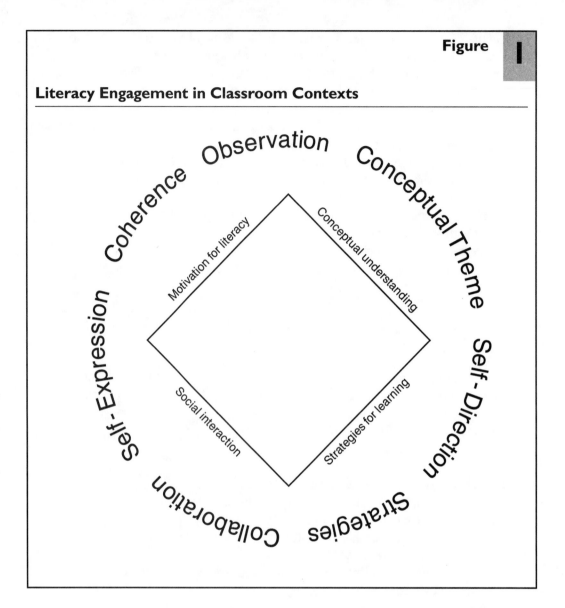

Figure I

Literacy Engagement in Classroom Contexts

Observation

Conceptual Theme

Self-Direction

Strategies

Collaboration

Self-Expression

Coherence

Motivation for literacy

Conceptual understanding

Social interaction

Strategies for learning

nizing frameworks for units of instruction lasting 14 to 16 weeks, and they represented topics that were academically significant and lent themselves to diverse reading, writing, and observational activities.

Conceptual learning is informed by at least three theoretical perspectives described in terms of enrichment, restructuring, and cumulative models (Chi et al., 1994; Chinn & Brewer, 1993; Vosniadu, 1994). Although space does not permit a full review of these models here, we adopt the enrichment perspective. In this view, conceptual learning consists of increases in several forms of knowledge. As students enhance their conceptual understanding, they gain increasing command of elements, features, and facts in a particular domain. As this information is accumulated, students construct principles to organize the particular elements into relations. At the highest levels of conceptual learning students possess interrelated explanatory principles for phenomena and events. At these levels of knowledge students can coordinate theories with evidence and express the connections among them (Alexander, Kulikowich, & Jetton, 1994; Chi et al., 1994).

The conceptual theme is the organizational focus for instruction. For example, real-life experiences and hands-on science activities are starting points for understanding concepts. As students ask questions and become curious, they are supported in their learning activities with informational resources and the cognitive strategies for using them productively. As students gain command of the available resources and strategies, they are encouraged to direct their own learning. The process of self-direction includes choosing topics, tasks, and means of learning. Collaborations among students are formed to help students move toward goals and subgoals to gain a more complete understanding of the conceptual theme of the unit. Toward the end of the integrated unit student self-expressions are increasingly emphasized. Students represent their knowledge of the principles relating to the theme through reading, writing, and performance. In sum, the social collaborations, cognitive strategies, and student self-expressions are educational objectives of the units, but they are organized around the broader goal of gaining principles and perspectives relating to the conceptual theme.

A conceptual theme used in one fifth-grade CORI classroom was adaptation. This theme emphasized general principles of species-biome relationships. The vignette in the introduction of this volume in which students participate in a cricket hunt is an illustrative case from this classroom. As mentioned in the vignette, after learning about crickets and their habitats, students selected an animal of their choice for in-depth reading, writing, and discussion regarding the principles of adaptation shown by their chosen specie. In addition to the expository trade books the children used for researching a subtopic within the thematic units, integrated instruction also was supported by texts from the literary genre. For example, the children in the fifth-grade classroom depicted in the vignette read *Tuck Everlasting* by Natalie Babbitt, a novel about the importance of the cycle of life and death for all creatures in nature. Native American folktales from *Keepers of the Earth* by Michael J. Caduto and Joseph Bruchac, about humans, animals, and their balanced relationships to the environment, were read and discussed. At the fifth-grade level, students were able to begin comparing the features of different literary and informational texts. Students could encounter alternative, and often contradictory, ideas and information on the conceptual theme that provided the impetus for higher level thinking.

Observation

Real-life experiences provide a vitally important introduction and a sustaining energy for instructional units. In science, observation may include hands-on activities with manipulatives. In history, observation may consist of encounters with artifacts or enactments of historical scenes. Real-life experiences provide an opportunity for learning that is usually sensory and concrete at first, opening the doors for more symbolic and abstract learning in the future (Metz, 1995).

Conceptual learning can be facilitated by experiences on a continuum from observational to symbolic (Brown, Collins, & Duguid, 1989). The observational end of the continuum consists of sensory experiences with concrete objects and events. A next level of experience is not directly sensory, but it is highly graphic and pictorial. At this level students view videos, read scenarios, and compose vignettes. At a less observational and more symbolic level, students learn principles, concepts, and rules that govern many particular instances. These principles require abstract thinking and represent experience in generalizations rather than in specific depictions. At the most abstract level, students interact with mathematical or conceptual symbols. These symbols capture complex relationships and represent a higher order of theoretical complexity than information from sensory observations. In the CORI context, students learn by participating in a hands-on activity at the beginning of an investigation, then learn by reading, writing, and discussing to advance their knowledge to a more abstract level. Students draw on this rich base and use what they learned to inform their subsequent hands-on opportunities. For students journeying along the experiential learning continuum, the trip is often recursive. As understanding is achieved at an abstract level, a more concrete representation of the concept can be revisited in a new light.

To be productive for conceptual learning, real-life experience requires instructional support. Students must be taught strategies for observing either scientific or historical phenomena. Strategies such as identifying critical features, noting the course of events, making representative drawings, and collecting quantitative information are needed by students. Strategies for making sense of real-life experience may be modeled by teachers, discussed among peers, and collected in journal reflections. Collaboration among students can be organized to support the analysis and use of these strategies. Working in pairs and small teams, students can work cooperatively to maintain their orientation to the observational activity, collect information thoroughly, and share the excitement of discovery.

Real-life observations play two key roles in CORI. The first role is motivational. In the vignette in the introduction of this book, one student on a cricket hunt captures his specimen and exclaims, "I caught one! I got it!" Direct encounters generate excitement for all students from preschool to high school. This excitement is highly situational, prompted by particular events or objects (Hidi & Anderson, 1992). When this initial interest is supported by discussion, informational resources, and conceptual learning, students personalize their learning. The situational interest evolves into a longer term personal interest in the topic. When situational interest is supported and extended through literacy activities and conceptual understanding, long-term intrinsic motivation for learning can be increased.

The second role of real-life experience is its contribution to student questioning. Immediately following real-life encounters, students ask a multitude of questions. Many of these questions are simple but answering them is complex. When they are taken seriously, the questions lead to conceptual pursuits. For example, in the earlier vignette, one student muses, "Why do crickets live here in the summer and where do they go in the winter?" which raises the topic of life cycles of insects. If student questions can be identified, articulated, and publicized, they can become goals for learning. Because student questions are expressed in their own language in terms of their background knowledge, they become compelling objectives for learning through science and language arts activities.

Self-Direction

In CORI, students are supported to take responsibility for their own learning. By giving students a significant amount of freedom to choose the topics, tasks, and media for learning, teachers enable students to take ownership of their growth as a learner. The choices provided to students are initially bounded, with an emphasis on selection among a few options and input into the teacher's decisions. Complete autonomy is not possible or desirable for elementary students working in a conceptual frame. However, students can participate in selecting the avenues for learning, peer-group structures, criteria for completion of projects, time of learning, and place for studying. When students can customize their learning environments, they become agents of their own engagement.

The contrast to a self-directed environment is one controlled by outside sources. Control of learning activities in classrooms can be found in many forms. Materials in which students follow a focused series of steps and answer a focused series of questions are directed material. Another source of control is the teacher, who may be highly prescriptive and procedural. Students' self-direction relies on their having a substantial amount of knowledge about the topic of learning and strategies for engaging with the content. When a topic is new and strategies are limited, teachers provide control and direction to initiate student engagement. As students gain more topic knowledge and increase their command of reading, writing, analysis, and interpretation, they can be encouraged to assume greater responsibility for their engagement in learning. To develop self-direction in students successfully, teachers scaffold strategies for learning, provide informational resources on the conceptual theme, and articulate clear goals for classroom activities.

The vignette of engagement depicted in the introduction illustrates that students can select subtopics within a conceptual theme and locate books relevant to the themes. These choices are empowering to learners. In the vignette, the students determine how they will show their learning. Robert and Kantu choose to make a video, and other students write informational stories about the animal of their choice. By choosing from among available subtopics, selecting appropriate books from the classroom collection, and composing a report in a form of their preference, these students exercise self-direction. While they gain conceptual knowledge about the theme of the unit, they also participate in the classroom discourse community and learn reading, writing, and interpretive strategies designated as goals by the teacher. Maintaining a balance between self-direction of learners and common goals for all students is attainable within the CORI framework.

Strategies

Within the CORI framework, teachers provide students the support needed to acquire powerful strategies for learning conceptual themes in many ways. Teachers select their approach to strategies from a repertoire that spans from explicit instruction to guided discovery. Strategies emphasized in CORI include problem finding (Collins-Block, 1992), using prior knowledge (Anderson & Pearson, 1984), searching for information (Armbruster & Armstrong, 1993), comprehending informational text (Dole et al., 1991), self-monitoring (Baker & Brown, 1984), and interpreting literary text (Graesser, Golding, & Long, 1991).

In pedagogical terms, the teachers' orientation to strategy instruction is analogous to coaching. Teachers first appraise the strategies that students possess by giving them an opportunity to learn in a complex situation. Following this appraisal, teachers engage students through modeling, peer tutoring, and whole-class discussion regarding the selection and use of strategies. Students are encouraged to think about their own strategies through self-questioning and maintaining journal entries that reflect self-assessment of strategy learning. The most critical feature of strategy instruction is that it is situated within the conceptual theme. Strategies such as summarizing text or drawing inferences from a graph are meaningless in isolation. Without a frame of reference, the accuracy of the summary or the inference cannot be judged. Consequently, a growing understanding that relates to a conceptual theme is an ideal milieu for strategy development. CORI teachers may introduce strategies, and students often invent strategies because they are useful for finding facts, constructing principles, and communicating understanding to others. Although strategies are best learned in context, students need help in using them in other areas. Transfer of strategies is facilitated through teachers explicitly bridging strategies across multiple text sources and providing many opportunities for learning strategies within the integrated thematic unit. Students discuss what strategies are effective for them, how they work, and when they are most useful.

Collaboration

CORI teachers support students in working together toward understanding the conceptual theme, gaining productive strategies, and learning how to communicate effectively in groups. Collaboration is a process with multiple goals relating to the content of the theme, cognitive processes of students, and social patterns of groups. To work productively in a collaborative team, students need to understand the purposes of the group. This development of goals can be fostered in whole-class discussion, but it is best for teachers to emphasize goal development at the team level. Teachers can help individual teams define the content of their learning goals by asking the teams to focus on questions such as, "What are we learning about?" and "What aspects of it are important?"

In elementary school, students need support to achieve levels of productive collaborative discourse (Almasi, 1995). Teachers in CORI classrooms guide students in developing the norms for their group activities. Teachers ask each team separately, "How will we work and talk together? What rules do we need?" As students generate a few rules and improve them during the unit, they make a commitment to a sense of positive interdependence among members. They develop an interactive discourse structure in which students build on one another's thinking. The ability of students to listen to others, respect perspectives, and use information from peers in their own conceptual constructions develops slowly and requires sustained monitoring by the teacher.

Goals of collaboration can be posted by the teacher and elaborated by the students. These goals emphasize answering student-generated questions, building toward thematic understanding, and composing reports for authentic audiences. Collaborative structures can include individual accountability and group goals by having students participate both in team projects and individualized tasks that may include writing in journals and self-publishing.

In CORI, students are likely to participate in social structures that include individual work, partnerships, small teams, and whole class activities. Two prominent instructional formats include literature circles and idea circles. In literature circles, students work in teams of four and five to interpret narratives and literary works. The teacher helps students initially to construct rules for interaction and interpretation by asking questions such as, "What will we talk about regarding this story?" Students bring their journal responses regarding a story to the circle for discussion and exchange. In idea circles, students work on a particular problem or develop a conceptual subtopic using multiple texts. For example, within a thematic unit on predation, students may read texts on different types of predators and bring their journal entries from their reading to the idea circle. The goal is to form general principles about predatory creatures from several different informational sources. To participate productively in these collaborative structures, students need some knowledge of the conceptual theme, a few useful strategies that enable them to learn efficiency about the theme, and a sufficient sense of self-direction to be a responsible member of a peer-led group.

Self-Expression

Students who learn in the integrated environment of CORI are supported in articulating their understanding of the conceptual theme to audiences that are personally and culturally relevant to them. Forms of expression may include performing, creating posters, making videos, and peer teaching, although the most widely used form is composition writing. Student expressions of their knowledge or viewpoints are self-expressive when individuals take responsibility for selecting the topic or style of communication. When students relate their personal experiences to their writing or permit their own viewpoints to be seen, they are sharing self-expression.

The opposite of self-expression is standard-based expression. When students display their knowledge or strategies for learning in ways that meet a fixed external criterion, they are engaging in standard-based expression. At the simplest level, looking up a word in a dictionary to spell it correctly is a form of standard-based expression. Composing a five-paragraph essay following an explicit model provided in a textbook also is a standard-based form of expression. CORI teachers attempt to attain a balance between self-referenced and standard-based expressions of knowledge. Students are encouraged to choose subtopics for deeper exploration, but the subtopics are elected within themes. Students also are encouraged to locate information of particular interest to them, but they are provided a structure outline for framing and organizing their collection and synthesis of information. At some stages of the writing process, standards for capitalizing, punctuating, and organizing information are emphasized. At other stages, quality of content and personal investment in the writing are considered the highest priorities.

Expressions of understanding about a conceptual theme depend on the other principles of CORI. For example, a successful self-expression depends on the learner's choice of topic and style. Too much prescription from a teacher will preclude students from tailoring their writing to their own ideas. In-depth understanding about the conceptual theme is vital; students do not write extensively about topics when they lack deep knowledge and interest.

Coherence

In addition to an integration of knowledge and strategies for learning, students in CORI experience a coherent set of activities that foster their development of self-direction, collaborative competence, and self-expression that link conceptual understanding with real-life experiences. The relation among these principles may be described as mutually transforming. When one dimension of the learning context is emphasized (for example, self-direction), the ramifications of this choice affect the presence and form of other characteristics such as the metacognitive strategies presented and the mode of strategy instruction. In another classroom where collaboration is emphasized, the metacognitive strategies that the students construct, discuss, and use could be very different in nature.

In the vignette in the introduction of this volume, students conduct hands-on science activities along with reading and writing activities. They participate in group discussions and in solo activities that permit both common-goal attainments and individual pursuits. This coherence is contrasted with curricula in which disciplines are departmentalized, skills are taught separately from content, and a social pattern emphasizes individual activity. We believe that contextualizing language arts within conceptual themes of science provides a disciplinary connection for all students. Learners who are in need of support due to their language background or previous instructional history benefit from integrated instruction. Further, all students gain a sense of expertise in the content domain and a command of strategies that enhance self-efficacy and provide a basis for productive acquisition of knowledge in new domains.

Effects of Concept-Oriented Reading Instruction on Literacy Engagement

An examination of whether the principles of CORI influence literacy engagement depends on at least two prerequisites. A first requirement is that the goals of instruction are clearly defined and measurable. In CORI the primary goal consists of enhancing literacy engagement. This goal entails the development of intrinsic motivations for learning, such as curiosity and involvement, and the acquisition of cognitive and volitional strategies. Measures of these aspects of literacy engagement include interviews with students, focus groups of teacher participants, videotapes of the classroom learning context, and performance assessments.

A second requirement for examining the effect of CORI on literacy engagement principles is the identification and documentation of classroom instruction embodying the principles of integrated teaching. The most powerful procedure for examining these principles is to design and support classrooms governed by them. When a set of instructional principles is implemented into a classroom program by a team of researchers and teachers, it is reasonable to trace any learning effects to the designed instructional practices. The alternative research strategy of locating extant classrooms that represent the principles of interest and relating the characteristics of these classrooms to learning is a less secure research approach. Even if an otherwise suitable classroom could be located, the key principles may be correlated with other instructional principles or classroom characteristics that have not been identified and measured.

Design and Implementation of Concept-Oriented Reading Instruction

During the first year of the design and development of CORI, we worked with one grade 5 teacher in a multicultural school, as mentioned earlier. The teacher integrated science and reading language arts in a year-long program. In language arts, trade books were used exclusively, and science emphasized a hands-on observational curriculum supported by multiple texts and video resources. The teacher implemented CORI in the following phases:

1. observe and personalize, in which students observed real-life science phenomena and composed their own questions as a basis for learning

2. search and retrieve, in which students located information in various book and video resources for addressing their questions and pursuing the conceptual theme of adaptation

3. comprehend and integrate, which consisted of explicit strategy instruction to support students' comprehension of reading multiple genres and of the transfer of ideas across contents

4. communicate to others, in which students wrote narratives, reports, and letters to various audiences to express their understanding about the conceptual theme.

The original principles of CORI were abstracted from our fieldnotes and videotapes of classroom instruction discussed at length with the teacher and the school's reading specialist.

After a satisfactory first-year implementation of CORI, a questionnaire about motivation was administered to students enrolled in the CORI classroom and to students that were instructed in reading and science using the traditional basal textbook approach. We found that the CORI students showed higher scores than the basal students on intrinsic motivations for reading such as curiosity, aesthetic enjoyment, social exchange, and challenge. In contrast, the students in the basal classroom were more likely to read and learn based on extrinsic motivations such as recognition, compliance, and work avoidance (Guthrie et al., 1996). This preliminary comparison suggested that students who received CORI were supported in developing their intrinsic literacy learning goals in reading and writing (see the table on page 143).

Growth of Motivations and Strategies During CORI

In the second year of CORI, the project was extended to four classrooms, including two grade 5 classrooms and two grade 3 classrooms. To assess growth of literacy engagement, we designed measurements of motivation and effective literacy strategy use. A performance assessment was administered during the fall and spring of the academic year to all students in the CORI classrooms. The assessment was a one-week unit of instruction in which we tracked students' performance on seven tasks. The assessment permitted us to examine students' ability to search for information from multiple texts and represent their conceptual understanding of science principles through drawing and writing. The topics in the assessment were counterbalanced in the fall and spring, which permitted us to infer students' levels of strategies and skills that were free of influence of a particular content area.

We appraised the students' motivations for literacy learning and their volitional strategies with the help of a 30-minute interview conducted in the fall and again in the spring with 20 CORI students. The students were selected by teachers to be representative of the range of levels of literacy engagement within their classrooms. Results of coding the interview data and the performance assessments for these 20 students revealed that strategy learning was highly dependent on the development of intrinsic motivations for literacy. We found that the majority of students (68 percent) increased in intrinsic motivation during the year. However, 100 percent of the students who increased in intrinsic motivation increased markedly in their command of cognitive strategies for searching multiple texts and comprehending information from them. In contrast, only 50 percent of the students who decreased in intrinsic motivation were observed to increase in the learning and use of literacy strategies. We infer from these findings that if the complex, effortful strategies needed for learning from multiple texts in integrated instruction are to be systematically facilitated, classroom contexts that support the enhancement of intrinsic motivations for reading and literacy must be initiated and sustained for substantial amounts of time.

We also investigated whether changes in intrinsic motivation of students were related to their actual reading practices. Within the interview, we asked students about their amount and breadth of reading, systematically covering the topics and the frequencies of their reading activities. The findings showed a high association between increases in intrinsic motivation and increases in amount and breadth of reading. These findings cor-

Benefits of Concept-Oriented Reading Instruction on Student Learning

Year	Classrooms	Measures	Results
1	1 grade 5 CORI 1 grade 5 traditional (one school)	motivation questionnaire	CORI students higher on intrinsic motivation
		motivation interview	CORI showed increases in intrinsic motivation.
2	2 grade 5 CORI 2 grade 3 traditional (across 2 schools)	performance assessment fall & spring	Motivation increases association with cognitive strategy, volition strategies, and amount of reading.
2	2 grade 5 CORI 3 grade 3 CORI 5 traditional (across 3 schools)	performance assessment spring	On search and conceptual learning: CORI 3 > traditional 3 CORI 5 > traditional 5 CORI 3 > traditional 5 CORI increased literacy engagement and conceptual learning with background controlled.

roborate high correlation between intrinsic motivations for reading and reading practices observed in other schools by Wigfield and Guthrie (1995).

Research has shown that intrinsic motivations for reading also influence the growth of volitional strategies (Corno & Kanfer, 1993). Students who are internally motivated to read must possess and coordinate strategies for finding books, managing time, locating places to read, and avoiding distractions. These volitional strategies enable students to initiate literacy events compatible with their interests. From the motivation interview data, we observed a high association between increases in intrinsic motivations for reading and volitional strategies for accomplishing reading goals. This implies that students who decreased in motivations also decreased in volitional strategies for reading. We believe these findings suggest that engaging classrooms must support not only the first occurrence of interest in learning or the opportunity for pursuing intrinsic goals, but also the long-term enhancement of intrinsic motivational goals such as curiosity, involvement, social exchange, and the enjoyment of challenge.

Comparison of CORI and Traditionally Organized Instruction

During the third year of the project we conducted a comparison between the CORI students and classrooms where language arts and science were taught using traditional basal text instruction. At this phase of our research, five classrooms, three grade 3 and two grade 5, were provided with CORI during the academic year. The basis for comparison data consisted of a performance assessment administered in the spring to all the classrooms.

Within the performance assessment there were three measures of particular importance: (1) search, which was the measure of students' ability to locate information on a broad question; (2) conceptual learning, which was indicated by a composite of students' drawing and writing to explain their understanding of a science concept; and (3) conceptual transfer, which consisted of students' writing a solution to a novel problem for which conceptual knowledge was useful. These tasks provided students opportunities to engage in multiple strategies for literacy learning and to display their knowledge. Student responses to the tasks were coded with highly reliable rubrics (these are described in Guthrie et al., 1996). The primary indicator of literacy engagement was the search score in the performance assessment chosen because it combined the elements of motivation and cognition most efficiently in an authentic learning context.

On the search score, grade 3 CORI students found and read more relevant materials and took more useful notes than grade 3 traditional instruction students. Grade 5 CORI students also scored higher than traditional instruction students. Most interesting was the finding that scores of grade 3 CORI students were significantly higher than grade 5 traditional students. These findings show that integrated instruction that embodies CORI principles can enable students to acquire searching, reading, and writing strategies at a level that surpasses not only same-age comparison students, but also comparison students who are two years older (see Figure 2).

The second measure in the comparison of CORI and traditional instruction was conceptual learning. On this indicator, CORI grade 3 students were able to express more sophisticated conceptual understanding through drawing and writing than traditional instruction grade 3 students. CORI grade 5 students also scored higher on the rubric than traditional instruction grade 5 students. CORI grade 3 students were not significantly different from traditional grade 5 students in this measure. The findings for conceptual transfer data reveal that CORI showed advantages over traditional instruction for grade 5 students but not for grade 3 students. Within our comparisons, conceptual transfer seemed to be more teachable for grade 5 than grade 3.

The finding from this comparison showed preliminary evidence for our model of engaged literacy development. This model (Figure 2) illustrates that CORI (a form of integrated teaching) enhanced literacy engagement (as indicated by search skills and reading comprehension in multiple texts), which increased conceptual knowledge (demonstrated by drawing and writing to explain a science concept). In this investigation, these relations were controlled for students' literacy level, science background knowledge, and topic-specific prior knowledge, thus eliminating potentially confounding variables.

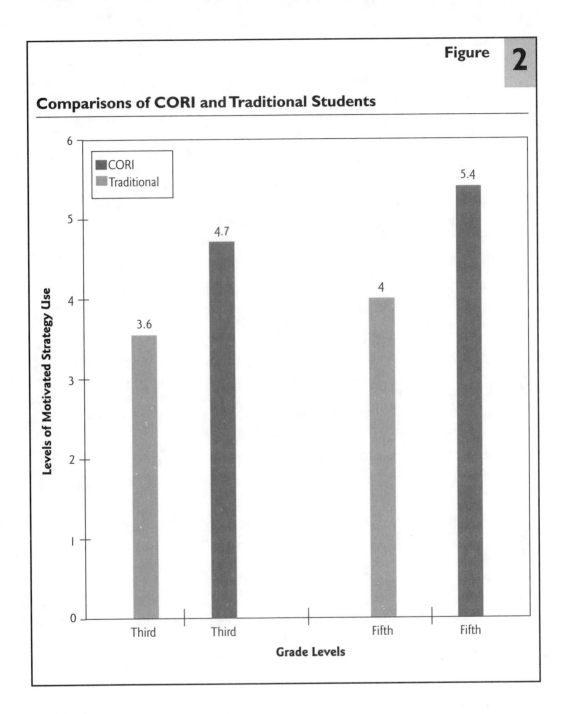

Figure **2**

Comparisons of CORI and Traditional Students

Levels of Motivated Strategy Use

- CORI
- Traditional

3.6

4.7

4

5.4

Third   Third   Fifth   Fifth

Grade Levels

Closing Comments

Our findings suggest that CORI has advantages over traditional instruction for enhancing the motivated use of strategies for learning, or literacy engagement. Students who learn and apply these strategies in an extended task gain conceptual understanding at a much higher level than students who do not apply them. The goals of helping students attain deep knowledge structures of important science concepts appear to be accomplished by enabling students to acquire skills of formulating questions, finding information, detecting important concepts, and integrating them into a set of higher order principles.

The past three years of data collection in the CORI environment have educated us about the benefits for learning that can emerge in a context where students are encouraged to direct their work, collaborate with classmates, develop new metacognitive strategies, and express their knowledge in innovative ways while studying an extended unit that integrates observational experiences with reading and writing about complex science concepts. Within this coherent learning context, students have exhibited strong intrinsic motivations and effective volitional strategies for engaging in literacy activities. They also gained higher order knowledge of science content that exceeds the skills and content knowledge of children learning in nonintegrated instructional environments.

As researchers concerned with the continued effort to improve classroom instructional practices, we feel cautiously optimistic about the contribution that CORI may provide to support other efforts at designing integrated teaching environments. While reviewing the available literature on support for curriculum integration, we found scant support that could be considered empirically compelling. We acknowledge the complexities of the CORI project, and we understand that the data presented here as generally supportive of integrated teaching more accurately reflects the many levels of differences between the CORI environment and the more traditional, basal text approach to teaching science and language arts. The positive learning effects from integration alone are very difficult to examine in isolation. We challenge the research community to devise methods to study the effectiveness of classroom-based interventions that include integrated teaching to further our collective understanding of its unique impact on learning.

Authors' Note

The characteristics of classrooms described in this chapter were derived from videotapes of instruction, fieldnotes, and discussion in an ongoing inquiry group consisting of the authors, teachers, and reading specialists who developed the CORI program.

References

Adams, M.J. (1990). *Beginning to read: Thinking and learning about print*. Cambridge, MA: MIT Press.

Alexander, P.A., Kulikowich, J.M., & Jetton, T.L. (1994). The role of subject-matter knowledge and interest in the processing of linear and nonlinear texts. *Review of Educational Research, 64*, 201–252.

Almasi, J.F. (1995). The nature of fourth graders' sociocognitive conflicts in peer-led and teacher-led discussions of literature. *Reading Research Quarterly, 30*, 314–351.

Anderson, R.C., & Pearson, P.D. (1984). A schema-theoretic view of basic processes in reading. In P.D. Pearson, R. Barr, M.L. Kamil, & P. Mosenthal (Eds.), *Handbook of reading research* (pp. 255–291). New York: Longman.

Armbruster, B.B., & Armstrong, J. (1993). Locating information in text: A focus on children in the elementary grades. *Contemporary Educational Psychology, 18*, 139–161.

Baker, L., & Brown, A.L. (1984). Metacognitive skills of reading. In P.D. Pearson, R. Barr, M.L. Kamil, & P. Mosenthal (Eds.), *Handbook of reading research* (pp. 353–394). New York: Longman.

Beane, J.A. (1995). Curriculum integration and the disciplines of knowledge. *Phi Delta Kappan, 76*, 616–622.

Blumenfeld, P.C., Soloway, E., Marx, R.W., Krajcik, J.S., Guzdial, M., & Palinscar, A. (1991). Motivating project-based learning: Sustaining the doing, supporting the learning. *Educational Psychologist, 26*, 369–398.

Bond, G.L., & Dykstra, R. (1967). The cooperative research program in first-grade reading instruction. *Reading Research Quarterly, 2*, 5–142.

Boyer, E.L. (1995). The educated person. In J.A. Beane (Ed.), *Toward a coherent curriculum: 1995 Yearbook of the Association for Supervision and Curriculum Development* (pp. 16–25). Alexandria, VA: Association for Supervision and Curriculum Development.

Brandt, R. (1991). On interdisciplinary curriculum: A conversation with Heidi Hayes Jacobs. *Educational Leadership, 49*(2), 24–26.

Brophy, J., & Alleman, J. (1991). A caveat: Curriculum integration isn't always a good idea. *Educational Leadership, 49*(2), 66.

Brown, A.L. (1992). Design experiments: Theoretical and methodological challenges in creating complex interventions in classroom settings. *The Journal of the Learning Sciences, 2*, 141–178.

Brown, J.S., Collins, A., & Duguid, P. (1989). Situated cognition and the culture of learning. *Educational Researcher, 18*(1), 32–42.

Bruner, J.S. (1969). *On knowing: Essays for the left hand.* Cambridge, MA: Harvard University Press.

Chi, M.T.H., DeLeeuw, N., Chiu, M., & Lavancher, C. (1994). Eliciting self-explanations improves understanding. *Cognitive Science, 18*, 439–477.

Chinn, C.A., & Brewer, W.F. (1993). The role of anomalous data in knowledge acquisition: A theoretical framework and implications for science instruction. *Review of Educational Research, 63*, 1–49.

Collins-Block, C. (1992). Strategy instruction in a literature-based reading program. *The Elementary School Journal, 94*, 139–151.

Corno, L., & Kanfer, R. (1993). The role of volition learning in learning and performance. In L. Darling-Hammond (Ed.), *Review of research in education* (pp. 301–341). Washington, DC: American Educational Research Association.

Dole, J.A., Duffy, G.G., Roehler, L.R., & Pearson, P.D. (1991). Moving from the old to the new: Research on reading comprehension instruction. *Review of Educational Research, 61*, 239–264.

Fogarty, R. (1991). Ten ways to integrate the curriculum. *Educational Leadership, 49*(2), 61–65.

Gamoran, A., & Nystrand, M. (1992). Taking students seriously. In F.M. Newman (Ed.), *Student engagement and achievement in American secondary schools* (pp. 40–61). New York: Teachers College Press.

Graesser, A., Golding, J.M., & Long, D.L. (1991). Narrative representation and comprehension. In R. Barr, M.L. Kamil, P. Mosenthal, & P.D. Pearson (Eds.), *Handbook of reading research, Volume II* (pp. 171–205). White Plains, NY: Longman.

Greene, L.C. (1991). Science-centered curriculum in elementary school. *Educational Leadership, 49*(2), 42–46.

Guthrie, J.T., McGough, K., Bennett, L., & Rice, M.E. (1996). Concept-oriented reading instruction: An integrated curriculum to develop motivations and strategies for reading. In L. Baker, P. Afflerbach, & D. Reinking (Eds.), *Developing engaged readers in school and home communities* (pp. 165–190). Hillsdale, NJ: Erlbaum.

Guthrie, J.T., Van Meter, P., et al. (1996). Growth of literacy engagement: Changes in motivations and strategies during concept-oriented reading instruction. *Reading Research Quarterly, 31,* 306–333.

Hidi, S., & Anderson, V. (1992). Situational interest and its impact on reading and expository writing. In K.A. Renninger, S. Hidi, & A. Krapp (Eds.), *The role of interest in learning and development* (pp. 215–238). Hillsdale, NJ: Erlbaum.

Jacobs, H.H. (1991). Planning for curriculum integration. *Educational Leadership, 49*(2), 27–28.

Lapp, D., & Flood, J. (1994). Integrating the curriculum: First steps. *The Reading Teacher, 47,* 416–419.

Lipson, M.Y., Valencia, S.W., Wixson, K.K., & Peters, C.W. (1993). Integration and thematic teaching: Integration to improve teaching and learning. *Language Arts, 70,* 252–263.

Meece, J.L., Blumenfeld, P.C., & Hoyle, R.H. (1988). Students' goal orientations and cognitive engagement in classroom activities. *Journal of Educational Psychology, 80,* 514–523.

Metz, K.E. (1995). Reassessment of development constraints on children's science instruction. *Review of Educational Research, 65*(2), 93–127.

National Assessment of Educational Progress. (1992). *Executive summary of the NAEP 1992 reading report card for the Nation and the states.* Washington, DC: U.S. Government Printing Office.

Pate, E.P., McGinnis, K., & Homstead, E. (1995). Creating coherence through curriculum integration. In J.A. Beane (Ed.), *Toward a coherent curriculum* (1995 Yearbook of the Association for Supervision and Curriculum Development, pp. 62–70). Alexandria, VA: Association for Supervision and Curriculum Development.

Perkins, D.N. (1991). Educating for insight. *Educational Leadership, 49*(2), 4–8.

Peters, T., Schubeck, K., & Hopkins, K. (1995). A thematic approach: Theory and practice at the Aleknagik school. *Phi Delta Kappan, 76,* 633–636.

Roth, K.J. (1994). Second thoughts about interdisciplinary studies. *American Educator, 18*(1), 44–48.

Stephenson, C., & Carr, J.F. (Eds.). (1993). *Integrated studies in the middle grades.* New York: Teachers College Press.

Vars, G.F. (1991). Integrated curriculum in historical perspective. *Educational Leadership, 49*(2), 14–15.

Vosniadu, S. (1994). Capturing and modeling the process of conceptual change. *Learning and Instruction, 4,* 45–49.

Wigfield, A., & Guthrie, J.T. (1995). *Dimensions of children's motivations for reading: An initial study* (Reading Research Report No. 34). Athens, GA: National Reading Research Center.

Integrating Science and Literacy Experiences to Motivate Student Learning

Roger Bruning and Barbara M. Schweiger

Beginning reading instruction emphasizes stories. Stories—narratives—describe life experiences and are linked closely to what children see and recall. Because of their familiarity with narratives, most students will have considerable facility with the narrative form by the time they reach the upper elementary grades. However, the upper elementary grades bring a significant new challenge to literacy learners: learning to comprehend expository writing. Through the remainder of most students' formal education, much of what they need to learn will be encountered in various expository forms such as reports, essays, and textbooks.

Science learning depends heavily on students' abilities to comprehend expository materials. This is not to say that observation and experimentation are unimportant for science learning. U.S. national science standards appropriately emphasize active, constructive learning that is often neglected in science instruction. However, reading is equally important; observation and experimentation engage students with scientific phenomena, but reading—especially comprehension of expository materials—is needed for students to fully understand scientific concepts.

Science programs that do not contain literacy activities provide an impoverished form of science learning. Observation and active involvement provide immediate, compelling, memorable sensory experiences (for example, watching bugs under a log or feeling the coolness of the forest). However, observation and activities alone cannot supply the detailed, organized knowledge that places information in a larger, conceptual framework (such as understanding how the log provides a habitat for the insects or learning how the forest is layered). We contend that deep understanding of scientific concepts and their interrelations is almost impossible without access to information available primarily or exclusively through exposition.

Many students are not well prepared for the challenge of comprehending exposition, in science or other areas. One reason for their ill preparedness is that reading expository text typically is not emphasized in the primary grades, as mentioned. In addition, several features of exposition itself make it difficult for many young learners. Expository texts are not as closely linked to direct experience as narratives. They typically are not organized around the familiar temporal and cause-effect relationships of real life, but instead around unfamiliar conceptual, logical, and hierarchical structures. As a consequence, students often need considerable encouragement and directed instruction to read expository materials with interest and comprehension.

The Explorers Program

The science-literacy learning link is the basis for the program described in this chapter. The Explorers program uses students' experiences in nature to energize literacy development. The goal is to take advantage of the power of observation and direct experience to engage students in long-term investigative projects requiring extensive use of expository text materials.

A collaborative program of the Omaha Public Schools and the University of Nebraska–Lincoln Center for Instructional Innovation, Explorers is offered to upper elementary students in some Omaha schools as an alternative to the regular summer school experience. Like other summer school classes, Explorers uses a half-day format, with students attending morning sessions over a six-week period in June and July. In contrast to the regular summer school students, Explorers students spend one of the half-days per week in a nature area to learn observation skills and identify topics of interest. In the classroom, students use expository books and other resource materials in long-term projects on their topics. They work on their projects individually and in groups. They also read literature for pleasure and, to help build connections between science and literacy, take part in whole-class and small-group discussions, make oral presentations, and write frequently throughout the summer.

The first Explorers program involved 6 teachers and approximately 60 students from an elementary school in a diverse Omaha neighborhood. Approximately half of the students were African American and the remainder European American. Our evaluation of the program showed that students learned to use books more effectively and increased the complexity of their thinking about plants and animals, as measured by semantic maps they created before and at the end of their summer experience (Bruning, Schweiger, & Horn, 1994).

In its second year, Explorers was expanded to include another school (from a diverse neighborhood in a different part of the city), 12 teachers, and approximately 180 students. About one-third of the students were African American, one-fifth Hispanic (mostly Mexican American), one-tenth Asian American, and the remainder European American. Project evaluation was substantially increased in the second year to include teacher and student data gathered in 12 Explorers classrooms and 6 comparison classrooms.

The Learning Sequence in Explorers

Trips to a nature area provide a focal point for learning in Explorers. The area, Gifford Point, is a heavily forested setting located in the Missouri River bottom lands just south of Omaha. On weekly fieldtrips to Gifford Point, students observe a rich array of animal and plant life ranging from millipedes and cattails to deer and trees. Teachers typically allow students wide latitude in their initial observations, but soon begin to help them focus and sharpen their observation skills. Students who notice waterbugs on the pond, for example, are encouraged to examine the waterbugs more closely with a magnifying glass, then perhaps to take notes and illustrate what they observed.

Classroom instruction builds on these observations. Teachers ask their students to discuss their observations and help them pose questions about what they have seen. Students might wonder how waterbugs move across the water, for example, or they might be curious about what they eat. The teachers help students sort the questions into categories and hint at further observations, experimentation, and text sources as ways students can answer these questions and pose new ones. The revised questions become the basis for short- and long-term projects.

Students soon realize that books are useful resources that they can use to complete their projects. As their projects progress, students monitor how they feel about their own learning and judge if they are achieving their goals. The teachers also help students organize themselves into work teams, share results of their investigations, and create products that will explain their findings to classmates, siblings, and parents.

The Explorers Curriculum

Explorers is organized around several instructional design dimensions, which include a comprehensive instructional model, student-selected thematic projects, expository text use, reading and writing strategies, and individualized student evaluation. The instructional design framework is calculated to take advantage of students' natural inquisitiveness, their personal interests, the attractiveness of text materials, and the motivational and cognitive effects of social interactions, goal setting, and student autonomy. Four goals are emphasized:

1. Increase student motivation for learning.

2. Improve students' reading and writing.

3. Help students learn to work cooperatively.

4. Develop students' science expertise.

The Explorers Instructional Model

Our learning model emphasizes both observation and text use. On the observational side, we assume that students will gain both literacy and science knowledge most rapidly if they directly observe interesting phenomena and learn to pose good questions about what they see. On the text-use side, teachers help students develop the skills they need to find answers to their questions. Long-term projects provide an overall structure by helping students organize their learning and by requiring them to communicate effectively with others.

In general, we take a social constructivist stance toward student learning, emphasizing the importance of both teacher scaffolding and classroom discourse in cognitive growth. In designing the specific features of the Explorers curriculum, we have drawn heavily on the Concept-Oriented Reading Instruction (CORI) model (Guthrie & Alao, in press; Guthrie, Van Meter et al., 1996; see also Chapter 7 in this volume), on the Project READ/Inquiring School model (Calfee & Patrick, 1995), and on our own previous developmental work with teachers and students in several Omaha Public School settings.

To aid in planning specific instructional activities, we have developed a set of design principles (and associated reflective questions). Among the most important of these principles are that students should always understand *what* they are learning (Is learning purposeful?) and reflect frequently on *why* they are learning it (Is learning examined?). Learning also should be project oriented (Is learning investigative?) and facilitated by teachers' coaching and explicit teaching (Is learning directed?). Finally, we emphasize social learning in a range of discourse-based methods that include classroom discussion, cooperative learning, and project-based activity (Is learning shared?).

To help students link their experiences to text materials, students work in two broad science-related areas, "pond life" and "forest life." These two topics match the resources available at Gifford Point and offer a wide range of possibilities for student investigation. For example, some students become interested in pond life, such as cattails, algae, dragonflies, and fish. Others are captivated by the forest and its many insects, trees, birds, and animals. Every student finds something interesting in the Gifford Point environment.

Concentrating on two topics also has allowed us to stock each classroom with a small library of trade books relating to what students observe. Thus, students can find excellent resources in their own classrooms about their topics. Also, because teachers select the books and are thoroughly familiar with their content, they can more effectively guide students in their reading and investigations.

Explorers Projects

Student activity in the Explorers program is organized around thematic projects. Projects provide a purpose for learning, help focus activities, and teach students to work toward long-term goals. Some students complete individual projects, others work in teams on group projects, and many take part in both individual and group projects. For example, several projects have been completed as displays for Parents' Day. These displays show what students learned during the summer and range from posters, murals, models, collections of leaves, and a classroom forest to dramatic presentations, class books, video productions, and a newspaper. The common features of these displays are that students chose a theme-related topic to learn about, asked and answered questions, organized information, and publicly shared their knowledge.

Explorers Books

Using books is the heart of the Explorers experience. Grants from local sources have enabled us to stock each classroom with a small but high-quality library of expository and narrative trade books keyed to the "pond life" and "forest life" themes, as mentioned. For example, most of the classrooms have several copies of illustrated science books, such as Eyewitness Books (published by Knopf) and field guides to help students identify animals and plants and learn more about them. A typical classroom library has expository trade books on specific topics such as butterflies, frogs, fish, deer, grasses, trees, beavers, and birds and also more general texts on topics such as pond life, forest life, photosynthesis, and ecology. Teachers help students find books on their topics, gather information from them, and use that information to plan and develop their projects. Each teacher also selects at least one narrative book that the students read and discuss as a class during the summer session.

Explorers Strategies

Explorers teachers have identified two reading strategies—using tables of contents and indexes, and summarizing—as most critical for their students. Throughout the term, teachers scaffold and model relevant skills for using both tables of contents and indexes. Students also receive extensive scaffolded instruction and guided practice in summarization. Students' summaries cover a wide range of materials and events, ranging from paragraphs and chapters in narratives and reports to synopses of field experiences.

Writing also is strongly emphasized. Every Explorers student writes daily, typically several times a day. Student writing includes taking notes; entering observations and reflections in journals; summarizing information; creating letters to parents, friends, and pen pals at another school; and labeling pictures and displays. All students receive explicit strategy instruction in writing summaries; students in a few classrooms have received some instruction in other writing strategies such as brainstorming, planning for writing, and writing for an audience (Graham & Harris, 1993; Harris & Graham, 1992).

Explorers teachers also have identified cooperation as an important social learning goal. To move students toward the goal of working cooperatively, teachers use various techniques including structuring multiple small-group and whole-class experiences, coaching students on cooperative learning approaches, and pointing out the utility of cooperative efforts.

Explorers Student and Program Evaluation

Students do not receive grades in the Explorers program. Instead, teachers keep anecdotal records of whether students are learning to use books effectively, enjoying learning about their topics, developing expertise in their topic areas, and working cooperatively. The most important evaluation principle is to encourage students to evaluate their own progress toward their goals and to adjust their approaches and strategies accordingly. For example, do students think that they have learned what they need to know about millipedes? If not, where can more information be found? Do they think they have written clearly enough for people to understand what they have learned? What else might be useful? This emphasis on student reflection and self-assessment necessitates teachers' meeting often with students about their progress and giving instruction as necessary.

To examine how well student goals are being met in Explorers, we have developed several techniques to measure students' motivation to read and write, how students use books, and their learning and conceptual growth. Most are authentic measures, taken as a regular part of the instructional day. At the beginning and end of the six-week Explorers session, for example, students draw semantic maps that reflect their concepts of "forest life" and "pond life"; we compare these to measure conceptual growth (Bruning, Schweiger, & Horn, 1994). To measure growth in reading comprehension, we have students read short segments of informational text, underline key words, summarize the text, and illustrate their summary. Samples of students' writing include research reports, daily journals, and copies of weekly letters students write to their parents and friends. During the most recent Explorers session, members of the evaluation team individually interviewed approximately 240 children in Explorers and comparison schools at the beginning and end of the summer to assess their reading and writing strategies, motivation to read, and ability to use books in research.

Teacher journals and notes, videos, and parental reactions complement the student data. Teacher journals contain their reflections about each day's activities, and teacher notes include specific evaluative comments about each student, recorded cumulatively two or three times a week. Video records are another source of evaluation information that can be used to analyze teacher-student and student-student interactions; the schools' media services have provided professional video footage for use in workshops. Finally, students' parents provide reactions to events in which they participate, such as open houses and fieldtrips. Other parents are sampled by a mail survey to provide overall reactions to the Explorers project.

Motivational Features of Explorers

Like most educational programs, Explorers has numerous features that affect student motivation. However, it is designed around a small set of motivational dimensions. The motivational dimensions most critical to Explorers are student observation, student interest, student autonomy, student goal setting, the text materials, and social interactions. Each motivational dimension falls generally under the rubric of intrinsic motivation.

Starting with Student Observation

Much of what we learn is learned from observation. Observation also has an extraordinary capability of energizing and directing further learning, including literacy learning (Guthrie & Alao, in press; Guthrie, Van Meter et al., 1996). The majority of literacy-related activities in Explorers are linked in some way to student observation. For example, a fifth-grade teacher, Mrs. Veit, describes how observations by her class led to questions they answered through reading:

> [On our second field trip], we collected pond water and tadpoles and small frogs...we ended up with [a larvae] in [the aquarium] that we didn't know what it was...it got huge over the weekend, which we noticed right away. And we also noticed that some of our tadpoles were gone. So we had to figure out what our [larva] was, what kind of tadpoles we had, what kind of frogs we had. So they were observing. They were looking at small details. Then they had to use informational books to make the connections to find out what these animals were, why there were fewer tadpoles, and why the larva was bigger.

Although the amount of time devoted directly to observation in Explorers is a small portion of the total instructional time, we see many examples like this one of observation energizing literacy learning.

Why is observation so powerful? One reason is that observational learning is a fundamental human ability. Human visual memory, for example, is exceptionally capable and stable (Standing, 1973). Also, visual experience has great immediacy and directness; what we see typically is quite important to us.

The language system, by contrast, is highly abstract and symbolic and is a much later product of human evolution. Literacy is an even more abstract and recent entry in human experience. The world of print is less accessible than spoken language to many people. Even if children's language-based systems were fully as capable as observational ones, the sequence of development suggests that children will be considerably more experienced with observation than with the symbols of language and literacy.

Capitalizing on children's responsiveness to observation as a resource for literacy learning requires considerable planning. In Explorers, we have attempted to create systematic links between observation and language activities by matching the observational setting and text materials. We also have tried to help students organize their observations into meaningful conceptual frameworks, so that their observations are not simply sequences of sensory impressions. We have searched for settings that have many interesting phenomena to observe. We also believe in the value of a continuous observational context; a stable setting allows students to build both declarative and procedural knowledge about the setting—knowledge we think provides a concrete experiential resource for grappling with the abstractions of language use and literacy. Familiarity with an observational setting also creates a level of emotional comfort in which learning can thrive.

Capitalizing on Student Interest

Student observation often is closely related to another important motivational factor in Explorers: student interest. Researchers working in the area of interest typically have distinguished between personal and situational interest, as mentioned in previous chapters in this volume. *Personal interest* is unique to an individual, topic specific, and long-lasting, and it exists in advance of a particular situation (Hidi & Anderson, 1992; Schiefele, 1991; Schraw, Bruning, & Svoboda, 1995). In contrast, *situational interest* is common across individuals, short-lived, and elicited in a particular context (Krapp, Hidi, & Renninger, 1992; Wade, 1992). Personal interest tends to be related to prior knowledge and intrinsic motivation (Deci, 1992), whereas situational interest usually arises spontaneously (Hidi & Anderson, 1992). Both personal and situational interest relate to reading comprehension, personal interest because of its relation to domain knowledge (Hidi, 1990) and situational interest because of its arousing and attention-focusing functions (Schraw, Bruning, & Svoboda, 1995). However, if situational interest is not focused on important learning goals, unimportant information can attract a disproportionate amount of a reader's attention (Wade et al., 1993), which is called the "seductive details" effect.

Most Explorers activities are calculated to take advantage of both personal and situational interest. For example, a fifth-grade teacher, Mrs. Nielson, describes in the following excerpt how her students' decisions about which animals to include in a classroom project were based on personal interest. The project was a huge "tree" built from floor to ceiling in their classroom, complete with surrounding habitat.

> Most of them tried to think of some of the things [to include in the habitat] that they saw out at Gifford Point or things that they were interested in that they saw in their backyards. For example, the rabbits came from the backyard...[and]...out at Gifford Point, the snake was just something [one student] was interested in.

Situational interest also proves to be a strong motivating force, as teachers are able to take advantage of happenings in the students' home and school environment and at Gifford Point. For instance, Mrs. Nielson describes how an opossum came to be included as one of the denizens of the classroom tree after one student noticed the creature during a road trip: "He had seen one [a possum], I think, that morning.... [It] was, of course, dead on the road and [the student] was kind of curious about them."

Another student, Brandon, wrote to his mother about what happened when his class encountered and then was followed in the woods by what they thought was a wolf: "We were having a great time until we saw a big wolf. So we ran about a mile. Some of us ran all the way to the bus!" Over the next several days, this highly arousing incident became the focal point of intense investigation and debate in the two classrooms involved as the teachers guided students into research on the habitat and habits of wolves, coyotes, and foxes. Students asked questions such as, "Was it really a wolf?" "Do wolves live in Nebraska?" "It was coyote colored, but are coyotes that large?" "Could it have been a fox or a dog?" To answer their questions, students consulted many sources, read about possible animals, and compared pictures with their memories of what they had seen. (Somewhat to students' disappointment, rangers at a nearby park identified the animal as a large coyote-colored feral dog!)

Mrs. Veit similarly describes the captivating effects of situational interest that are created by observation in the following excerpt.

[My students] happened to see a plant out at Gifford Point that looked like somebody had spit on it, and that was really disgusting to them. But what was neat is one of the kids had heard [of] a spittle bug. Now two people are doing this project on spittle bugs. The whole fieldtrip today—"Maybe we'll find a spittle bug!"

Situational interest also seems to be aroused by displays of live creatures in Explorers classrooms. Here Ms. Marshall, a third-grade teacher, describes what happened motivationally when her class brought a frog into the classroom and placed it in an aquarium.

A living animal adds so much.... I didn't realize—I've never had a live animal in my classroom...just seeing them interact with this living thing and knowing that we can't learn anything about it unless we research...they've told me that so I know that we've gotten across something to them about how important the research is. We can't just assume that we know everything that there is to know about a frog—we have to research it.

It is apparent from these and the many other examples we have observed that interests are powerful motivators. Because long-term personal interests often are connected to preexisting declarative and procedural knowledge, they give students a chance to develop greater expertise on topics with which they already are familiar. Because they are based on arousing incidents, observations, and content, situational interests offer more potential for creating *new* areas of interest and investigation. Taking advantage of either personal or situational interest requires teachers to be strongly committed to an interest-based, flexible instructional model.

Creating an Environment of Student Autonomy

Deci and Ryan (1987) have identified two kinds of environments, *autonomy-supporting* and *controlling*, as mentioned in a previous chapter in this volume. In autonomy-supporting environments, individuals are intrinsically motivated—that is, they perform tasks for internal reasons such as satisfaction or pleasure, rather than for external reasons such as rewards, obligations, or threats. In controlling environments, individuals feel pressure to conform to a set standard or to meet a particular expectation. In Deci and Ryan's view, the degree of perceived choice that individuals have is a critical factor in how they will respond in a given context. Some of the factors that affect students' perceived choices are their own expectations, the teacher's expectations, the tasks they engage in, the materials they encounter, the type of evaluation, and how rewards are used (Bruning, Schraw, & Ronning, 1995; Corno, 1993).

The overall design of Explorers is intended to foster intrinsic motivation based on both the perception and reality of student autonomy and choice. The process begins with students' selecting topics for their projects, which helps generate several autonomy-increasing factors. Students decide what project they will pursue, determine resources they need, and make their own judgments about the adequacy of their projects. When teachers give feedback, they try to provide information-oriented feedback, which stresses how performance can be improved, rather than performance-oriented feedback about how students compare to others.

Teachers' experience in the project generally seems to build their faith in an autonomy-supporting model of intrinsic motivation. In interviews at the end of the second summer that focused on student motivation, *none* of 12 Explorers teachers mentioned extrinsic rewards. In contrast, there were repeated references to the intrinsic motivation generated by autonomy-supported purposeful activity and by students' pursuing their interests and making choices. A fourth-grade teacher, Mr. Cramer, speaks of how he organized his class projects around student interests and choices:

> [The students made] the decision to choose whatever topic in the area [we] were studying. For example, we did the pond unit or pond theme study for the first three weeks. They were able to choose something that was most interesting to them in that habitat, and from there they were able to make the decision [about] which method of sharing or project they'd like to do. I had a variety from mobiles to making models with clay and a newspaper/magazine type activity all the way to just illustrated poster.

Ms. Marshall also illustrates her students' autonomy in making the decision to do further research on the frog:

> And they're always telling me that "Oh, we need more research, we don't know the answer to that." In fact, they were really worried because his skin was changing colors and we all thought he was sick and we were going to take him back to the pond immediately. [Then] they said, "Let's don't do that right away. Let's research and find out why."

Mrs. Veit describes how students' involvement in a purposeful task—becoming more "expert" in their interest area—can promote skill acquisition.

> They can use their reading skills to gain science knowledge to become science experts. They need the summarizing—they need all of the other reading abilities because they want to know so much more about their interest.

She further indicates how student interest and choice are integral to her students' projects.

> It's not that I said, "I want you to do a report on frogs and I think you should do your report on snakes." I have said, "Let's do a project, I want you to find something that will interest you." So we initially set up a project and they had a topic. They set it out in note cards.... They developed questions. We talked about developing questions to be not too big and not too small.... They have changed some of their topics because they were inspired by something that they found in a book or something that they found while we were out in the woods. I think the [girl who] is doing the spittle bugs project started out with moths. But then when she found her spittle bug, that was what she needed to do research on....

Overall, Explorers teachers try to nurture intrinsic motivation by allowing students to make meaningful choices. The goal is to create an autonomy-supporting environment in which student opinions and decisions matter, rather than an environment where control is exerted through instructional objectives, assessment systems, or extrinsic rewards. However, the process is not one of pure discovery. Teachers guide student decision making, often providing considerable conceptual scaffolding for student responses. Learning is purposeful: students acquire new information and skills in order to complete tasks meaningful to them. At the same time, students have considerable latitude and ultimate authority to choose the topics of their investigations and the forms their projects will take.

Setting Mastery Goals for Learning

Much attention has been focused on Dweck and Leggett's (1988) theory of motivation, which proposes two orientations toward learning: a *learning* orientation, characterized by a concern for personal improvement or mastery, and a *performance* orientation, in which learners are more concerned with how they compare with others or with external standards. Dweck and Leggett have argued that these orientations have potent, causal influences on learning in classrooms. Students who adopt learning orientations tend to be more adaptive, strategic, and persistent. In contrast, a performance orientation tends to lead to maladaptive behaviors such as lack of persistence and learned helplessness (Ames, 1992; Blumenfeld, 1992; Roedel, Schraw, & Plake, 1994). In Explorers, we strongly emphasize goals aimed at personal improvement and mastery, while attempting to minimize concern for performance goals.

Nurturing student goal setting has become a major focus of Explorers. Before the program begins in the summer, teachers and staff plan specific methods for involving students in setting learning goals. There seems to be general agreement that it is important to begin this process the first day. Some teachers, especially those working with younger students, are initially concerned about their students' ability to set realistic goals for the short summer session. This concern has led to consideration of both short-term and long-term goals. By the time the session begins, all the teachers will have prepared lessons or activities to assist students in setting realistic, achievable learning goals.

The overall Explorers goals are posted in classrooms. Many teachers use them as a way to describe the program and monitor the summer's events. As part of the orientation to Explorers, teachers talk with students about their understandings of what reaching a goal means. One fifth grader in Ms. Allen's class showed a strong learning orientation, stating, "It means I decide what I really need to do, and then do it!" More often, however, students' initial conceptions of goal attainment are performative, such as "doing what I need to do," "getting my work finished," and "being the first one to get my work done." At the outset, most students seem to reflect an educational history of having been rewarded for completing assigned tasks and pleasing the teacher.

At the beginning of each summer, some of the teachers question the ability of their students to set their own learning goals, suggesting that it might work best if "we (the class) all did it together." However, as they become more comfortable with the idea of students' setting their own goals, they emphasize student choice and mastery goals. Most students clearly rise to the challenge. For example, when individual students describe their projects to one another during the last week of classes, there is almost no reference to performative goals. Comments such as, "My goal was to find out more about butterflies" or "Studying about frogs fits into my plan to know more about pond life" are much more common.

Classroom projects provide a natural arena for goal setting and for shaping a mastery orientation toward learning. Teachers and students can agree on the desired complexity of the project as well as the time required for completion. Structuring investigation around themes appears to be particularly helpful in guiding goal setting, allowing students to concentrate on their research topic. The goals of completing their projects successfully and "becoming an expert" encourage students to plan how they will allocate their time. One teacher commented,

> I find it really more effective if they (students) set a time line within a set of guidelines. They really can get it done on their own time. And they know that there is an end goal and there's something beyond this end point. There's something more exciting to do or something more to do if they want to get it done.

In postsession interviews, students are asked to describe how they knew if they were doing a good job and accomplishing their goals. Lydia, an insightful fourth-grade student, commented, "Well, if I know I have done my best and succeeded, I know it in my head and feel it in my heart. If things haven't turned out, my head tells me, but I feel it in my stomach, too." This mastery-oriented view of learning and classroom activities (Ames, 1992) is a fundamentally different framework for judging school achievement than the performance-oriented view that dominates many classrooms. Accomplishing learning goals serves as the basis for determining the next steps in learning. Goal attainment is not an end product, but a way to determine what students have learned so far.

Using Books in Enjoyable and Functional Ways

For some elementary students, a visual display or an especially interesting-looking book may be all that is necessary to draw them into literacy activities. For others, however, mere contact with books will not provide adequate stimulation for engagement in reading. Thus, Explorers teachers systematically seek to expose their students to multiple levels of experiences with books.

Because we believe that access to books is a key to building motivation to read (see also Palmer, Codling, & Gambrell, 1994), we have created a classroom library of approximately 100 books in each Explorers classroom. Most are well-illustrated expository texts focusing on the Explorers target concepts. They range from easy to fairly difficult. Students are encouraged to use multiple text sources to develop their projects and to find answers to their questions. Students also have access to the school library. Some classrooms have computer technology available for student use as well. Encyclopedias are present in most classrooms but are not used extensively.

Explorers teachers try varied approaches to help students see books as enjoyable and useful. On the first day of classes, for instance, Mrs. Gonzales, a fourth-grade teacher, held up books about frogs from the classroom library and asked the students to generate questions they had about frogs. Ms. Faust, a third-grade teacher, shared highlights from some of her favorite books, and Mrs. Veit displayed her classroom's books and let students browse, listening to their comments about what they found in the books. In general, the teachers' purpose is to spark students' interests and to help them quickly see how books will help them achieve their goals. Mrs. Gibson, a fifth-grade teacher, commented,

> The experiences with books the first day got us off to a good start, and the students' curiosity, interests and motivation for using text continued the entire six weeks. I had students who did not want to leave, even the last day of classes, and that's something different, especially for a summer session!

In several classes, teachers have had students decide how to organize the books for quick access to various topics. In one class, a fifth grader named Melissa said, "We have to decide together a way that will work the best, when we need to find something real quick to answer our questions." Interestingly, we have observed that as the session progresses, the approach to categorizing the books can change. This seems to be the result of the students' becoming more sophisticated about their topics and setting higher goals.

For some students, the transition from becoming acquainted with books to organizing and using them effectively is an easy one. Others, however, need considerable guidance to become effective text users. Teachers often model text use and share ideas about using books as informational sources. They also help students form cooperative groups to answer questions raised during field observations. Students who are not risk-takers or who are less experienced in making decisions often select topics or text materials that have been the focus of a lesson or teacher demonstration. For this reason, the teachers try to model using several different texts in group lessons.

More advanced readers concentrate on the print content of multiple texts, whereas less experienced readers tend to use strategies such as closely examining pictures and labels to gain the desired information. Generally, students do not see their supply of books as becoming "used up" during a six-week summer session nor do they reject books because they have read them before. Instead, they become noticeably more adept at using multiple texts and aware of the strengths and weaknesses of particular sources. Many students develop highly adaptive ways of finding the needed pages, which range from getting help from peers to using identifiable features of the books. Their willingness to share their book-using expertise with their classmates seems to be a visible sign that books serve as motivators for discovering and exploring science concepts.

Each teacher also incorporates several narrative selections during the term to complement and balance the focus on using expository texts for research. Often the expository text provides information useful for understanding some of the events illustrated in the stories. Occasionally, this information leads students to challenge their literary texts. For example, Rob, a fifth grader, had been highly involved in learning about butterflies and had carefully studied several informational texts about butterflies. His expertise led him to question the author of a narrative text, who portrayed butterflies with "non-butterfly" characteristics that Rob knew to be unrealistic.

In summary, having an array of books readily available, coupled with teachers' previewing the texts and directing strategy instruction, seems to greatly affect students' initial motivation to use books. In the longer term, however, students seem most affected by books' functional characteristics—namely, whether students see particular books as useful and interesting. Their choices and judgments about a book's worth are affected by how well the book matches their needs and provides answers to their questions. Under conditions in which students are goal oriented, clarity of exposition and how well expository text links to students' goals seem to be primary values.

Managing Social Interactions and Discourse

Classroom discourse—the talk that goes on in classrooms—increasingly is recognized as important not only to literacy development, but also for effective schooling in general (Calfee, Dunlap, & Wat, 1994; O'Flahavan, 1994). A major goal of Explorers has been to create settings in which *authentic discourse*—interactions that are purposeful, open to participation, and in which students share alternative perspectives—can thrive (Nystrand & Gamoran, 1991). The general framework guiding our attempts to create authentic discourse is social constructivism, in which social exchanges between individuals are seen as sources of cognitive growth (Rogoff, 1990; Vygotsky, 1978).

Explorers teachers use a wide variety of mechanisms to generate authentic discourse, such as cooperative learning ventures, goal-oriented writing, "jigsaw" activities (in which groups contribute unique information, group brainstorming), and decision making. Ms. Saunders, a fourth-grade teacher with a strong science background, describes a classroom environment in which authentic classroom discourse seems almost certain to develop.

> [At Gifford Point] every time we found a log that was decaying and could be turned over, we'd turn it over to see what was there. And we found [several] rather large millipedes, about as big as your little finger...and so we put [them out] where everybody could see them and we just looked at them for a long time and asked questions. "What do you see?" We paid attention to how the legs moved and tried to figure out if we could count them—which was an impossibility! We looked at their antennae and noted that they were pointing down instead of up.
>
> We made all of these observations and [then]...said, "All right, now how many things do we know about the millipede?" "What did we know before we started?" We listed the things we knew. And then we asked some questions about what we don't know...what do we need to find out?... From there, we went into the books and answered the questions...we [were] grouped into small groups of maybe three or four students per book so they can read and take notes and answer the questions.... Then they all had to come back

to the group and share the information they had. And by sharing that, we were able to answer the questions....

Sometimes, the spirit of authentic investigative activity seems to affect the teachers as much as it does the students. Here is a comment from Mrs. Gonzales, a fourth-grade teacher.

I think I've learned more than the kids sometimes. So a lot of times when I'm asking them questions, it really is that *I* don't know the answer and sometimes, when I do know the answer, we're trying to use all the books and the resources we now have.

Effective discourse patterns do not necessarily occur automatically. A significant challenge in Explorers is helping students learn to work together effectively. One mechanism is to take advantage of group expectations for performance. For example, one teacher noted the positive effect of social norms and expectations on his third graders' work patterns.

The other students...inspire their classmates in group activities. With my class, [it sometimes is] very difficult for these kids to work cooperatively.... There's always...some type of friction...but their classmates are pushing them within the group.... "No, this is your turn, you must do this," and it gets the other students involved without me pushing so much.... [One project] basically started out as an individual type of thing and then we brought it into the group activity where each student [needed to] participate...that's where the students, the ones [who are] reluctant to participate or reluctant to even illustrate or to write or to do anything except play—you can see them eventually coming around. "Nope, you must illustrate this—this is your job."

Written communications provide another arena for authentic discourse. Ms. Faust, another third-grade teacher, describes how she used a pen pal arrangement with another teacher to develop writing skills.

We're doing pen pals, the two of us, and it really is working out well with observations, too. Writing down what we had seen that week and asking the kids [at the other school] about what they have seen...they tell their peers different things than they tell their parents, you know.

Writing letters home creates another excellent opportunity for students to communicate about important issues with an interested audience. In a letter to his mother, James nicely summarizes the results of his class's investigation of the "wolf incident" described earlier.

Mom, when I came home and told you we go(t) chased by a wolf, it wasn't. Then we thought it was a coyote, it wasn't. Then we found out that it was a wild stray dog.

Overall, we consider classroom discourse to be one of the most important dimensions of Explorers. The skills learned in authentic classroom talk not only are vital to the learning process, but also will be important later for participating in a democratic society (Calfee & Patrick, 1995; Johnston & Nicholls, 1995). Explorers teachers take classroom talk and discussion seriously. They attempt to create a spirit of joint adventure in their classrooms, where students' questions are encouraged and their viewpoints are valued. They also create work environments in which students must communicate what they know, listen to others, and work together toward shared goals.

The Future of Explorers

Although our initial data suggest that conceptual and literacy growth occur reliably under the motivational conditions of Explorers (Bruning, Schweiger, & Horn, 1994), data analysis currently underway will provide a more definitive description of the relation between the motivational framework of Explorers and this growth. At this point, however, our observations provide several firm conclusions about conditions that are likely to enhance literacy learning.

Promising Findings for Literacy Learning

First, we have little doubt about the utility of intrinsic motivation for literacy learning. We have seen students working purposefully toward goals in almost all our classrooms, with the absence of external rewards. Students' descriptions show that they understand clearly what they are working on and why they are doing it. When students understand the purpose for their learning, they find it valuable (Wigfield, 1994). In addition, although the Explorers model to date has been used only in a summer school science learning setting, teachers have easily adapted many of its motivational and instructional features to the regular school year and to various content areas.

Second, we believe a literacy-learning approach that builds on personal interests can be highly effective. Students not only learn content relating to their interests, but also acquire more general learning strategies, self-regulatory approaches, and positive beliefs about learning. Learning based on longstanding personal interests seems to lead to a desire to increase competency. Students want to learn about topics in which they have an interest, not simply perform better than others or meet an arbitrary standard (Ames, 1992; Dweck & Leggett, 1988).

Third, children's observations can motivate literacy learning (Guthrie & Alao, in press; Guthrie, Van Meter et al., 1996). The situational interest generated by an interesting phenomenon can be the first step in a lifetime of learning. We have seen that children's experiences with "live" phenomena, such as plants and animals in a forest and pond, set in motion a chain of events that energizes and maintains a tremendous range of literacy-related activity. Student reactions to observations become the basis for questions; questions result in answers; finding answers requires skills in locating resources; and using resources effectively means being able to understand the information.

Finally, our beliefs about the power of books to motivate literacy learning have been reinforced. Finding books, handling books, sorting books, leafing through books, sharing books, trying to understand the messages in books, telling others about books, and arguing about what books say create a culture for literacy. In Explorers, books are available to students in their own classrooms, they match the themes of the project, and they are mostly new and attractively illustrated. These conditions combine to create extraordinary motivation for seeking out, reading, talking about, and writing about books. When books are relevant to important tasks and readily available, even the most reluctant literacy learner is likely to become interested in them.

Challenges for the Future

We have been heartened by the motivation we have seen for literacy learning in Explorers. Students in the project, including many who have not previously experienced much success in literacy learning, are motivated to engage in literacy-related activities ranging from searching for information in expository texts to writing fantasies, poetry, and short stories. Motivation seems to relate to several program features including capitalizing on interest, allowing students autonomy while helping them choose meaningful learning tasks, creating opportunities for direct observation, and making attractive, functional text materials available. At the same time, however, we have experienced substantial challenges to implementing the motivational and literacy-learning model in Explorers. The most significant of these challenges are outlined following.

First, it is not easy for teachers to adopt the student-centered approach that a literacy program based on intrinsic motivation demands. Many teachers have learned to use an instructional model that emphasizes direct teaching, close behavioral supervision, and extrinsic rewards for performance. As a consequence, they have learned to manage classroom behavior using systems based on carefully dispensed extrinsic rewards and punishments. However, a strong focus on classroom management can result in excessive energy being spent on managing a few students at the expense of instructional time and energy for the rest of the class. The alternative, adopting an instructional model based on student autonomy, requires substantial risk taking. Considerable experience is required before most teachers feel comfortable in adopting a student-centered instructional and motivational model.

Second, many students will not have well-developed skills in self-regulation. A sudden transition from a teacher-centered model of instruction to one guided by student interests, choices, and learning is unsettling to some students. Freedom to make choices does not mean that students automatically make good choices. For our students, we have found pure discovery models to be ineffective for both literacy learning and classroom decision making. Teachers have found it more productive to provide students with frameworks for literacy learning and decision making. Many students also will be challenged by the social interactions required by the Explorers instructional model. Explorers students, for example, have needed to acquire listening, turn-taking, and cooperation skills to benefit from discourse with their peers or teacher. Some students bring their outside-of-school habits such as strongly challenging differing opinions into school. These habits can interfere with effective group contexts for learning. Emphasis needs to be placed on build-ing an overall climate of respect for others.

Finally, it has become evident that ensuring student success is critical to an intrinsic motivation model of literacy instruction (Bandura, 1993). Teacher scaffolding is one fac-tor that seems to promote student success. Left completely on their own, students typi-cally will not have the motivational and cognitive resources to perform successfully, es-pecially at first. Guidance from a skilled teacher, however, helps students move ahead steadily. Another factor that promotes student success is student acquisition of specific strategies for reading and writing. Explorers teachers work hard to develop their students' skills in summarizing expository and narrative texts. Having these skills enables students to achieve their project goals more easily and at a substantially higher level. These and related skills (such as planning for writing) build confidence not only in reading and writ-ing, but also for learning in general.

Authors' Note

The teachers' and students' names used in this chapter are pseudonyms.

References

Ames, C. (1992). Classrooms: Goals, structures, and student motivation. *Journal of Educational Psychology, 84,* 261–271.

Bandura, A. (1993). Perceived self-efficacy in cognitive development and functioning. *Educational Psychologist, 28,* 117–148.

Blumenfeld, P.C. (1992). Classroom learning and motivation: Clarifying and expanding goal theo-ry. *Journal of Educational Psychology, 84,* 272–281.

Bruning, R., Schraw, G., & Ronning, R. (1995). *Cognitive psychology and instruction.* Englewood Cliffs, NJ: Prentice Hall.

Bruning, R., Schweiger, B., & Horn, C. (1994, December). *Explorers: Developing engaged reading through observation, text use strategies, and classroom talk.* Paper presented at the 44th Annual Meeting of the National Reading Conference, San Diego, CA.

Calfee, R., Dunlap, K., & Wat, A. (1994). Authentic discussion of texts in middle grade schooling: An analytic-narrative approach. *Journal of Reading, 37,* 1–14.

Calfee, R., & Patrick, C. (1995). *Teach our children well* (Portable Stanford Series). Stanford, CA: Stanford University Alumni Association.

Corno, L. (1993). The best-laid plans: Modern conceptions of volition and educational research. *Educational Researcher, 22*(2), 14–22.

Deci, E.L. (1992). The relation of interest to the motivation of behavior: A self-determination theo-ry perspective. In K.A. Renninger, S. Hidi, & A. Krapp (Eds.), *The role of interest in learn-ing and development* (pp. 43–70). Hillsdale, NJ: Erlbaum.

Deci, E.L., & Ryan, R.M. (1987). The support of autonomy and control of behavior. *Journal of Per-sonality and Social Psychology, 53,* 1024–1037.

Dweck, C., & Leggett, E. (1988). A social-cognitive approach to motivation and personality. *Psy-chological Review, 95,* 256–273.

Graham, S., & Harris, K.R. (1993). Self-regulated strategy development: Helping students with learn-ing problems develop as writers. *The Elementary School Journal, 94,* 160–181.

Guthrie, J., & Alao, S. (in press). Designing contexts to increase motivations for reading. *Educational Psychologist*.

Guthrie, J.T., Van Meter, P., et al. (1996). Growth of literacy engagement: Changes in motivations and strategies during concept-oriented reading instruction. *Reading Research Quarterly, 31,* 306–332.

Harris, K.R., & Graham, S. (1992). *Helping young writers master the craft: Strategy instruction and self-regulation in the writing process.* Cambridge, MA: Brookline.

Hidi, S. (1990). Interest and its contribution as a mental resource for learning. *Review of Educational Research, 60,* 549–572.

Hidi, S., & Anderson, V. (1992). Situational interest and its impact on reading and expository writing. In K.A. Renninger, S. Hidi, & A. Krapp (Eds.), *The role of interest in learning and development* (pp. 215–238). Hillsdale, NJ: Erlbaum.

Johnston, P., & Nicholls, J. (1995). Voices we want to hear and voices we don't. *Theory into practice, 34,* 94–100.

Krapp, A., Hidi, S., & Renninger, K.A. (1992). Interest, learning, and development. In K.A. Renninger, S. Hidi, & A. Krapp (Eds.), *The role of interest in learning and development* (pp. 3–25). Hillsdale, NJ: Erlbaum.

Nystrand, M., & Gamoran, A. (1991). Instructional discourse, student engagement, and literature achievement. *Research in the Teaching of English, 25,* 261–290.

O'Flahavan, J. (1994). Teacher role options in peer discussions about literature. *The Reading Teacher, 48,* 354.

Palmer, B., Codling, R.M., & Gambrell, L. (1994). In their own words: What elementary students have to say about motivation to read. *The Reading Teacher, 48,* 176–178.

Roedel, T., Schraw, G., & Plake, B. (1994). Validation of a measure of learning and performance goal orientation. *Educational and Psychological Measurement, 54,* 1013–1021.

Rogoff, B. (1990). *Apprenticeship in thinking: Cognitive development in social context.* New York: Oxford University Press.

Schraw, G., Bruning, R., & Svoboda, C. (1995). Sources of situational interest. *Journal of Reading Behavior, 27,* 1–17.

Schiefele, U. (1991). Interest, learning, and motivation. *Educational Psychologist, 26,* 299–323.

Standing, L. (1973). Learning 10,000 pictures. *Quarterly Journal of Experimental Psychology, 25,* 207–222.

Vygotsky, L.S. (1978). *Mind in society: The development of higher psychological processes.* Cambridge, MA: Harvard University Press.

Wade, S. (1992). How interest affects learning from text. In K.A. Renninger, S. Hidi, & A. Krapp (Eds.), *The role of interest in learning and development* (pp. 281–296). Hillsdale, NJ: Erlbaum.

Wade, S., Schraw, G., Buxton, W., & Hayes, M. (1993). Seduction of the strategic reader: Effects of interest on strategies and recall. *Reading Research Quarterly, 28,* 3–24.

Wigfield, A. (1994). Expectancy-value theory of achievement motivation: A developmental perspective. *Educational Psychology Review, 6,* 49–78.

Ownership, Literacy Achievement, and Students of Diverse Cultural Backgrounds

9

Kathryn H. Au

Mrs. Nakamura, a second-grade teacher, had copied Nathan's report on sharks on chart paper for a minilesson on the qualities of effective writing. The report began:

Hello, I'm Mr. Fernandez. I'm your leader to the undersea world of sharks. Today we will all follow the great white shark. Everybody put on your suits and tanks and goggles and fins.

Nathan had gotten the idea for writing his report as a guided tour from his classmate Moana, who had written about stars. Moana had been inspired by science books written by children's author Joanna Cole, in which students in Ms. Frizzle's class journey on a magic school bus.

Mrs. Nakamura pointed out Nathan's use of humor: "Sharks like meat and you are meat." His classmates noticed that he had chosen his phrases with care: "The part you have to worry about is...." Nathan said he had borrowed this phrase from a videotape, *The Fox and the Hound.*

Like many of Mrs. Nakamura's students, Nathan is of Native Hawaiian ancestry, comes from a low-income family, and speaks Hawaii Creole English as a first language. Students with these background characteristics frequently achieve at low levels in school (Kamehameha Schools Bishop Estate, 1993). However, at the time Nathan had completed his report, he and the other students in Mrs. Nakamura's class seemed to view writing in surprisingly sophisticated ways. For example, Nathan had incorporated wording from a videotape viewed at home in his research report. He and other students knew how to draw upon ideas from children's literature and their classmates' writing. Entries in their notebooks showed that they had closely observed the world around them: for example, entries described the sound of the wind and a conversation between a father and an uncle.

Mrs. Nakamura and her colleagues had been following the whole literacy curriculum developed at the Kamehameha Elementary Education Program (KEEP), an effort to improve the literacy achievement of Hawaiian students, in operation from 1971 to 1995 (Au et al., 1990). The whole literacy curriculum required teachers to grapple with a new philosophy of literacy and learning as well as new forms of instruction, classroom organization, and assessment. The 160 teachers who worked with the whole literacy curriculum taught at 9 public schools in low-income communities on 3 of the Hawaiian Islands. The teachers varied considerably in years of classroom experience, ranging from zero to more than 20. All were volunteers with an interest in improving their students' achievement. Teachers were encouraged to adopt new ideas and practices through extensive opportunities for staff development. KEEP consultants stationed in the schools conducted workshops, facilitated discussions among small groups of teachers, provided individual consultation, and assisted teachers with portfolio assessment.

The overarching goal of the curriculum was ownership of literacy. Ownership was defined as students' valuing of literacy, including holding positive attitudes toward literacy and having the habit of using literacy in everyday life. Students display positive attitudes by willingly engaging in reading and writing, showing confidence and pride in their own literacy, and taking an interest in the literacy of others (for example, by writing on the comment page of another student's published book). Students show that they have the habit of literacy when they read books at home, write in journals or diaries, maintain books of addresses and phone numbers, make lists, create greeting cards, and correspond with friends and relatives. Some of these activities (such as journal writing) may have been introduced by teachers, but students who have the habit of literacy engage in these activities outside of school when they are not required. These actions show that students routinely engage in literacy even when not being supervised by teachers.

In the whole literacy curriculum, a reciprocal relationship was assumed between ownership of literacy and proficiency in reading and writing. Students who have ownership of literacy are motivated to learn to read and write well because literacy plays a central and meaningful role in their lives. Also, as students become more proficient at reading and writing, these activities can be carried out with greater ease and success, so they become more motivating.

Throughout the year, Mrs. Nakamura conducted a writers' workshop nearly every day, giving students time to write on self-selected topics. During the second semester, she began the workshop by having students discuss experiences they might want to write about in their notebooks. Ten minutes of sustained silent writing followed, then the students gathered on the carpet, and five or six of them read their notebook entries. Mrs. Nakamura taught them to comment on what was effective about the writer's approach. After the students read their entries, Mrs. Nakamura conducted a minilesson. Most often, as with the minilesson based on Nathan's writing, she taught about the author's craft and the qualities of effective writing, although she also covered skills such as spelling, punctuation, and capitalization. After the minilesson, students worked on their projects. Mrs. Nakamura taught them to read through their notebooks and mark entries that might serve as the basis for projects, following the approach described by Calkins (1991).

The writers' workshop in Mrs. Nakamura's classroom, like the vignette featuring Robert and Kantu presented in the introduction of this volume, serves as an example of the kind of highly engaging experiences that promote literacy learning in school. Although such experiences are beneficial to all students, they play a crucial role in the school literacy learning of students such as Nathan, who are of diverse backgrounds. The phrase *students of diverse backgrounds* is used here to refer to students within the United States who are from low-income families; African, Asian, Hispanic, or Native American in ethnicity; and speakers of a home language other than standard American English.

A gap between the literacy achievement of students of diverse backgrounds and students of mainstream backgrounds has long been documented. For example, the results of the National Assessment of Educational Progress show that the reading and writing performance of African American and Hispanic American students lags behind that of their European American peers, beginning in the primary grades and continuing through high school (Applebee, Langer, & Mullis, 1985; Mullis & Jenkins, 1990). Educators face the challenge of bridging this gap. This chapter addresses the relationship between motivation and the literacy achievement gap.

Anthropological Perspectives

The ideas of two educational anthropologists, John Ogbu and Frederick Erickson, serve as useful starting points for thinking about issues of motivation and their relation to the literacy achievement gap between diverse and mainstream students. Ogbu's (1990, 1993) theory is based on comparative research that addresses the question of why some students of diverse backgrounds succeed in school, while others do not. Of relevance here are Ogbu's ideas about the achievement of students that he terms "castelike" or "involuntary minorities." He asserts that involuntary minorities became part of American society against their will through processes of enslavement, conquest, or colonization. Examples of such groups are African Americans and Native Hawaiians. Ogbu questions why involuntary minorities may not be motivated to overcome barriers to school success in the same way as immigrant or voluntary minorities. It should be noted that Ogbu's research addresses broad patterns of achievement and that other researchers (such as Achor & Morales, 1990; Hayes, 1992) have identified exceptions to these patterns and argued in favor of other theoretical perspectives.

In research conducted in Stockton, California, Ogbu (1981) identifies economic incentive as one source of this lack of motivation. He documents the existence of a job ceiling that consigned the African Americans in the study to low-paying, low-status jobs regardless of the level of education they had achieved. In other words, education did not seem to yield the same benefits to African Americans as it did to European Americans in the study. African American parents told interviewers that they thought education to be important to their children's success in life. However, according to Ogbu, parents did not believe their children had the same chance to succeed as European Americans. For this reason, they did not strongly support their children's efforts to perform well academically.

Another barrier noted by Ogbu is the distrust of the public schools among some involuntary minorities. This distrust, grounded in historical conditions of discrimination, leads some parents to conclude that public schools, particularly in the inner city, cannot provide their children with a proper education. These parents believe that public schools represent the same mainstream interests that have discriminated against involuntary minorities in the past.

Over time, discrimination and distrust may contribute to the development of cultural practices that oppose ways of thinking common in the American mainstream, a phenomenon Ogbu (1993) terms "cultural inversion." Failing to do well in school appears to be an example of cultural inversion among involuntary minority students. To be successful in school, some African American high school students find that they must adopt a European American perspective or "act white" (Fordham, 1991). Many students appear unwilling to drop the markers of cultural identity that they associate with being African American, as the price for school success. They generally believe that remaining part of the peer group and retaining ties with the community require that they not "act white" and, therefore, not be successful in school.

The research of Ogbu and his colleagues suggests that some involuntary minority students and their families have come to perceive schooling as a process of giving up their cultural identity without the guarantee of the social and economic rewards available to members of the mainstream. In this context educators must work to gain students' trust, so that students become willing to acquire the strategies and attitudes necessary for academic success.

While Ogbu's research addresses factors in the larger society, Erickson's (1993; Erickson & Mohatt, 1982) research looks at interactions in classrooms. Erickson argues that the school success or failure of students of diverse backgrounds is not simply predetermined by broad societal factors but results from the day-to-day interactions of students and teachers in the classroom. He suggests that students will be motivated to learn in school if teachers use communication patterns responsive to or compatible with the norms, beliefs, and values of students' home cultures. The use of such communication patterns is one form of *culturally responsive instruction* (Erickson, 1993; Ladson-Billings, 1995). Students' motivation increases because they understand the rules for participation and are able to engage comfortably and successfully in classroom activities.

An example of cultural responsiveness in communication patterns is seen in research on the use of talk story-like participation structures in reading lessons with young Hawaiian children. Mason and I (Au & Mason, 1981, 1983) compared the lessons given by two teachers similar in professional background and years of teaching experience, with the notable difference that one (Teacher HC) had previously taught Hawaiian children and the other (Teacher LC) had not. Each teacher taught two lessons on reading comprehension to the same group of six Hawaiian second graders. Teacher HC, as expected, conducted her lessons following interactional rules similar to those in talk story, a Hawaiian community speech event (Watson, 1975). She did not tightly control turn taking but allowed the children to determine who would answer her questions. Although she occasionally called on a particular child to speak, she did not prevent others from adding to that child's answer. The tone of the lessons was conversational, and there was considerable overlapping speech. The high level of collaboration shown in the lessons, which centered on group rather than individual performance, seemed consistent with the importance placed on cooperation versus competition in the students' home culture.

In contrast, Teacher LC conducted her lessons according to interactional rules typical in mainstream classrooms. She taught following the initiation-response-evaluation (IRE) pattern (Cazden, 1988; Mehan, 1979) in which the teacher initiates the topic, often through a question, and calls on a single student to respond. The chosen student is understood to have exclusive speaking rights, and others are not supposed to answer. The teacher evaluates the student's response, indicating whether it is correct.

Although this pattern for organizing interaction runs smoothly in mainstream classrooms, it did not work well in Teacher LC's lessons with Hawaiian children. When Teacher LC called on a student to respond, others would add their ideas. It took Teacher LC a great deal of time to stop the other students from answering. As a result, she spent considerable time managing the lesson and little time discussing the story. The lessons moved forward fitfully, as the teacher attempted to enforce her rules for turn taking, which the students persisted in ignoring. The rules for the IRE pattern are rooted in norms of individual achievement and competition, values more important in mainstream culture than in the Hawaiian children's home culture.

The results showed that the students were much more attentive and involved in the lessons with the culturally responsive, talk story-like participation structures than in the lessons with the IRE structure. Further, they discussed many more text ideas and made more logical inferences during the talk story-like reading lessons. Reading lessons in which interaction was structured in a culturally responsive manner seemed to confer motivational and academic benefits on Hawaiian children that conventional reading lessons did not.

Erickson (1993) discusses why an adaptation as simple as changing the structure of turn taking in a lesson might promote the motivation and academic learning of students of diverse backgrounds. From an anthropological perspective, such adaptations may reduce the cultural shock in the classroom, as students find that familiar ways of speaking are accepted in an otherwise unfamiliar setting. In a symbolic sense, students may perceive the teacher's acceptance of their norms for interaction as affirming their own worth and the worth of their community.

Students always are doing some kind of learning, whether they are in school or in the community. According to Erickson, when educators say that students are "not learning," they mean that students are not learning the academic content being presented by teachers. Erickson views students' not learning—or more accurately, refusal to learn—as a form of political resistance. Students resist because they do not trust their teachers to exercise authority in a fair manner. Students must believe that assenting to the authority of teachers will prove beneficial rather than harmful to them, and they must feel that they can trust the teacher to respect their identities.

In situations where mutual trust is lacking, students become increasingly alienated from school, as Erickson (1993) suggests:

> It is no longer a matter of difference between teacher and student that derives from inter-generationally transmitted communicative traditions. It is also a matter of cultural intention as a medium of resistance in a situation of political conflict. As students grow older and experience repeated failure and repeated negative encounters with teachers, they develop oppositional cultural patterns as a symbol of their disaffiliation with what they experience (not necessarily within full reflective awareness) as an illegitimate and oppressive system. The more alienated the students become, the less they persist in doing schoolwork. Thus they fall farther and farther behind in academic achievement. The student becomes either actively resistant—seen as salient and incorrigible—or passively resistant—fading into the woodwork as an anonymous well-behaved, low-achieving student. (p. 41)

Erickson relates Ogbu's notion of cultural inversion to students' resistance to school and highlights the reflexive nature of school failure. Teachers' constant repetition of detrimental classroom situations triggers resistance, and students refuse to engage in the academic work that leads to school success. Teacher and students thus collaborate to perpetuate a cycle of failure (McDermott & Gospodinoff, 1981).

In short, Erickson (1993) argues that school failure is not a faceless process carried forward by the grand sweep of social and economic forces. Rather, the alienation of students of diverse backgrounds comes about through daily interactions between teachers and students in classrooms, which tend first to lower students' motivation to do well in school and then to foster resistance. Teachers may carry out hegemonic practices without conscious awareness or intent, but if they are inadvertently engaging in practices that put students of diverse backgrounds at a disadvantage, they also can decide to engage in alternative practices that build toward school success.

Findings from Research with Native Hawaiian Students

Native Hawaiians fit Ogbu's (1990) characterization of involuntary minorities. Following the overthrow of its monarchy in 1893, Hawaii ceased to be an independent kingdom and was annexed to the United States in 1898. As a result, the curriculum and instruction experienced by Hawaiian children during the 20th century have tended to reflect the beliefs and practices of the American mainstream. The consequences have not been positive. As a group, Hawaiian students in public schools in Hawaii score in the bottom quartile on standardized tests of reading achievement (Kamehameha Schools Bishop Estate, 1993). Not surprisingly, they often exhibit negative attitudes toward reading and writing in the classroom.

Yet some teachers, such as Mrs. Nakamura, who worked with the KEEP whole literacy curriculum, have been able to create classrooms in which Hawaiian students show positive attitudes and considerable proficiency in literacy. Details of the five years of research with the whole literacy curriculum are reported in the following works: Au and Asam, 1996; Au and Carroll, in press; Au and Scheu, 1996; and Carroll, Wilson, and Au, 1996.

The remainder of this chapter highlights findings from this research regarding issues of motivation and their relation to the literacy achievement gap.

Ownership as the Overarching Goal

As seen in the figure on page 175, the whole literacy curriculum incorporated six aspects of literacy, with ownership as the overarching goal (Au et al., 1990), as mentioned earlier.

The second aspect of literacy was the writing process. In keeping with the process approach to writing, described by Graves (1983), Atwell (1987), Calkins (1994), and others, writing was viewed as a dynamic, recursive process involving planning, drafting, revising, editing, and publishing. Teachers conducted writers' workshops similar to that described in Mrs. Nakamura's classroom. Students wrote on self-selected topics, engaged in conferences with the teacher and with peers, and often published three or more books during the academic year.

Reading comprehension, the third aspect of literacy, was seen as a dynamic interaction among the reader, the text, and the social context in which reading took place (Wixson et al., 1987). The view of reading comprehension in the whole literacy curriculum followed reader response theory, particularly the ideas of Rosenblatt (1978, 1991). Teachers organized instruction around readers' workshops and encouraged students to develop personal responses to literature and to read from both aesthetic and efferent stances. Students wrote in response to literature and engaged in literature discussions, some teacher led and others peer guided.

The treatment of word reading and spelling strategies, the fourth aspect of literacy, was based on Clay's (1985) idea that effective word identification requires using information from three cue systems: meaning (passage and sentence context), structural, and visual. Teachers taught word-identification lessons based on opportunities afforded by the literature students were reading. For example, a particular text might present students with several compound words, words beginning with blends, or verbs ending with -ing. Spelling was taught primarily as part of editing during the writing process.

The fifth aspect of literacy, language and vocabulary knowledge, referred to the ability to understand and use appropriate terms and structures in both spoken and printed English. Vocabulary was viewed in terms of knowledge of various topics (Mezynski, 1983), and teachers taught students the meanings of sets of words drawn from literature. For a work of fiction, there might be a set of words describing the characters' feelings, and for a work of nonfiction, a set of words associated with a topic such as volcanoes.

Voluntary reading, the sixth aspect of literacy, emphasized students' willingness to read independently from self-selected materials. Teachers promoted voluntary reading through read-alouds, book talks, and daily periods of sustained silent reading. Classrooms contained well-stocked libraries with books of varying difficulty levels. Many teachers also encouraged students to read books of their own choosing at home.

In brief, the whole literacy curriculum encompassed both cognitive and affective dimensions of literacy and traditional skill areas as well as processes of meaning making

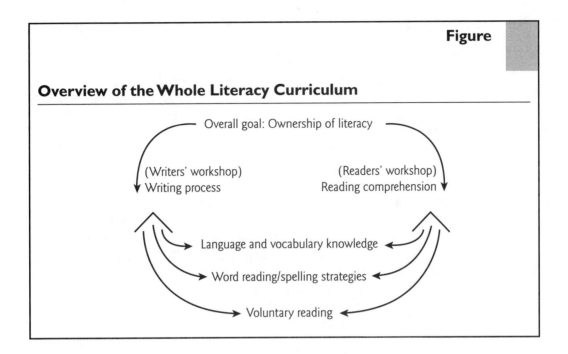

Figure

Overview of the Whole Literacy Curriculum

and interpretation. Proficiency in literacy was desired, but ownership was considered the primary goal.

Each of the other aspects of literacy was thought to relate to ownership in the manner indicated by the arrows shown in the figure. The arrows pointing upward reflect the notion that ownership could be bolstered by the writing process and reading comprehension, which were reinforced by language and vocabulary knowledge, word-identification and spelling strategies, and voluntary reading. The arrows pointing downward highlight the reciprocal nature of the relationship, the idea that ownership could increase student interest and commitment to engaging in the other five aspects of literacy.

The whole literacy curriculum proved highly effective in bringing issues of motivation to the forefront. Before this curriculum was adopted, KEEP teachers and staff members had focused on proficiency in reading and writing as the endpoint. In implementing the whole literacy curriculum, they agreed that they would work toward helping students see literacy as a personally meaningful, significant part of their everyday lives, outside of school as well as within.

Using Motivating Classroom Activities That Preserve Cultural Identity and Peer Relationships

In classrooms where the majority of students are Hawaiian and from low-income families, resistance to schooling is common. D'Amato (1988) describes the phenomenon of "acting," a playful form of protest that can escalate to a tense, year-long stand-off between teacher and students. D'Amato points out that Hawaiian and other students of diverse backgrounds lack a structural rationale for complying with teacher's requests. Either they do not understand the structural relations between schooling and later opportunities, or they do not believe that doing well in school will affect their opportunities. As Ogbu (1981) notes, a strong connection between doing well in school and obtaining a good job often has not been illustrated in their own family histories. Students who lack a structural rationale for cooperating with their teachers do not fear the consequences of poor academic achievement or disruptive behavior.

When a structural rationale is unavailable to students, D'Amato argues, teachers must provide a situational rationale. They must give students good reasons, within the classroom situation, for being cooperative and gaining proficiency in academic content and strategies. D'Amato endorses culturally responsive instruction as a means teachers can use to give students a situational rationale. Like Ogbu and Erickson, he recognizes the importance students attach to their cultural identities and peer group relationships.

In his research, D'Amato witnessed extraordinary efforts by Hawaiian students to maintain relationships of equality within the peer group. Students continually strived to show that they were just as good as everyone else, not to show that they were better. D'Amato notes that teacher use of the IRE structure forces students to perform and be judged as individuals, putting them in a situation in which they must show that they are better than their peers. The use of talk story-like participation structures is more effective with Hawaiian students because it allows them to cooperate to produce answers and to maintain equality in peer relationships.

By using culturally responsive forms of instruction, teachers signal to students that they are in tune with them. Trust begins to develop as students realize that teachers are making it possible for them to succeed in school without having to violate cultural or peer group norms.

In addition to using culturally responsive forms of instruction, teachers can give students another kind of situational rationale: authentic, personally meaningful classroom experiences with literacy. In this regard, the process approach to writing has proved particularly effective in classrooms with Hawaiian students. An example of a writers' workshop following the process approach to writing is shown in the earlier description of Mrs. Nakamura's classroom. During whole-class and small-group discussions, Mrs. Nakamura often used talk story-like participation structures. Students wrote on self-selected topics, first in their notebooks and then in the drafts of pieces they intended to publish. Mrs. Nakamura had students read aloud their drafts and published pieces in the "author's chair" (Graves & Hansen, 1983), so that students could be recognized as authors by the whole class. A bulletin board showed a photo of each student with the titles of his or her published books.

KEEP teachers such as Mrs. Nakamura took to heart Graves's (1990) notion that teachers must explore and share their own literacy with their students. Mrs. Nakamura shared her own writing with students: childhood memories of trying to trap mynah birds and recent events such as getting a flat tire on the freeway. She conducted minilessons in which she shared her drafts and revisions with students, pointing out how she crossed out words or whole sections and sometimes even had to start over again. She asked students for suggestions about how she might improve her drafts. Through these actions, Mrs. Nakamura showed that she too was a writer and put herself in the same vulnerable situations as her students. Trust developed as she and the students learned more about one another through sharing their writing, and students' motivation to write increased.

Assessing Growth in Students' Ownership of Literacy

The KEEP whole literacy curriculum included portfolio assessment of the six aspects of literacy. Although affective aspects of literacy such as ownership and voluntary reading are not typically assessed, KEEP staff members decided to do so. They reasoned that ownership might not receive much attention unless it was assessed because what gets assessed is often what gets taught.

KEEP staff members created grade-level benchmarks for ownership of literacy, based on classroom observations and teacher judgment about the kinds of habits and attitudes that should be expected at each grade level. The ownership benchmarks for kindergarten through grade 6 are shown in the table on page 178. The benchmarks represent the habits and attitudes desired of the average student at the end of each grade level. Benchmarks also were created for the other five aspects of literacy (Asam et al., 1993).

KEEP staff members and teachers devised various means of assessing students' accomplishment of the ownership benchmarks. They used checklists or anecdotal records and kept artifacts (for example, notes children had written at home). They interviewed younger children or had older ones complete questionnaires. As they gathered evidence to document students' progress in meeting the benchmarks, KEEP teachers and staff members gained a keen awareness of the habits and attitudes associated with ownership of literacy. They then passed this awareness on to students.

Leading Students to High Degrees of Ownership
with a Whole Literacy Curriculum

By the second year of implementation of the KEEP whole literacy curriculum, improvements in the children's ownership of literacy were apparent to teachers and observers. Teachers had succeeded in engaging students in the full processes of reading and writing. Students discussed novels with the teacher and their peers, wrote in response to literature, and had time to read books they had chosen. They wrote on self-selected topics and shared their writing with others. They were actively engaged in meaningful literacy activities within classroom communities of learners.

During the second and third years of implementation of the whole literacy curriculum, results were collected for all KEEP students in kindergarten through grade 3, a total of about 2,000 at the 9 schools. About two-thirds of the students were of Native Hawaiian ancestry,

Table

Benchmarks for Ownership of Literacy

				Grade Level			
Ownership of Writing	K	I	2	3	4	5	6
Enjoys writing	*	*	*	*	*	*	*
Shows confidence and pride in own writing	*	*	*	*	*	*	*
Shares own writing with others	*	*	*	*	*	*	*
Shows interest in others' writing	*	*	*	*	*	*	*
Writes in class for own purposes			*	*	*	*	*
Writes outside of class for own purposes				*	*	*	*
Makes connections between reading and writing					*	*	*
Sets goals and evaluates own achievement of writing					*	*	*
Gains insights through writing						*	*

and the majority were from low-income families. During the school year, portfolios were assembled for each student, containing evidence of progress in meeting the grade-level benchmarks in each of the six aspects of literacy. For example, observational checklists, interviews, and anecdotal records were collected as evidence of ownership, and written summaries and reading logs were collected as evidence of reading comprehension.

By referring to the evidence in students' portfolios and the grade-level benchmarks, KEEP teachers and staff members could rate students as below, at, or above grade level in the aspects of literacy. Students received a rating of *below grade level* in a particular aspect of literacy if their portfolios did not show evidence that they had met all the benchmarks for their grade level. They received a rating of *at grade level* if there was evidence that they had met all the benchmarks. To be rated *above grade level*, a student had to have portfolio evidence meeting all the benchmarks for the next higher grade. Baseline portfolio data had not been collected before implementation of the whole literacy curriculum, so it was not possible to make comparisons to students' previous levels of achievement. However, the results for each classroom were audited for the adequacy of evidence in students' portfolios and for the accuracy of ratings.

Observers' impressions of the classrooms were confirmed in the assessment results for ownership of literacy, which indicated that about two-thirds of the students in kindergarten through grade 3 had met the benchmarks at their grade level. The KEEP whole literacy curriculum appeared to be leading to high levels of engagement in literacy among

Au

students of diverse backgrounds. As explained following, however, this finding is only part of the overall picture.

Understanding That Ownership Does Not Automatically Lead to Proficiency

The two years of data previously discussed indicated that KEEP students had not reached adequate levels of proficiency in reading and writing, as measured by grade-level benchmarks. Across all grade levels, approximately two-thirds of the students were rated below grade level in the writing process and in reading comprehension. Students also remained below grade level in vocabulary and language development; assessment in this area was tied closely to assessment of reading comprehension. These aspects of literacy required complex forms of higher level thinking that did not develop simply as a consequence of students' high engagement with literacy. Interestingly, proficiency in word identification did reach acceptable levels, perhaps due to high levels of voluntary reading (for complete results, refer to Au & Asam, 1996; Au & Carroll, in press).

These findings indicated that students appeared to require extensive instruction in the complex kinds of thinking involved in the writing process and reading comprehension. Although ownership and proficiency were undoubtedly related, the two were not perfectly correlated. Proficiency in literacy did not follow naturally as a consequence of high degrees of ownership.

Attending to Ownership While Aiming Toward High Standards

In the fourth and fifth years of work with the whole literacy curriculum, KEEP staff members focused on achieving implementation of the curriculum in just a few demonstration classrooms, to determine whether better achievement results could be attained. Thirteen demonstration teachers participated in the fourth year and 30 in the fifth year. (Mrs. Nakamura became a demonstration teacher in the fifth year, when the observations reported here were made.) The demonstration teachers were asked to concentrate on implementation of either the writers' workshop or the readers' workshop, and the majority chose the writers' workshop. The following discussion will address the work of the writing-oriented teachers (11 in the fourth year and 26 in the fifth year).

The demonstration teachers provided instruction in the writing process within the context of having students write on self-selected topics. For the most part, the teachers knew how to conduct minilessons and conferences. However, they had difficulty making their own writing part of instruction. The teachers who, like Mrs. Nakamura, had the courage to use samples of their own writing in minilessons, discovered that they were better able to motivate students to learn and apply the targeted concepts, strategies, and skills. By revealing their own struggles as writers, teachers made the minilessons meaningful to students (Au & Scheu, 1996).

The teachers also worked on portfolio assessment. As they monitored students' progress toward the benchmarks, teachers gained information that led to adjustments in instruction. For example, a second-grade teacher noticed that most of her students were not meeting the benchmarks for editing. She realized that she had been taking much of the responsibility for editing on herself. To remedy the situation, she began conducting a series of minilessons on editing skills. At the same time, she required students to attempt to edit their own pieces and to work with a peer editor before she met with them for an editing conference.

The teachers engaged older students (from the second grade and higher) in the process of gathering evidence to show that they were meeting the benchmarks. A fifth-grade teacher identified the benchmarks she would focus on for the first quarter, second quarter, and so on. For example, benchmarks for planning and drafting seemed achievable during the first quarter, while those for publishing were put off until later in the year. Near the end of the first quarter, the teacher showed a group of six students how to label evidence in their portfolios to show that they had met the first quarter benchmarks. These students worked with small groups of classmates to teach them the same process. In two days, all students in the class had assessed their own progress toward meeting the first quarter benchmarks. They knew which benchmarks they had achieved and which still required work. The teacher had the students repeat the process of self-evaluation toward the end of the second, third, and fourth quarters. Not surprisingly, most of her students succeeded in meeting all the fifth-grade benchmarks for ownership of writing and the writing process by the end of the year.

During the fourth and fifth years, the demonstration teachers achieved outstanding results. Both years, more than 80 percent of their students received ratings of at or above grade level in ownership of writing. More important, during both years about 66 percent of the students were rated at or above grade level in the writing process. These results were the opposite of those obtained during the first three years of implementation, when about 67 percent of the students had been rated below grade level in the writing process (for details of the results, see Au & Asam, 1996; Au & Carroll, in press.)

Through a combination of intensive instruction and close monitoring of student progress toward the benchmarks, the demonstration teachers showed that a whole literacy curriculum could be effective in improving students' literacy achievement, in terms of the quality of students' writing and their ownership of literacy.

Conclusion

Students of diverse backgrounds may lack the motivation to do well in school because, in their family histories, success in school has not led to better life opportunities. Further, students may decide not to be successful in school if they have to give up their cultural identities. To motivate students of diverse backgrounds, teachers must explore alternatives that allow students to be successful in school while maintaining their cultural identities. Two interrelated approaches appear promising: culturally responsive instruction and instruction centered on authentic literacy activities.

Making ownership of literacy the overarching goal of the curriculum can be a first step toward improving the literacy achievement of students of diverse backgrounds. However, high levels of motivation will not automatically lead to increased achievement. Efforts to increase students' ownership of literacy must be combined with high standards (for example, in the form of grade-level benchmarks) and intense instruction in the higher level thinking processes required in the writing process and in reading comprehension. Only then can the literacy achievement gap be bridged.

References

Achor, S., & Morales, A. (1990). Chicanas holding doctoral degrees: Social reproduction and cultural ecological approaches. *Anthropology & Education Quarterly, 21*, 269–287.

Applebee, A., Langer, J.A., & Mullis, I. (1985). *The reading report card: Progress toward excellence in our schools*. Princeton, NJ: National Assessment of Educational Progress, Educational Testing Service.

Asam, C. et al. (1993). *Literacy curriculum guide*. Honolulu, HI: Kamehameha Elementary Education Program, Kamehameha Schools/Bernice Pauahi Bishop Estate, Early Education Division.

Atwell, N. (1987). *In the middle: Writing, reading, and learning with adolescents*. Portsmouth, NH: Heinemann.

Au, K.H., & Asam, C.L. (1996). Improving the literacy achievement of low-income students of diverse backgrounds. In M.F. Graves, P. van den Broek, & B.M. Taylor (Eds.), *The first R: Every child's right to read* (pp. 199–223). New York: Teachers College Press.

Au, K.H., & Carroll, J.H. (in press). Improving literacy achievement through a constructivist approach: The KEEP Demonstration Classroom Project. *Elementary School Journal*.

Au, K.H., & Mason, J.M. (1981). Social organizational factors in learning to read: The balance of rights hypothesis. *Reading Research Quarterly, 17*, 115–152.

Au, K.H., & Mason, J.M. (1983). Cultural congruence in classroom participation structures: Achieving a balance of rights. *Discourse Processes, 6*(2), 145–167.

Au, K.H., & Scheu, J.A. (1996). Journey toward holistic instruction: Supporting teachers' growth. *The Reading Teacher, 49*, 468–477.

Au, K.H., Scheu, J.A., Kawakami, A.J., & Herman, P.A. (1990). Assessment and accountability in a whole literacy curriculum. *The Reading Teacher, 43*, 574–578.

Calkins, L.M. (1991). *Living between the lines*. Portsmouth, NH: Heinemann.

Calkins, L.M. (1994). *The art of teaching writing* (2nd ed.). Portsmouth, NH: Heinemann.

Carroll, J.H., Wilson, R.A., & Au, K.H. (1996). Explicit instruction in the context of the readers' and writers' workshops. In E. McIntyre & M. Pressley (Eds.), *Balanced instruction: Skills and strategies in whole language* (pp. 39–63). Norwood, MA: Christopher-Gordon.

Cazden, C.B. (1988). *Classroom discourse: The language of teaching and learning*. Portsmouth, NH: Heinemann.

Clay, M.M. (1985). *The early detection of reading difficulties* (3rd ed.). Auckland: Heinemann.

D'Amato, J. (1988). "Acting": Hawaiian children's resistance to teachers. *The Elementary School Journal, 88*, 529–544.

Erickson, F. (1993). Transformation and school success: The politics and culture of educational achievement. In E. Jacob & C. Jordan (Eds.), *Minority education: Anthropological perspectives* (pp. 27–51). Norwood, NJ: Ablex.

Erickson, F., & Mohatt, G. (1982). Cultural organization of participation structures in two classrooms of Indian students. In G.B. Spindler (Ed.), *Doing the ethnography of schooling: Educational anthropology in action* (pp. 132–174). New York: Holt, Rinehart & Winston.

Fordham, S. (1991). Peer-proofing academic competition among Black adolescents: "Acting white" Black American style. In C.E. Sleeter (Ed.), *Empowerment through multicultural education* (pp. 69–93). Albany, NY: State University of New York Press.

Graves, D. (1983). *Writing: Teachers and children at work.* Exeter, NH: Heinemann.

Graves, D. (1990). *Discover your own literacy.* Portsmouth, NH: Heinemann.

Graves, D., & Hansen, J. (1983). The author's chair. *Language Arts, 60*(2), 176–183.

Hayes, K.G. (1992). Attitudes toward education: Voluntary and involuntary immigrants from the same families. *Anthropology & Education Quarterly, 23*(3), 250–267.

Kamehameha Schools Bishop Estate. (1993). *Native Hawaiian educational assessment 1993.* Honolulu: Kamehameha Schools Bishop Estate, Office of Program Planning and Evaluation.

Ladson-Billings, G. (1995). Toward a theory of culturally relevant pedagogy. *American Educational Research Journal, 32,* 465–491.

McDermott, R.P., & Gospodinoff, K. (1981). Social contexts for ethnic borders and school failure. In H.T. Trueba, G.P. Guthrie, & K.H. Au (Eds.), *Culture and the bilingual classroom: Studies in classroom ethnography* (pp. 212–230). Rowley, MA: Newbury House.

Mehan, H. (1979). *Learning lessons.* Cambridge, MA: Harvard University Press.

Mezynski, K. (1983). Issues concerning the acquisition of knowledge: Effects of vocabulary training on reading comprehension. *Review of Educational Research, 53,* 253–279.

Mullis, I.V.S., & Jenkins, L.B. (1990). *The reading report card, 1971–88: Trends from the nation's report card.* Princeton, NJ: National Assessment of Educational Progress, Educational Testing Service.

Ogbu, J.U. (1981). School ethnography: A multilevel approach. *Anthropology & Education Quarterly, 12*(1), 3–29.

Ogbu, J.U. (1990). Minority status and literacy in comparative perspective. *Daedalus, 119*(2), 141–168.

Ogbu, J.U. (1993). Variability in minority school performance: A problem in search of an explanation. In E. Jacob & C. Jordan (Eds.), *Minority education: Anthropological perspectives* (pp. 83–111). Norwood, NJ: Ablex.

Rosenblatt, L. (1978). *The reader, the text, the poem: The transactional theory of the literary work.* Carbondale, IL: Southern Illinois University Press.

Rosenblatt, L. (1991). Literature—S.O.S.! *Language Arts, 68,* 444–448.

Watson, K.A. (1975). Transferable communication routines: Strategies and group identity in two speech events. *Language in Society, 4,* 53–72.

Wixson, K.K., Peters, C.W., Weber, E.M., & Roeber, E.D. (1987). New directions in statewide reading assessment, *The Reading Teacher, 40,* 749-754.

Starting Right: Strategies for Engaging Young Literacy Learners

Julianne C. Turner

L earning to read is difficult. Some children approach this formidable task strategically, with resolve and persistence. They regard literacy as a means for communication and self-expression. However, others lose interest while mechanically executing tasks and putting forth minimal effort; they tolerate reading and writing as schoolwork that must be done. What influences such behaviors? How are these behaviors related to children's understanding of the goals of literacy instruction?

This chapter examines how the classroom context, specifically the activities that children complete during literacy instruction, influences their cognitive engagement in reading and writing. Different types of literacy activities offer distinctly different opportunities for children to engage in such motivated learning behaviors as strategy use, persistence, and attention control. In addition, activities may dispose children to adopt different notions of the purposes and value of literacy. By exploring the relations between classroom activities and children's motivation, teachers can better understand how to design classroom instruction so that it engages and supports literacy learning.

The first section of this chapter discusses the importance of literacy contexts, especially instructional activities, and their potential to influence learning and motivation. The second section describes three characteristics of literacy activities that influence literacy engagement and uses specific examples of students' responses to instruction for illustration. The third section explains how teacher support enables students to take advantage of the opportunities that activities offer. Finally, the chapter concludes with a discussion of motivated literacy learning and how it differs from conventional views of learning.

The Importance of Literacy Contexts

As mentioned in this volume's introduction, early views of literacy learning focused mostly on students' cognitive processes with the goal of teaching sound-symbol relations and comprehension. The assumption was that literacy is a collection of skills to be mastered. Although they do not downplay the importance of cognitive skills, more recent social-constructivist views of literacy learning have argued that cognitive processes are neither predictable nor identical; rather, they are qualitatively influenced by the social context of the classroom (Santa Barbara Classroom Discourse Group, 1994; Moll, 1993; Turner, 1995). From this perspective, the *what* of literacy learning is intimately intertwined with the *how*, transforming literacy from a cognitive to a socially constructed and motivated phenomenon.

Socioconstructivist interpretations of literacy learning are based on certain tenets. First, the society or culture of the classroom helps create shared understandings about meanings, forms, and uses of literacy. For example, in some classrooms, students are asked to demonstrate correct application of literacy skills by completing practice exercises, whereas in other classrooms, students interpret and compose texts. These opportunities influence students' understanding of what it means to read and write.

A second tenet is that literacy is constructed in holistic activities rather than in the practice of isolated skills. Vygotsky (1978) emphasizes that learners should be engaged in the whole activity, rather than a discrete part, and that cognitive processes are best learned when situated in specific, meaningful contexts. For example, students should practice reading comprehension by interpreting the meaning of a text with others, not by underlining main idea sentences.

Third, social-constructivist theorists contend that social contexts are the appropriate settings for learning literacy, that literacy cannot really be learned in isolated, individual activities. Through language and discourse, teachers model an approach to learning. Teachers and students demonstrate not only cognitive processes, but also affective and self-regulatory strategies. Thus cognitive and social processes cannot be separated because they are socially constructed by teachers and students as they engage in activities and participate in classroom discourse. For example, Dahl and Freppon (1995), DeFord (1984), and Kantor, Miller, and Fernie (1992) studied the influences of different literacy contexts and children's responses to them. They determined that specific values and beliefs about written language are constructed and communicated by teachers and children in classroom environments.

The Influence of Literacy Activities on Learning Goals

Studies of classroom contexts suggest that students' most frequent, and perhaps most powerful, interactions with literacy may occur during their daily activities. Academic tasks or activities are distinct units of academic work and can be identified when either their products (such as a story, a worksheet, or a game) or their processes (for example read, discuss, or select the correct answer) change. Literacy lessons, which are often skill- or theme-driven in elementary school, may include three to five supporting tasks. Tasks may influence the social interaction among students by encouraging them to seek help, share resources, or provide explanations. Research on academic tasks (Doyle, 1983) suggests that activities are a crucial influence on student cognition and motivation in literacy because they represent to students what literacy is, why it is important, and what it can do.

Tasks influence learning goals in two ways. First, academic tasks encourage students to associate certain cognitive processes with reading and writing activities (Doyle, 1983). Depending on the cognitive processes required by activities, students may link literacy to thoughtful, critical, stimulating processes or to repetitive, rote, mechanical ones. For example, students who are frequently engaged in more cognitively complex activities, such as responding to literature or writing, are more likely to associate literacy with higher level thinking processes such as synthesizing information and making decisions. In contrast, those who perform mostly low-level tasks such as sequencing the events of a story, may regard literacy primarily as an algorithmic process. For instance, Fisher and Hiebert (1990) investigated literacy tasks in skills-oriented (SO) and literature-based (LB) classrooms. They found a remarkable consistency within the two types of instruction across the elementary grades in that teachers in LB classrooms were much more likely to emphasize higher order processes than those in SO classrooms. Fisher and Heibert speculate about the cumulative effects of such tasks over many years of schooling, wondering whether students whose literacy instruction consists mainly of low-level cognitive skills might eventually dissociate literacy from higher level cognitive processes and opportunities for problem solving.

The second way that tasks influence learning goals is by communicating messages about the purposes and uses of reading and writing. Edelsky (1991) contends that students will not develop a value for literacy activities unless the activities are authentic and are attractive enough for learners to pursue of their own volition. In other words, meaningful and purposeful tasks are "the ordinary practices of the culture," pursued in actual, rather than simulated, situations (Brown, Collins, & Duguid, 1989, p. 34). Critics of traditional literacy instruction assert that when students learn skills separate from their social and functional contexts, they will have little understanding of their real use and value. In summary, both the cognitive processes that students use during literacy instruction and the way they perceive the purposes of tasks influence their understanding of literacy.

Motivational Consequences of Literacy Activities

Literacy activities also may affect students' motivation. One way to view literacy activities is by the opportunities they offer students to engage in motivated behaviors such as strategy use (Paris, Lipson, & Wixson, 1983; Paris, Wasik, & Turner, 1991; Pressley et al., 1992), persistence (Diener & Dweck, 1978), and self-control (Corno, 1992; Rohrkemper & Corno, 1988). From this perspective, activities may be classified as *open* or *closed* (Willems, 1981). Open activities are those in which students select the literacy processes they use or the products they create. For example, in reading a text, students may use various strategies such as picture, title, graphophonemic, and contextual cues. They may predict, ask questions, or reread to construct meaning. Students' interpretations of text may be similar to those of other group members, but they also may contain some personal meanings based on interest or past experiences. In this example, the activity of constructing meaning from text requires planning, execution, monitoring, and evaluation of strategies for the student to comprehend. An open activity facilitates strategic action because the student must set a goal and decide how to meet it; it supports persistence because the student, having chosen a goal, is more committed to meeting it. Finally, open activities are more likely to encourage volitional control because students want to protect the goals they set. They may monitor attention better, avoid distractions, or encourage themselves in order to meet a valued goal.

Closed activities are those in which either the process to be used or the solution is constrained. For example, in many drill-type activities students are directed to use one process (such as blending sounds or matching rhyming words) or to find one right answer. Often the goal of such activities is practice rather than application. Closed activities may be helpful for teaching skills and strategies, but when literacy instruction comprises mostly closed tasks, students may be deprived of opportunities for problem solving and may be encouraged to regard literacy as inert rather than flexible knowledge (Bransford et al., 1989). For instance, setting a narrow writing topic such as "write about what we saw at the farm today" might lead students to simply list objects with no organization or theme. In such cases, children would be evaluated on whether they met the teacher's goals, and savvy students might direct their energies more toward following directions than to devising and evaluating writing plans. In this example, the assignment constrains opportunities for students to use motivated behaviors, so there is low incentive to take charge of the activity. The same writing activity could be opened by asking children to use the farm as a starting place to compose. In addition to selecting, planning for, and limiting their topic, children would be required to select vocabulary, decide whether to compose expository or narrative text, and evaluate if they met their goal.

Although teachers may want to balance open and closed tasks in classroom instruction, activities designed to encourage student decision making about products or processes can provide important opportunities for students to use motivated behaviors. In a study of the influence of classroom context on first-grade students' motivation for literacy (Turner, 1995), I observed a striking relation between classroom instruction and tasks, and students' motivated behaviors. Classrooms were evenly divided between those following a whole language philosophy and those using a traditional basal approach to literacy learning. I observed the literacy instruction in each classroom for five consecutive days. Both groups of teachers demonstrated highly skilled teaching consistent with their instructional orientation.

Literacy activities were one indicator of the differing philosophies of literacy and teaching in the classrooms. In whole language classrooms, 73 percent of all the activities I observed were open. These included trade book and partner reading, games or constructive activities, and composition. The remaining tasks included drill exercises such as use of worksheets and flash cards. In basal classrooms, 77 percent of all the literacy tasks observed were closed. Most of these were worksheet activities in which the goal was skill practice, including matching exercises, selecting answers from options, or filling in the blanks. The rest of the activities included open tasks such as those described in whole language classrooms.

Observations of the students during their literacy activities and interviews with them afterward indicated a significant difference among students. The more students participated in open activities, the more likely they were to use motivated behaviors such as reading strategies, persistence, and attention control during their classwork. Students in the basal classrooms who participated in open activities showed the same behaviors.

Why do open activities provide incentives for students? What is it about an open activity that encourages students to try hard, to persist even if they are discouraged, and to take personal control of their literacy learning?

How Literacy Activities Foster Motivation

Theories of intrinsic motivation describe three characteristics of open activities that promote student engagement: they provide opportunities for challenge and self-improvement, autonomy, and social collaboration.

Challenge

One hallmark of good instruction is offering activities that advance, but do not overwhelm, learners' development. However, it may be difficult for teachers to design these types of tasks. Teachers may reason that if activities are initially complex or confusing or if they cause students to pause, reflect, plan, or rethink, students will become frustrated and give up. However, the most motivating activities are moderately difficult ones because they give learners information about their progress. Unlike repetitive or practice tasks, they help students assess their progress toward goals and, when accomplished, provide evidence of substantial accomplishment (Schunk, 1989). Succeeding at a challenging task enhances student efficacy and interest and conveys to students that teachers have confidence in their ability to learn (Weiner, 1992).

Support for the value of challenge can be found in research on motivation and learning. As mentioned in the first section of this book, Csikszentmihalyi (1975) contends that successful and motivated persons owe their success to constantly extending their skills to meet new challenges. In the ideal situation, these elements are cyclical: individuals improve skills to meet challenges, and then, equipped with greater skills, they seek new challenges. The result is synchrony between the demands of the activity and the individual's ability to respond. When challenges and skills are out of balance, students may feel either frustration or boredom—familiar motivational problems in classrooms.

Vygotsky (1978) also advocates the use of challenge as an optimal learning strategy. He claims that "learning that is oriented toward developmental levels that have already been reached is ineffective" and "the only 'good learning' is that which is in advance of development" (p. 89). These statements imply that knowledge and skills are dynamic rather than static and that they should constantly be applied to new settings. Moreover, Vygotsky believes that challenging tasks are accomplished with the help of social supports (see also the section on social collaboration later in this chapter). Another way of conceiving challenge is through Vygotsky's concept of the zone of proximal development. In this view, the child is enabled to move to a higher level of skill with the assistance of mentors who model and share a new task until the child's skill level matches the challenge.

Optimal difficulty is necessary but not sufficient to ensure the motivational quality of open tasks. Even moderately difficult tasks are limited unless they provide opportunities for students to adjust strategy use or alter tasks or environmental factors (Rohrkemper & Corno, 1988). Clifford's (1984) theory of "constructive failure" explains that what sustains learners as they reach for difficult accomplishments is the knowledge that they can learn from their mistakes by trying other strategies. In open tasks in which the means and goals are flexible, students can use their errors constructively by reappraising strategies. If students value a goal, they will interpret confusion or temporary failures not as evidence of low ability but as less than optimal use of strategies. When students are moderately challenged and they have opportunities for self-regulation, they are likely to show positive responses to difficulty such as increased persistence, more varied strategy use, greater interest in the activity, and increased performance. In contrast, if the processes or products are controlled as in closed tasks, students may become trapped in a failed tactic or give up before reaching the assigned goal.

Challenging tasks encourage students to strive for self-improvement.
Open activities promote self-improvement by providing students with opportunities to actively engage literacy. For example, in the observational study of average-achieving first graders described earlier (Turner, 1995; Turner & Paris, 1995), composing was presented to students as an opportunity for them to define topic, style, and goal. This allowed students to evaluate their own progress and improvement. In one lesson, the teacher read the students a book about the life cycle of butterflies. The teacher did not assign a topic but encouraged students to use the story as a beginning point in their own compositions. Thomas wrote,

> I was once a caterpillar. I was eating breakfast. I was old. The next day, I made a cocoon and till winter I would stay in my cocoon. Then I would get out and dry my wings and fly away and have fun.

In response to the question, "What are you supposed to learn from the activity?" Thomas answered, "To write more gooder and for people to read my story." When asked what he was thinking about as he wrote, he replied, "I would learn more and I know how to write letters more." He valued the activity because "you get to write two or three pages."
In response to the same activity, Marissa wrote,

> One day I was outside in the yard. I saw a butterfly. It flew away from me. It was colorful. It had egges (sic). The dad butterfly is going to guard him for a while so he won't get hurt.

When interviewed about the activity, Marissa said the work was interesting to her because she "never did a butterfly story before." She also mentioned thinking about "caterpillars' changing" and about "butterflies' laying eggs and things." She acknowledged the challenge of the activity when she commented, "You have to think hard about what you're going to write." These students appeared to view their writing activity as an opportunity to learn new information (they both incorporated knowledge gained from the text), to improve skills, and to meet new goals, such as writing a butterfly story for the first time.

Students in the study appeared to respond critically and creatively to the assignment rather than simply to list information about the topic verbatim from the text. In the open activities I observed there were no compulsory standards, yet the majority of students strove to meet personal challenges. One of the advantages of open tasks is that they can accommodate students of diverse levels. The stories children wrote were original, displayed student choices about using expository and narrative modes, and showed evidence of paragraph structure and sequence with beginning, middle, and ending sentences.

In contrast, when writing activities in the lessons I observed were less challenging, student compositions were less varied and there was less evidence of self-improvement or recognition of progress. For example, one teacher asked the class to write about the school secretary, Mrs. Robinson, for secretary's week. Kathleen, a very able student, wrote, "Mrs. Robinson. A secretary. A secretary helps us. She is a nice secretary." When asked what she was supposed to learn, Kathleen replied vaguely, "The words." She added that there was nothing hard about the assignment for her. In the class in which the teacher assigned the topic "what we saw at the farm yesterday," the teacher and the students generated a list of 28 words (such as milking, silo, hen, and calf) that students could use in their writing. Belinda wrote, "We wate (went) to the farm. (We) had some food." After writing five words, she stopped to count them, perhaps to ensure that she was meeting the requirement of the assignment. She did not use any words from the list. Although Belinda described a good purpose for writing ("telling your parents what you did at the farm"), she did not relate the activity to her own progress. She said the activity was easy, and she "finish(ed) when I run out of things to say."

There is little evidence from these comments that either student considered the compositions as opportunities to improve or to measure their growth as writers. More likely, they were simply complying with the assignment. The differences in quality and length between the products written in response to the open and closed writing assignments are striking, and they illustrate how more challenging assignments in which students have to plan, monitor, and evaluate their progress may encourage higher quality writing.

Challenging tasks encourage strategic behavior.   In one classroom I observed, the students were playing a game in which they were to decode words starting with either hard or soft "c" and place them correctly on a chart. When the students did not know how to pronounce a word, they had to devise a strategy. Mike explained, "I started with *cat* because I knew it," and he avoided the words *city* and *ceiling*, which he did not know. These strategies helped Mike persist even when he did not know all the words. He also used self-knowledge: "These three are hard for me," he commented as he pushed some aside. In response to the word *candy*, he said, "I saw this at a gas station." At the end, when he still had not decoded all the words, he used a help-seeking strategy: "I need a clue," he said to the teacher.

When activities are not challenging, there are few opportunities for students to respond strategically. For example, on the day I observed Ryan, she was completing two worksheet activities. The first was a crossword puzzle with *pl-*, *fl-*, *gl-*, and *sl-* words—a pattern-matching rather than a thinking activity. Two of the words already had first and last letters (for example, p_ _ n), so students simply had to match and copy. It took Ryan an effort-less one and a half minutes to complete this exercise. The second worksheet required her to find the target words at the top of the page (for example, words such as *flat*) in longer nonsense words such as *sflatp*. Ryan also completed this activity in less than two min-utes. In neither activity were there any opportunities to use spelling, graphophonemic, personal experience, or organizational strategies as Mike had done. In these closed ac-tivities, both the low-level processes (matching) and the product (the right answer) were controlled so that Ryan did not need to draw on her own literacy resources. In addition, she seemed to have difficulty relating this activity to any meaningful use of reading. When I asked her what she was thinking about during this activity, her reply of "not much" seemed to indicate her disinterest and lack of engagement in literacy learning.

Challenging tasks present opportunities to learn from others.   When ac-tivities are within students' zones of proximal development, students can learn concepts and strategies that otherwise would be beyond their reach. One frequent opportunity for peer scaffolding I observed in first-grade classrooms was partner reading. In one class-room, Crystal was alternating reading pages with Samantha. Crystal read first, and Saman-tha helped her with four words. Then Crystal helped Samantha when she lost her place during her turn and corrected Samantha twice during her next turn. Samantha helped Crystal sound out the word "sifted." The girls supported each other by supplying infor-mation that would help them continue to see reading as meaningful. This support is es-sential for students to meet challenges successfully.

Autonomy

Another quality of motivating activities is that they promote learner autonomy or control. When learners feel that they can make decisions about their academic work such as plan-ning, organizing, goal setting, and evaluating, they are likely to be more interested in and committed to those decisions (Deci et al., 1991). Students may interpret classroom activi-ties as either informational (providing useful competence information) or controlling (pres-sure to perform, think, or feel in particular ways). Open activities, in which students make decisions about processes and products, are typically perceived as informational because students can learn both about themselves and the task. In contrast, closed activities may undermine intrinsic motivation by removing the elements of student participation, standard setting, and decision making. In closed activities, students must conform to the required processes and products (even if they are low level) because of evaluation criteria.

When classroom environments support student autonomy, students perceive them as more intrinsically motivating (deCharms, 1968; Grolnick & Ryan, 1987). For example, Ryan and Grolnick (1986) found that children who perceive their classrooms as promoting autonomy reported more interest in their schoolwork and more perceived competence at school. Similarly, Csikszentmihalyi (1990) suggests that literature and activities that provide choices are more likely to pique intrinsic interest in literacy than "textbooks that illustrate abstract principles" (p. 135). Allowing students to participate in decision making and evaluation teaches them to set high standards and helps them gain ownership of their own literacy learning. In this regard, rigid rules, procedures, time constraints, and competition can threaten opportunities for engagement. These findings suggest that teachers who share their role as instructional leaders with students may boost their students' intrinsic interest in literacy.

Autonomous tasks allow student choice.   In the classrooms I observed in the study mentioned earlier (Turner, 1995), activities were set up at centers, and students selected two to four activities during literacy time. Teachers used multiple "quality-control" strategies so that students would benefit from the activities. For example, teachers selected only activities that were instructionally appropriate, or activities that were adaptable to many levels. One common activity was to read with the teacher so that the teacher could guide the choice of an appropriately challenging text, if necessary. Activities that involved reading books and composing were adaptable to students' developmental level.

Another way that teachers used choice effectively was to allow students to sequence required activities. Some teachers designated one "teacher's choice" that all students were required to do and allowed students to select other activities themselves. Examples of literacy activities done during a thematic week entitled "Bears" included reading stories about bears, writing in response to the stories, listening to a book on tape, describing a bear book to a friend, and making a bear puppet to use with stories. In another classroom, students chose the "words of the day," the books to read to their teacher, and their own writing topics. These practices were typical in the classrooms where teachers used primarily open activities.

I also observed first-grade teachers altering or reinventing traditional activities such as sequencing tasks in order to offer students opportunities for autonomy. Instead of asking students to number sentences or events, as in typical workbook activities, teachers took text from familiar stories or nursery rhymes and cut it into individual words or sentences. Students were asked to reassemble the text and sometimes to illustrate it. This task required students to design a plan, monitor strategy use, and evaluate the outcome. The drawing was a creative outlet that provided another way to construct meaning. The task was accessible to students at various developmental levels; it could be solved through various strategies (for example, students could use meaning, capitalization and punctuation clues, or memory for text); and there were several solutions (students could re-create the original text or make up an original text with individual words). For instance, Megan cut out four strips of text that told the story, selected the first strip, and illustrated it. Using her memory of how the text proceeded (the text described the order of family members), she said, "Now the mommy" when she read the third strip. At the end of the activity, she reread her entire text to ensure meaning, and she went to the classroom library to compare her text with the original.

Students had fewer choices in the classrooms I observed that used primarily closed activities. In many classrooms, teachers listed the morning work in order, and students proceeded through the work systematically. Students may have perceived these activities as controlling because they did not have a choice about which activities to complete or input into how they could approach the activities. Perhaps a contrast with another sequence task will illustrate the differences I often saw in student behaviors when they completed closed rather than open activities. In one activity, Kristin and her partner were directed to sequence four sentences from *Little Mermaid* by Hans Christian Andersen. Rather than using meaning clues to order the sentences, these students tried to assign numbers to sentences without first reading them. Kristen asked her partner, "Do you think this might be second?" The students focused on completing the task rather than on thinking about *why* one sentence would precede another. Students had little choice about how to approach tasks in this classroom and little input into the tasks' final outcome. There were limited opportunities for students to participate meaningfully, so it is not surprising that they regarded this sequencing task as mechanically as they did many others.

One way the teacher in this classroom could have increased the motivational potential of the sequencing task would have been to ask students to draw and label the four or five most important events in the story. This approach would have promoted autonomy by having students select important events and decide how to order and portray them. Closed activities, through their reliance on separate, automatic skills, not only discourage strategy flexibility, but also deny students the opportunity to integrate multiple strategies (Pressley et al., 1992).

Autonomous tasks allow diverse student interests. In the first-grade classrooms I observed, most teachers who used open tasks went beyond simply giving students choices. They reasoned that if students could see literacy as a way of pursuing interests and solving personally relevant problems, they would be more willing to engage in reading and writing and would value it more highly. These teachers tried to design literacy activities that students could find personally meaningful.

How does interest affect motivation for literacy? As discussed in the first section of this book, when students are interested in texts and tasks, they attend to them longer and remain involved with them even if they are somewhat difficult (Hidi, 1990). In addition, interest influences the goals that students set: when students are engaged by ideas, they are more likely to set "learning goals," or those aimed at self-improvement (Elliott & Dweck, 1988). Thus, they come to see literacy not as schoolwork, but as a way of communicating and seeking information and enjoyment. Allowing young students to satisfy personal quests, tell about compelling ideas, and relive enjoyable stories encourages engagement in reading and writing.

In the classrooms I observed, open activities proved to encourage students to integrate their own goals and interests with the instructional goals of the literacy tasks. For example, when students wrote "bear stories," some wrote narratives, some wrote expository text, and others integrated information from related texts or media into their stories (Short, 1992). Jenny coupled the bear theme with ideas from a book recently read in class called, *Who's in the Shed?* by Brenda Parkes. She wrote,

The Bear Who Was Stuck
One day there was an old woman and an old man. They had four animals. One was a chicken. The other was a rooster and a cat and a dog. One niet (night) the animals were crying and frightened. The animals went outside. The chicken went to the shed. He looked in a hole. He saw a circus bear. Everyone was trying to get the bear out and they did, but then they were afraid of it.

Because the assignment of writing stories about bears was not overly defined, it encouraged student interest and goal setting; it also supported students by suggesting that they could use information gleaned from the week's activities about the bear theme. Jenny integrated several experiences then added her own ideas.

The first-grade classroom in which I observed the most writing was one in which book making and publishing their work were regular activity choices. Students always chose their own topics, and their published books were strong indicators of topics students were interested in that year. When the teacher thought that students had exhausted the potential of their favorite topics, she attempted to interest them in other topics.

One final and powerful example of how teachers helped students combine their interests with instruction was the use of thematic interdisciplinary activities. Teachers selected themes that they believed would appeal to their students, such as holidays, animals, how other people live, chocolate, and natural phenomena like "wind." Then they designed multiple literacy activities around these themes similar to those described in Chapter 7. Often, the teachers incorporated science, math, and art activities. For example, in many open activities, art was an integral part of making meaning. I mentioned previously that Megan illustrated the text of the book as she sequenced the sentence strips. In another classroom, students colored bear masks to use in a play they created from a story, and they illustrated alternative endings to a story read in class. They constructed sheds with mysterious creatures in them and then wrote their own versions of *Who's in the Shed?* As an accompaniment to the butterfly story mentioned earlier, children colored pictures of butterflies to illustrate the mathematical concept of symmetry. They used these illustrations as the covers for their own butterfly stories. In all these cases, teachers tried to incorporate opportunities for students to use their talents and interests as part of their literacy activities.

In classrooms where closed activities predominated, the sameness of the children's literacy work was striking. Predictable tasks and the skills required to complete them (such as matching, underlining, or numbering) were familiar. Even the writing topics were limited, sometimes seeming more like dictation than composition. In several of these classrooms, I saw students who tried to diversify their activities, perhaps with the goal of making them more interesting and motivating. For instance, when students were allowed to color their phonics sheets, they would often spend 80 percent of work time on coloring and a only 20 percent on completing the task; or, students would rush through their instructional work so that they could color. Although these art activities were pleasant for the children, they had little educational substance. In contrast, the teachers who were able to incorporate art as an integral and meaningful part of literacy activities were able to use it as an enjoyable and creative tool in constructing meaning rather than as a reward for finishing work. By involving students' interests, art encouraged persistence and served as another way for children to make sense of reading and writing.

Autonomy and interest influence students' attitudes.   In addition to the differences I observed in students' behaviors during open and closed activities, I also found differences in how they talked about their literacy learning. When asked to comment on what they were supposed to learn from their activities, students who completed mostly closed, low-autonomy tasks often responded that they were supposed to learn word parts or that they "didn't know" what they were supposed to learn. Conversely, students who completed a large number of open tasks reported that they were supposed to learn specific information or to become better readers. After reading a book about a barefoot bear with her partner, Rosie explained that the purpose was to learn "about bears—they don't like wearing shoes...he wanted his own feet...." The responses of children like Rosie reflect their perceptions of the meaningfulness of the assignments and of the greater opportunities they had in defining learning goals themselves. Students who had to select and define activities knew more about them, reported more strategic behavior, and reported genuine literacy goals such as communication.

   I also asked children how they handled any difficulties they encountered during their activities. Students who participated in open activities with more opportunities for autonomous actions were more knowledgeable about the source of their difficulties and were also likely to mention effort as a strategy they used to overcome their problems. For example, Rosie explained the source of one of her comprehension problems: "I didn't know that the bear wasn't paying a lot of attention...I've never heard of it before." However, students who completed mostly closed activities more often responded that they guessed when they had comprehension or other difficulties or "just did it." These replies reflect the automatic responses that closed activities encourage rather than the more thoughtful and strategic responses that greater autonomy might support.

Social Collaboration

   A third motivational characteristic of activities is the potential they offer for social interaction. It is not surprising that children enjoy working with one another, but research on both learning and literacy has shown that collaboration can also increase understanding, self-regulation, and self-efficacy (Brown, Collins, & Duguid, 1989; Slavin, 1987; Stevens

& Slavin, 1995). When children know that they have resources to increase their learning, they are more willing to expend effort and to persist. Similarly, when children succeed at reading and writing, they are more likely to continue to pursue these activities.

One way that children collaborate is by asking for help from peers and teachers. Investigations of help seeking (Newman, 1990; Newman & Goldin, 1990) indicate that children who believe that they are competent learners and who have intrinsic interests in learning are more likely to seek help. Children are aware of both the costs (such as comparing unfavorably to others or having to admit they do not understand) and benefits of help seeking, although younger children seem to focus more on benefits. Contextual aspects of the classroom that may influence students' willingness to work together are whether the teacher explains how to work together, whether she emphasizes the benefits of collaboration, whether the physical set up and activities allow or encourage collaboration, and the perceived helpfulness of peers. For example, teachers can use more self-confident students as models of help seeking and help giving so that less competent students can see how to request and use help.

Research in the Vygotskian tradition views all learning as "assisted performance" rather than the achievements of individuals (Moll, 1993; Rogoff, 1990). From this perspective, learning is not simply aided by others, but is inseparable from the social context in which it occurs. Several useful behaviors occur in social situations that assist children both cognitively and motivationally (Tharp & Gallimore, 1993). They include modeling, offering intrinsic and extrinsic rewards for successful performance, giving feedback for improvement, providing instructions, questioning, and providing cognitive structures, such as giving the theme of a story as "heroes" or reminding students to use strategies. This assistance can come from teachers or more capable peers. Social guidance and cooperation in classrooms has been recognized as fundamental to both learning and motivation.

Social interaction is motivational in several ways. First, peer comments and ideas introduce elements of surprise that pique students' curiosity and encourage further interest (Berlyne, 1960). Second, peers provide models of expertise that others can emulate; when children observe the progress of others like them, it may increase confidence in their own ability to succeed (Bandura, 1982; Schunk, 1989). In addition, peer models provide benchmarks for students' own self-evaluations, helping them to set proximal goals and gauge improvement (Brown, Collins, & Duguid, 1989). Third, working with others, as research in cooperative learning has shown, promotes student engagement in work (Slavin, 1987). Working with others forges a group consciousness and responsibility that aids effort allocation and persistence.

Collaborative activities. In the first-grade classrooms I observed, open tasks provided opportunities for students to interact through modeling, advising, and offering feedback to one another. Many teachers designed activities so that students would work on them together by locating the activities in designated areas where diverse groups of students worked side by side. Each day, more able students were available to assist less able peers, which made visible many models, approaches, and strategies to children. In addition, teachers often reconceptualized traditional individual activities as shared experiences, such as partner reading, collaborative flash card practice, and shared comprehension exercises.

Several activities provide examples of how students collaborated. Tyrone and Jamie were working on a set of flash cards together. When Jamie did not know a word by sight, he asked Tyrone for a clue. Tyrone gave him contextual cues by reading the sentence on the back of the card or by questioning him (he asked, for example, "What number comes after eight?" and "What is the opposite of fast?"). He also provided graphophonemic clues such as, "Does this have an -s in it?" Not only did Tyrone model decoding strategies, which Jamie used successfully, but he also encouraged Jamie to continue with the activity, despite a high error rate.

As another example, when Maria was writing her "bear" story, she did not know the spelling of all the words she wanted to use. Instead of simply eliminating the vocabulary and using words she could spell, she asked another student for help in spelling. Maria said that the other student had helped her by "telling her what to write." She commented that she liked this activity because she "got to make the words big." Maria's comments illuminate well the reciprocal nature of learning and motivation. The collaborative assistance from a more capable peer not only helped Maria learn to spell, but it also enabled her to meet an interesting and important challenge. Although some teachers might fear that allowing peers to supply words that students do not know might discourage strategy use and setting high goals, this did not occur in Maria's case. How teachers establish climates of collaboration may help explain this phenomenon.

Collaboration fosters peer teaching and learning. For collaboration to facilitate learning, classrooms must become communities of learners rather than collections of competing individuals. In cooperative classrooms, students contribute to a collective expertise. In addition to designing activities in which students are explicitly encouraged to help one another, teachers also should model helping behavior. In one class I observed, students were preparing to complete a word search using words related to their theme, chocolate cake. The teacher asked the children to predict and help her spell words that might be in the puzzle such as *stir, frosting,* and *spoon.* All the students had ideas, but not all of them could spell their contributions. When the students needed assistance, the teacher would "write" the letters on their backs, which helped students spell their words. The students beamed with pride as the teacher wrote their spellings on the chart. This teacher sanctioned help giving by demonstrating that providing just enough help enabled all students to succeed. It is important that teachers model instrumental help, or giving clues, rather than executive help, in which they simply provide answers (Nelson-LeGall, 1986).

In another example of a teacher modeling helping behavior, a teacher provided clues or "cognitive structures" (Tharp & Gallimore, 1993) in a sequence activity. The teacher had cut five sentences from *Noisy Nora* by Rosemary Wells into individual words and had color coded the sentences so students could select appropriate words for each sentence. As the teacher observed one group of three boys working with all five sentences, she provided some strategic advice: first, sort the sentences by color; second, do the sentences

196

one by one; third, use the noises that Noisy Nora made as clues; and fourth, remember the first word of each sentence begins with a capital letter.

When teachers model collaborative behavior, students are more likely to adopt it. Because they observe the kinds of instrumental help that teachers give, students can more readily provide their peers with hints rather than answers. Notice how students helped one another in the following activity. Holly was calling out words for two students in a Bingo game. Diana could not decode the words easily, and she needed some support. Holly showed the word to Diana so that she could match the letters, or she spelled it out for her. Diana also asked for help when she needed it. Thinking she had found a word, she asked for confirmation, "Is it spelled *l-i-s-t-e-n*?" She also spelled words aloud to herself while she looked for them on her card. When another child had difficulty, Holly said, "Jess, do you want to help Marie?" The children entered into the game with the intention of helping everyone learn and win, and they provided assistance rather than answers to their less capable peers. The children had adopted the teacher's goal for playing the game; they used helping strategies that promoted learning the words rather than concentrating only on winning.

Practices that discourage collaboration and learning.   In classes I observed where closed tasks were used, the focus was on the product, not the process, of the tasks. Although students often sat in groups of four, collaboration was rare. Because right answers were indicators of achievement in these classes, giving or receiving help could easily be construed as either cheating or incompetence. As a result, students who were unsure often resorted to behaviors that produced answers but hindered learning. For example, Joey's class worked on a rhyming activity in which students were to arrange rhyming words to read *Sam put grape jam on the ham*. Joey wrote, *Sam put grape ham on the jam*. When asked to explain how he handled the "hard parts" of the activity, Joey said, "I just wrote them. Sam was first because it was a person, ham was second because it was meat, and jam third because it's jelly." Whether Joey invented this rationale for the benefit of the interviewer or whether he believed it a viable solution, the closed task may have stifled a more effortful and meaning-based approach.

Lack of varied teacher modeling also may have affected students' strategic choices in some of the classrooms I observed. Although teachers demonstrated decoding strategies effectively, they did not model or encourage helping behaviors. Activities were used more often as evaluations than as indicators of what students could do with assistance from more able peers. Therefore, students did not take advantage of others' expertise.

In addition, students who routinely worked on collaborative activities showed quite different motivational orientations from those who did not. When asked what she was supposed to learn when doing partner reading with Samantha, Crystal responded, "For both of us to learn the words. Since you read every other page, you can learn the words from the other person." After observing Diana play Bingo, I asked her what she did if she had problems with her work. She responded that she might ask friends because "they might help me sound them out." In contrast, one student who was having trouble with filling in cloze sentences with spelling words commented that when she had problems with her work, "I wouldn't tell anyone. I would just get it." She seemed to be ashamed that she did not understand her work, and she did not appear to know that she could ask for help.

Summary

Motivational research and observations in first-grade classrooms have shown that activities that provide appropriate challenges, genuine choices, some student control over learning, and opportunities to collaborate with others all enhance students' determination, effort, and thoughtful engagement. However, open activities are most effective when they are supported by teacher instruction and a classroom climate that fosters meaningful learning.

How Teacher Practices Support Motivation

The activities I described in the previous section took place in typical first-grade classrooms, yet they suggest the kinds of skills and self-regulation of older children (Paris, Wasik, & Turner, 1991). Studies of young children indicate that they often have only rudimentary understandings of the task of reading, so they may have difficulty understanding what reading is or what makes it difficult. For example, younger and less able readers often focus on decoding, not realizing that they need to expend extra cognitive effort to gain meaning. Young children also have limited knowledge about monitoring, managing, and regulating their own reading. For instance, they often fail to detect inconsistencies in text and fail to self-correct. When they do detect a problem, they may not know how to solve it. In addition, young children are generally effortful, but they are unaware that trying harder is not as fruitful as using various strategies. Finally, young children are not used to monitoring their own attention; they can be unaware of when their attention strays, how to harness it for academic tasks, and how it affects learning. They need to develop the ability to subdue emotional preferences such as responding to distractions or giving in to frustration in order to take responsibility for school learning.

These metacognitive characteristics—low task awareness and inability to self-regulate—can hamper young children's attempts to learn to read and write. If children cannot deduce the reason to learn literacy skills, they may have little interest in literacy tasks, reducing effort and persistence. Even if they are aware of learning goals, beginning readers inevitably encounter difficulties in such tasks as decoding and comprehension. If students do not have meaning-construction or repair strategies, they may lose confidence in their own ability to control learning, which will decrease their sense of efficacy and will to try again. Children feel successful when they can meet the goals set for the group such as completing tasks and mastering skills; however, if they do not know how to meet goals and learn, they may feel helpless and decide that literacy is not useful or valuable.

If children are taught what is needed to perform more effectively, they can take steps to meet the demands of literacy learning (Baker & Brown, 1984). The first-grade teachers I observed who skillfully executed open tasks with their classes were aware that they needed to help children develop into strategic readers. By supporting children's ability to learn, not only did teachers teach students the skills they needed to be successful learners, but they also nurtured their motivation by enhancing children's competence and autonomy as readers and by helping them gain a mature understanding of literacy.

Emphasizing Metacognition and Motivation

In observing teachers who used open activities effectively, two characteristics of their practices were apparent. First, teachers supported the cognitive curriculum with a metacognitive and motivational one. From the metacognitive perspective, they helped students identify knowledge that would be useful in reading and writing, and they emphasized planning, monitoring, and evaluating for all activities. Teachers routinely introduced new texts by asking students to tell what they knew about a topic or to predict, based on their experiences, what might happen. For instance, during the week devoted to the bear theme, the teacher wrote on an easel: *What do you know about bears?* The students responded by writing sentences such as, "Thar bron and black and woet [white]", "taye grat" [they're great], "they have long claws", and "they hibernat." In preparation for reading a book about birds, another teacher asked students to talk about what they knew about birds so that "When we finish we'll check our sentences to see if we were right. Then we can study what we don't know."

In addition, teachers reminded students about what they knew about reading and writing strategies and why they worked. As a result, students who engaged in open activities were more likely to provide thoughtful analyses of their strategies. In response to the question "How do you handle the hard parts?" Lee responded, "I sound them out, skip words, and read on, and I use my head; my brain is in there," and Eric replied, "You read on, and from that the sentence is still going and you start to get the new words. The old word is still in the sentence, so they [the new words] help you figure it out." The teacher's emphasis on how to solve learning problems had helped these students recognize that reading required decision making, not just the application of rote processes.

Teachers also helped students learn and use self-regulation strategies. In contrast to many primary classrooms where the emphasis is on following the teacher's rules, the teachers who used open tasks sought to teach children to be responsible for their own learning. Thus, these children had more opportunities to establish personal, intrinsic goals in reading and writing. For example, one teacher labeled the activities for the day as "reading, writing, thinking, and planning" to help students understand the purposes of the activities. Teachers provided explicit reminders about the importance of planning, monitoring, and evaluating activities. For example, one teacher helped students plan how to assemble and illustrate sentence strips to make a book: "Who can tell me what to do? How could you illustrate the first sentence strip? What is another way to do it?" This approach differs from simply outlining the steps in a worksheet activity in its emphasis on planning and individual decision making.

Teachers also assisted children in monitoring their work. As a group of students walked into one of the classrooms one morning, they read this message on the board from their teacher: "This is the last day for center work. Use your time wisely." Another teacher supported student self-regulation by asking, "Are you focused?" or "Is that the best place to work?" Finally, teachers encouraged students to evaluate their work. In several classrooms, teachers conducted "wrap-up" sessions at the end of morning literacy time by asking students to think about what they had done, what strategies they had used to approach their work, and if they were successful. When students reported dissatisfaction or confusion, the teachers asked other students how they had handled the same problems. Often young learners gained valuable insights from these exchanges. The metacognitive emphasis on knowledge awareness and self-regulation differed from more traditional classrooms because the focus was on enabling students to take responsibility, rather than on socializing children to do schoolwork correctly and on time. The metacognitive curriculum supported the motivational aspects of the instruction such as meeting challenges, making choices, pursuing interests, and working collaboratively with others. These motivational aspects encouraged students to engage in more self-regulatory activities.

Setting High Expectations

The second characteristic of teachers I observed who used open activities effectively was that they set high expectations. For example, when one teacher assigned students to write bear stories, she provided students with 8½" × 11" paper. Although she did not insist that the students use the entire page, her action suggested that developing a real story required a certain length. This type of expectation was in contrast to teachers who set composition lengths for students, which may have communicated low expectations.

Lessons that required students to integrate reading strategies rather than to execute isolated skills were more challenging for students. One teacher created a cloze exercise with the big book text of *Clifford's Birthday Party* by Norman Bridwell by covering key instructional vocabulary with adhesive notes. As the class read the book together, the teacher asked students to predict what the hidden word might be. She repeated students' predictions and directed them to start with the context, then she gradually uncovered the word letter by letter. This tactic helped students narrow their choices and practice using several strategies simultaneously. It also promoted discussions about how certain strategies may be more appropriate in certain situations. As the teacher led students through the decoding process, she also integrated comprehension strategies such as prediction, vocabulary instruction, and story structure into the lesson.

Another example of teachers' high expectations was their use of activity centers in the classrooms. In these rooms, first-grade students were expected to select activities, keep track of their completion, and evaluate their own success. If students did not choose wisely, if they wasted time, or if they did not understand their work, they were held accountable. In fact, one student commented that she had to complete the activities that she had chosen because if she did not, "they circle [the choice] for you and [you] don't get to choose [yourself]."

Teachers spent time teaching students to use the activity centers through instruction, modeling, practice, and whole-class discussions. Similarly, they integrated decoding and comprehension strategies in whole-class activities daily so that students could learn to use them. They also communicated that it was all right not to know something or to make a mistake. Recall how one teacher supported her students' participation in the chocolate cake activity by "spelling" words on their backs.

Teachers also encouraged children to evaluate their own work. Although teachers still evaluated students, they encouraged students to set personal standards to make the attainment of goals more meaningful and falling short less devastating.

Perhaps the most important strategy teachers used was to cast errors as opportunities to learn rather than as indications of incompetence. One teacher asked a student, "Jessica, does it matter that you got this wrong? Or is it more important than you learned something?" The constant emphasis on meaningful learning helped students focus on their own improvement, and many learned to look at errors as deficits in their strategy use rather than as failures in themselves (Clifford, 1991). As one first grader said, "I just try and try and try." Knowing that failure was not final or disastrous allowed students the freedom to take on challenging tasks.

Reflections and Conclusions

I have illustrated in this chapter how open activities and the strategies that teachers use to support them offer students many opportunities for motivated literacy engagement. In contrast to closed activities that promote mostly automated behaviors, open tasks give students a role in choosing how they will go about a task and what they want to accomplish. Open tasks have three characteristics that seem to encourage student strategy use, persistence, and volitional control. First, they are challenging, offering opportunities and feedback for student improvement. Second, they give students some control, allowing them to use reading and writing to pursue personally interesting and important goals. Third, they offer opportunities for collaboration. Although all students approach open tasks differently, they have much to share about strategies for planning, organizing, and evaluating their work. In addition, students can share knowledge about word meanings, spelling, story structure, and content that is useful to their peers. Modeling and help giving have the potential to increase students' skills and to encourage them that they can be successful readers and writers.

Open tasks enrich a literacy curriculum both in terms of what students learn and also in terms of their interest and willingness to engage in reading and writing. The student behaviors and attitudes that I have reported in this chapter reflect the opportunities that students were given to engage in holistic, meaningful reading and writing activities. These activities should not be interpreted as merely letting students choose what, when, or whether to learn. Nor should they be interpreted as rejecting the need to instruct students in sound-symbol correspondences and to provide sufficient practice for automaticity of word recognition (Adams, 1990; Fisher & Hiebert, 1990). In fact, most of the teachers who used open tasks also provided closed activities to the students. The criticism of closed tasks reflects not a position that they should never be used, but a caution that they can be easily overused. The consequences of such overuse are fewer opportunities for literacy engagement.

The findings described in this chapter, gathered in first-grade classrooms, also have implications for extending our theoretical understandings of intrinsic motivation. Theories of intrinsic motivation (Csikszentmihalyi, 1975; Deci et al., 1981) predict that when tasks are challenging yet attainable, and when classrooms support students' autonomy, students will report higher intrinsic motivation and perceived competence. Previous studies have shown that these relations exist, but there has been a dearth of information about *how* they are created. The data from my study (Turner, 1995) provide some clues about how teachers use autonomy support to foster engagement and self-efficacy and how students develop a need for challenge. In the classrooms I observed, students had multiple opportunities each day to set goals and make decisions. They made decisions about which tasks to complete, what their purposes would be, how to use resources such as books and environmental print, how to respond to text, and how to use social structures for learning. To help students make good decisions, teachers taught and modeled strategies and conducted whole-class discussions of time and effort management. Rather than telling students what to do, teachers offered flexible literacy tools that they helped students use effectively. Even when teachers asked students, "Are you focused?" they appeared to regard the question as informational, a cue that they needed to redirect attention. Repeated opportunities and successes in making decisions helped students acquire a strategy orientation. They learned that there are many ways to solve literacy problems and that if one failed, another could be tried. Learning that they could be in control of such complex processes as reading and writing empowered the students. Consequently, students' self-confidence and their effort and interest in literacy increased.

In addition to autonomy support, the teachers who used open tasks effectively fostered challenge seeking. One way students met challenges was by incremental and flexible goal setting. Although goals may not have always been explicit, students could select and change processes and products as they worked; they could adjust tasks to fit their interests or a skill just mastered; they could include intertextual references or personal preferences; and they could work alone or collaboratively. These options supported challenge seeking by allowing students to match their skills with the challenges. Autonomy support may have enlivened students' challenge seeking because they knew that they had genuine options, could infuse projects with personal meaning, and would receive support for trying to achieve their goals. As Csikszentmihalyi (1990) points out, it is unlikely that a person would strive for greater competence if the goal were not interesting or valuable. Thus, many students did not appear to complete work simply for the sake of completion. Students' expressions of their desire to improve, to use "big" words, and to learn interesting content are evidence that they had adopted intrinsic goals and that they felt competent.

In sum, the provision of information through autonomy support and challenging activities can influence learner outcomes such as behaviors, beliefs, and attitudes. The successful first-grade teachers I observed demonstrated that by creating a context in which learning and effort are their own reward, teachers can help students develop both the strategies and the interest needed to continue engagement in literacy.

References

Adams, M.J. (1990). *Beginning to read: Thinking and learning about print*. Cambridge, MA: MIT Press.

Baker, L., & Brown, A.L. (1984). Metacognitive skills and reading. In P.D. Pearson, M. Kamil, R. Barr, & P. Mosenthal (Eds.), *Handbook of reading research* (pp. 353–394). New York: Longman.

Bandura, A. (1982). Self-efficacy mechanism in human agency. *American Psychologist, 37*, 122–148.

Berlyne, D.E. (1960). *Conflict, arousal, and curiosity*. New York: McGraw-Hill.

Bransford, J.D., Franks, J.J., Vye, N.J., & Sherwood, R.D. (1989). New approaches to instruction: Because wisdom can't be told. In Vsniadou & Ortony, (Eds.), *Similarity and Analogical Reasoning*. Cambridge, England: Cambridge University Press.

Brown, J.S., Collins, A., & Duguid, P. (1989). Situated cognition and the culture of learning. *Educational Researcher, 18*, 32–42.

Clifford, M.M. (1984). Thoughts on a theory of constructive failure. *Educational Psychologist, 19*, 108–120.

Clifford, M.M. (1991). Risk taking: Theoretical, empirical and educational considerations. *Educational Psychologist, 26*, 263–297.

Corno, L. (1992). Encouraging students to take responsibility for learning and performance. *The Elementary School Journal, 93*, 69–83.

Csikszentmihalyi, M. (1975). *Beyond boredom and anxiety*. San Francisco, CA: Jossey-Bass.

Csikszentmihalyi, M. (1990). Literacy and intrinsic motivation. *Daedalus, 119*, 115–140.

Dahl, K.L., & Freppon, P.A. (1995). A comparison of inner-city children's interpretations of reading and writing instruction in the early grades in skills-based and whole language classrooms. *Reading Research Quarterly, 30*, 50–74.

deCharms, R. (1968). *Personal causation*. New York: Academic.

Deci, E.L, Schwartz, A.J., Sheinman, L., & Ryan, R.M. (1981). An instrument to assess adults' orientation toward control versus autonomy with children: Reflections on intrinsic motivation and perceived competence. *Journal of Educational Psychology, 73*, 642–650.

Deci, E.L., Vallerand, R.J., Pelletier, L.G., & Ryan, R.M. (1991). Motivation and education: The self-determination perspective. *Educational Psychologist, 26*, 325–346.

DeFord, D.E. (1984). Classroom contexts for literacy learning. In T.E Raphael (Ed.), *The contexts of school-based literacy* (pp. 162–180). New York: Random House.

Diener, C.I., & Dweck, C.S. (1978). An analysis of learned helplessness: Continuous changes in performance, strategy, and achievement cognitions following failure. *Journal of Personality and Social Psychology, 36*, 451–462.

Doyle, W. (1983). Academic work. *Review of Educational Research, 53*, 159–199.

Edelsky, C. (1991). *With literacy and justice for all*. Bristol, PA: Falmer.

Elliott, E.S., & Dweck, C.S. (1988). Goals: An approach to motivation and achievement. *Journal of Personality and Social Psychology, 54*, 5–12.

Fisher, C.W., & Hiebert, E.H. (1990). Characteristics of tasks in two approaches to literacy instruction. *The Elementary School Journal, 91*, 3–18.

Grolnick, W.S., & Ryan, R.M. (1987). Autonomy in children's learning: An experimental and individual difference investigation. *Journal of Personality and Social Psychology, 52*, 890–898.

Hidi, S. (1990). Interest and its contribution as a mental resource for learning. *Review of Educational Research, 60,* 549–571.

Kantor, R., Miller, S.M., & Fernie, D.E. (1992). Diverse paths to literacy in a preschool classroom: A sociocultural perspective. *Reading Research Quarterly, 27,* 185–201.

Moll, L.C. (Ed.). (1993). *Vygotsky and education.* Cambridge, England: Press Syndicate of the University of Cambridge.

Nelson-LeGall, S. (1986). Help-seeking behavior in learning. *Review of Research in Education, 12,* 55–90.

Newman, R.S. (1990). Children's help-seeking in the classroom: The role of motivational factors and attitudes. *Journal of Educational Psychology, 82,* 71–80.

Newman, R.S., & Goldin, L. (1990). Children's reluctance to seek help with schoolwork. *Journal of Educational Psychology, 82,* 92–100.

Paris, S.G., Lipson, M.Y., & Wixson, K.K. (1983). Becoming a strategic reader. *Contemporary Educational Psychology, 8,* 293–316.

Paris, S.G., Wasik, B.A., & Turner, J.C. (1991). The development of strategic readers. In R. Barr, M.L. Kamil, P. Mosenthal, & P.D. Pearson (Eds.), *Handbook of reading research: Volume II* (pp. 609–640). White Plains, NY: Longman.

Pressley, M. et al. (1992). Beyond direct explanation: Transactional instruction of reading comprehension strategies. *The Elementary School Journal, 92,* 513–555.

Rogoff, B. (1990). *Apprenticeship in thinking.* New York: Oxford University Press.

Rohrkemper, M.M., & Corno, L. (1988). Success and failure on classroom tasks: Adaptive learning and classroom teaching. *The Elementary School Journal, 88,* 297–312.

Ryan, R.M., & Grolnick, W.S. (1986). Origins and pawns in the classroom: Self-report and projective assessments of individual differences in children's perceptions. *Journal of Personality and Social Psychology, 50,* 550–558.

Santa Barbara Classroom Discourse Group. (1994). Constructing literacy in classrooms: Literate Action as Social Accomplishment. In R.B. Ruddell, M.R. Ruddell, & H. Singer (Eds.), *Theoretical models and processes of reading* (4th ed., pp. 124–154). Newark, DE: International Reading Association.

Schunk, D.H. (1989). Social cognitive theory and self-regulated learning. In B.J. Zimmerman & D.H. Schunk (Eds.), *Self-regulated learning and academic achievement* (pp. 83–110). New York: Springer-Verlag.

Slavin, R.E. (1987). Cooperative learning: Where behavioral and humanistic approaches to classroom motivation meet. *The Elementary School Journal, 88,* 29–37.

Short, K. (1992). Researching intertextuality within collaborative classroom learning environments. *Linguistics and Education, 4,* 313–333.

Stevens, R.J., & Slavin, R.E. (1995). The cooperative elementary school: Effects on students' achievement, attitudes, and social relations. *American Educational Research Journal, 32,* 321–351.

Tharp, R.G., & Gallimore, R (1993). Teaching mind in society: Teaching, schooling, and literate discourse. In L.C. Moll (Ed.), *Vygotsky and education* (pp. 175–205). Cambridge, England: Press Syndicate of the University of Cambridge.

Turner, J.C. (1995). The influence of classroom contexts on young children's motivation for literacy. *Reading Research Quarterly, 30,* 410–441.

Turner, J.C., & Paris, S.G. (1995). How literacy tasks influence students' motivation for literacy. *The Reading Teacher, 48,* 662–675.

Vygotsky, L.S. (1978). *Mind in society: The development of higher psychological processes.* Cambridge, MA: Harvard University Press.

Weiner, B. (1992). *Human motivation: Metaphors, theories and research.* Newbury Park, CA: Sage.

Willems, J. (1981). Problem-based (group) teaching: A cognitive science approach. *Instructional Science, 10,* 5-21.

Incentives and Intrinsic Motivation to Read

Linda B. Gambrell and Barbara Ann Marinak

M any teachers and administrators believe that extrinsic rewards or incentives spark students' development of reading motivation. To increase reading motivation, they organize or adopt programs that provide students with incentives for attaining specified reading goals. Moore and Fawson (1992) surveyed five diverse public school districts in a U.S. southwestern metropolitan area and found that 95 percent of elementary teachers conducted some variation of a reading incentive program in their classrooms. Teachers involved in the survey reported that the main reason they implemented an incentive program was to develop students' intrinsic motivation to read.

However, there has been growing concern about the use of incentive systems in educational settings (Deci et al., 1991; Kohn, 1993a, 1993b). Specifically, the concern centers around the possibility that incentives may have a detrimental effect on intrinsic motivation to read. For example, some researchers have suggested that if a child who enjoys reading is externally reinforced with incentives such as points or money, the child may choose to read less frequently when the incentive is discontinued (Deci et al., 1991; Lepper & Greene, 1978).

This chapter focuses on what is known about the use of incentives and how they affect intrinsic motivation. A brief review of the research on intrinsic and extrinsic motivation and the use of incentives is presented. The next section provides an overview of several reading incentive programs that are being implemented in classrooms throughout the United States. The chapter concludes with research-based insights about the effective use of incentives to enhance intrinsic motivation to read.

Motivation to Read

What motivates individuals to read in the absence of incentives? Much of the recent research of the Literacy Motivation Project at the National Reading Research Center (Codling & Gambrell, in press; Codling, Gambrell, Kennedy et al., in press; Gambrell,

Codling, & Palmer, 1996; Gambrell et al., 1996) has drawn heavily on the work of Csikszentmihalyi (1975; 1991) to identify and emphasize the specific conditions in classrooms that foster intrinsic motivation to read and write. As mentioned by others in this volume, Csikszentmihalyi's view of motivation is based on the concept of "flow," the mental state in which an individual is so completely engrossed in a task, such as reading, that he or she loses track of time. Readers experience flow when they enjoy or are satisfied by what they are reading, and the reading experience becomes its own reward (Csikszentmihalyi & Csikszentmihalyi, 1988). Of primary importance in flow theory is how learners respond to academic expectations. Children continually respond to stimuli in the classroom that are interpreted as either challenges or obstacles: a child who is intrinsically motivated will view reading as a meaningful challenge, whereas a student who lacks intrinsic motivation will view reading as an obstacle.

Another consideration in flow theory is the possession of goals. According to Csikszentmihalyi, many teachers know that the best way to help students achieve instructional goals is to enlist their interest. They do this by offering what might be termed "redefined" incentives that include being sensitive to students' goals and desires, offering choices, and providing clear and helpful feedback. It also is clear that in many classrooms tangible incentives—reinforcement and reward systems—are used to enlist students' interest in learning (Fawson & Fawson, 1994; Moore & Fawson, 1992).

Intrinsic Versus Extrinsic Motivation

Dichotomous theories of motivation that contrast learning as a self-initiated process and learning as a conditioning process provide a context for viewing motivation as either intrinsic or extrinsic. According to Deci (1972; 1992) and Csikszentmihalyi (1975), intrinsically motivated actions are performed out of interest and require no incentive other than the experience of enjoyment, interest, and satisfaction that accompanies them. Extrinsically motivated behaviors are performed for the external incentive or consequence that follows from their performance (Bandura, 1977; Skinner, 1953).

Theories of intrinsic motivation view learning as the lifelong process of making contact with and assimilating information from the environment (Piaget, 1952, 1971; Rigby et al., 1992). Thus, learning is viewed as the most natural of psychological processes because "the tendency to explore and to assimilate is an innate endowment of the human being" (Rigby et al., 1992, p. 166). Piaget (1971) considers the tendency to develop through contact and assimilation to be innate and intrinsic; he also contends that learning is spontaneous and that it serves as the very essence of life. Other theorists support this notion of intrinsically motivated learning and believe that innate intrinsic motivation represents our greatest human resource (Dewey, 1938; Montessori, 1967; Rogers, 1963).

In contrast, theories of extrinsic motivation maintain that learning is made to occur by forces from outside the individual; it is something that is imposed on the individual (Bandura, 1977; Skinner, 1953). This view of extrinsic motivation suggests that the reasons for learning are based on incentives and social controls. Numerous studies have explored the effects of both nontangible (verbal praise and feedback) and tangible incentives (Deci, 1971; Lepper, 1981; Lepper & Greene, 1978; Lepper, Greene, & Nisbett, 1973; O'Leary & Drabman, 1971; O'Leary, Poulos, & Devine, 1972).

Nontangible Incentives and Intrinsic Motivation

Teacher praise and feedback are nontangible extrinsic incentives that have been shown to positively influence student attitudes and behavior. One of the most profound findings in the research on motivation and learning is the facilitating effect of teacher praise and feedback on student performance (Cameron & Pierce, 1994; Deci, 1971). For example, Lepper and Cordova (1992) investigated whether verbal rewards (praise) could produce an increase in learning and subsequent interest. They carried out a series of four studies with upper elementary students. The tasks the students were asked to complete involved several problem-solving activities using a computer and several using a board game. Each of the studies resulted in verbal rewards having positive effects on immediate interest; generalization of learning; and, to some degree, subsequent motivation. Specifically, Lepper and Cordova found that verbal rewards in the form of praise that provided verbal scaffolding, support, direction, and additional information led to more motivated, confident, problem solving. In addition, elaborated or embellished praise was found to be more motivational than tangible incentives.

Tangible Incentives and Intrinsic Motivation

Research is less clear about the effects of tangible incentives on student performance. Some studies report a decrease in intrinsic motivation following the receipt of a tangible reward, and others report an increase in motivation.

Studies suggesting that tangible incentives undermine intrinsic motivation.
Widely cited early research on intrinsic motivation has yielded replicable findings showing that offering people tangible rewards for performing an intrinsically motivating activity leads to a decrease in intrinsic motivation for engaging in the activity (Deci, 1971, 1972, 1975; Lepper & Greene, 1978). These studies and many that followed support the notion that intrinsic and extrinsic motivation are antagonistic.

Deci (1971) conducted research to investigate the effects of rewarding students with money and other tangible incentives for engaging in an already intrinsically interesting task. Students who engaged in a task in one session and were paid during a second session tended to show less intrinsic motivation toward the task than did the comparison groups that had not been paid. The results of this study suggest that offering students money and other tangible rewards results in a decrease in their subsequent interest in engaging in an already interesting task in the absence of such rewards. Based on this research, Deci (1971) developed the "overjustification hypothesis"—the perception that an individual has undertaken an activity to receive some extrinsic reward.

Lepper, Greene, and Nisbett (1973) explored the overjustification theory in educational settings. Their investigation used tangible incentives that are used regularly in classrooms such as grades, stickers, and token economies in which children are offered redeemable tokens in exchange for exhibiting a desired behavior. The study involved preschool children who showed an intrinsic interest in drawing. The children were exposed to three conditions. In the expected-reward condition, children agreed to draw in exchange for an extrinsic reward (a certificate with a gold seal and ribbon). In the unexpected-reward condition, children had no knowledge of a reward until the drawing was complete (the same certificate with a gold seal and ribbon). In the no-reward condition, children neither expected nor received a reward. In the expected-reward condition, children showed less interest in drawing after receiving the reward. However, in the unexpected-reward condition, some children showed increased interest in drawing.

Studies suggesting that tangible incentives enhance intrinsic motivation.
Several studies have demonstrated that, under certain conditions, tangible rewards can enhance intrinsic motivation. Brennan and Glover (1980) found that subjects in an expected-reward condition showed an increase in intrinsic motivation relative to subjects in a control condition; however, Deci (1971) and Lepper, Greene, and Nisbett (1973) reported a negative effect when rewards were expected. Karnoil and Ross (1977) found a positive effect when rewards were given contingent on a specified level of performance.

There is considerable evidence in the research on token economy systems that supports the use of extrinsic rewards in specific situations (Fargo, Behrns, & Nolen, 1970; O'Leary & Drabman, 1971). Lepper, Greene, and Nisbett (1973) suggest that extrinsic rewards should be particularly useful when the level of initial interest is low and when the attractiveness of the activity becomes apparent only through engaging in it for a long time or only after some minimal level of mastery has been attained.

A classic study by McLoyd (1979) provides clarification of the conditions under which tangible incentives increase or decrease children's intrinsic interest in reading. The study examines the effects of a high-value versus low-value reward on second and third graders' intrinsic interest in reading a high-interest versus low-interest storybook. Both the reward value and storybook interest were inferred based on individual choices made by each child participating in the study. Children in the high-interest group received their first-choice storybook to read, and children in the low-interest group received their last choice. Children also identified high- and low-value rewards by rating the following list of incentives: good reader award (a certificate with ribbon and star), finger ring, animal eraser, pencil sharpener, metal washer, and plastic peg. Children read from a book (either high-interest or low-interest, depending on treatment condition), and at the conclusion of the reading period they received either a high- or a low-value reward or no reward. The results of this study reveal that when the amount of time spent reading and the approximate number of words read were used as indexes of intrinsic interest in reading the book, both high- and low-value rewards decreased children's interest in reading the high-interest book. In contrast, high-value rewards significantly increased children's interest in reading the low-interest book. This study supports Deci's findings (1971, 1972, 1975) that giving tangible rewards for engaging in an already interesting activity may prove to be detrimental to subsequent interest in the task. However, highly valued rewards may enhance subsequent interest and involvement in tasks that children find relatively uninteresting. The findings of this study point to the importance and relevance of the incentive in motivating students to read, particularly if they do not already find reading to be intrinsically rewarding.

The Reward Proximity Hypothesis: Using Incentives in Educational Settings

An extensive meta-analysis conducted by Cameron and Pierce (1994) provides perhaps the most definitive evidence to date that carefully chosen incentives can enhance intrinsic motivation. The meta-analysis included 96 experimental studies that compared rewarded subjects to nonrewarded subjects on measures of intrinsic motivation. Cameron and Pierce found that although tangible incentives produced no effect when delivered unexpectedly, they were not detrimental when they were expected and delivered contingent on a level of performance or completion of a task. They also found that tangible rewards produced a decrease in intrinsic motivation when given to individuals for simply engaging in an activity. Decreases in intrinsic motivation also were found when expected rewards were given regardless of the level of students' performance. The findings of Cameron and Pierce's meta-analysis support the following conclusions:

1. Verbal praise and positive feedback increase intrinsic motivation because of their informational value.

2. Tangible incentives do not undermine intrinsic motivation if offered as a result of completing a task in accordance with a set of standards.

In addition, it appears that individuals who receive tangible incentives are not less willing to work on activities, and they do not display less favorable attitudes toward tasks than people who do not receive incentives.

One notable characteristic of both teacher praise and feedback is that they are always closely linked to the desired student behavior, whereas tangible incentives (such as gold stars and stickers) are usually unrelated to the desired behavior. The "reward proximity hypothesis" (Gambrell, 1996) suggests that intrinsic motivation is enhanced when the incentive is linked to the desired behavior. In other words, a person's intrinsic interest in an activity is fostered when the incentive not only rewards the desired behavior, but also reflects the value of and encourages future engagement in the behavior. For example, if a teacher wants to foster a student's intrinsic motivation to read, appropriate incentives that are clearly linked to the desired behavior of reading might include books, bookmarks, or extra time allowed for reading.

Following is a brief overview of four reading incentive programs that have been implemented in classrooms throughout the United States. Most of these programs have been designed to encourage children to increase the amount of time they spend engaging in reading. The four programs have in common the specific goal of increasing the reading experiences of students and the use of tangible incentives for meeting specified reading goals.

All American Reading Challenge

The All American Reading Challenge (AARC) is sponsored by McDonalds, the American Library Association, and Scholastic, Inc. It is open to children in kindergarten through sixth grade. The program is designed to encourage elementary students to read for pleasure and to complete reading required for school assignments. Children choose a reading partner (a parent, sibling, neighbor, or friend), and they read 10 books together. Younger participants may have the books read to them, and older children may read aloud to their partner. After reading and discussing 10 books, participants complete a reading log, listing the titles read. The log is signed by a parent, teacher, or librarian. Children can then take their completed log to McDonalds for a free "All American Meal."

After completing 10 books, children are challenged to do it again. After completing three reading logs for a total of 30 books, the children become All American Readers. The reading logs distributed by the three sponsors contain reading tips and information on other programs designed to promote family reading such as the McDonalds Family Theater (a series of primetime network shows that profile children's literature) and The Busy World of Richard Scarry (an animated children's series based on books by Richard Scarry).

To summarize, the motivational characteristics of the All American Reading Challenge are as follows:

- Children read to meet specified goals (10 books or 30 books).
- Children choose the books they read for pleasure, or they read to complete school assignments.
- The major incentive is the McDonalds meal.

Book-It!

Book-It! is a reading incentive program for kindergarten through sixth grade and is sponsored by Pizza Hut, Inc. Children are rewarded with pizza for their reading accomplishments. Teachers set the monthly reading goals; they can set a different goal for each child in the class, and the goal can vary from month to month. The type of goal also can be decided by the teacher. For example, the goal can be the number of books read, the number of pages or chapters read, or the amount of time spent reading. For children who have not learned to read, teachers can set monthly goals for the child to be read to by others. When the child meets a monthly goal, as verified by the teacher, he or she receives a Pizza Award Certificate for a free pizza. On the first visit to Pizza Hut, the child is personally congratulated by the manager for reaching the monthly goal and receives a Book-It! button and sticker in addition to the free pizza. If a child meets the reading goal five times, he or she qualifies for the Reader's Honor Roll, a classroom record of achievement signed by the teacher and principal. If all the children in a class meet their reading goals in any four of the five months of the program, the entire class and teacher receive a pizza party. Pizza Hut, Inc., provides all necessary materials for participating in the program.

The motivational characteristics of Book-It! are as follows:

- Children are rewarded for reaching specified goals.
- Reading goals can be individualized.
- Choices are provided for identifying goals (for example, the number of books or pages read).
- Options are provided for reaching the goals (children can be read to or can read independently).
- The major incentive is free pizza

Bucks for Books

Earning by Learning is an educational volunteer program funded by the Earning by Learning Foundation, a nonprofit corporation in Delaware. One of the Earning by Learning programs, Bucks for Books, is designed to reward children with cash incentives to motivate them to read. Participants are paid US$2.00 for each book they complete while enrolled in the program. The program primarily targets youths who are at risk of school failure in grades three through six, and children are identified for participation by their teacher. Those who have the ability to read but are not motivated are the target group.

Children can be enrolled for the program through various community organizations including schools, libraries, and summer recreational programs. If the project is not connected with a school, a social worker or adult supervisor at the site has the responsibility for identifying children within the broad definition of "at risk." The program varies in length from several weeks to several months depending on the site. Reading for the program takes place mainly at the school or community center where the project is conducted. An adult volunteer, teacher, or librarian must verify, after discussion with the child, that each book was completed. Payment to readers can occur during the program, or sites may choose a pay-off day at the conclusion of the program. Adult volunteers are recruited from the private sector, and they receive an orientation to the program. All necessary materials and training are provided by the Earning by Learning Foundation.

To summarize, the motivational characteristics of Bucks for Books are the following:

- The program targets students who are not motivated to read.
- Children choose what they read.
- The major incentive is money.

RUNNING START

The RUNNING START (RS) program was developed by Reading Is Fundamental, a nonprofit organization that promotes reading and is funded by Chrysler Corporation. RS is designed to help first graders get off to a running start in reading. In keeping with the theme of the program, "Developing Readers for the 21st Century," first graders are challenged to read (or have someone read to them) 21 books in 10 weeks. Each classroom is provided with approximately 60 to 80 high-quality children's literature books that are selected by the classroom teacher. Teachers support children in reaching the goal of reading 21 books by having parent volunteers and older students listen to or read to the children. Children also are encouraged to take books home to share with family members. When children reach the goal of reading 21 books, they select a book of their choice as a reward. Reading Is Fundamental provides the necessary materials to participate in the program.

The motivational characteristics of RUNNING START are as follows:

- Children read to meet a specified goal (21 books).

- Children choose what they read.

- Options are provided for meeting the specified goal (children can be read to or can read independently).

- The major incentive is a book selected by the child.

Effective Use of Incentives in Reading Motivation Programs

The four programs described in the preceeding section are representative of the broad range of reading incentive programs that have been developed and implemented in U.S. classrooms in recent years. Despite the well-intentioned goals of these programs, there has been little documentation of their overall effectiveness. From 1990 to 1994, we conducted a series of studies as part of the Literacy Motivation Project at the National Reading Research Center that explored the effects of one of these programs, RUNNING START, on the reading motivation and behaviors of first-grade children and their parents (Gambrell et al., 1995). These studies included quasi-experimental designs, interviews with children and parents, and extensive classroom observations. The major findings reveal the following:

- Participation in the RUNNING START program increased the reading motivation and behaviors of the children and parents who participated in the program as compared to a control group.

- There were long-term positive effects for both children and parents that extended beyond the 10-week program and into second grade.

- There were substantial differences between the classroom context of the RS classrooms and the control classrooms in terms of book access and social interactions about books and reading.

This section highlights findings from the RS studies and from research and presents four research-based insights about the effective use of incentives in reading motivation programs. These insights provide information that may be helpful to educators to evaluate, select, and implement nationally sponsored reading incentive programs. In addition, these research-based insights may help guide the effective implementation of classroom-based reading incentive programs that are designed to foster intrinsic motivation to read.

Teacher Praise and Encouragement Are Powerful Incentives

Several findings from the RUNNING START studies suggest that both teacher praise and feedback are powerful incentives. One question we asked in our interviews with children who participated in the RS program is, "What did you like best about the RS program?" Children frequently mentioned talking with the teacher about the books they had read, and they referred to specific teacher praise and feedback comments by saying, "My teacher thinks I choose good books" and "I know I'm a good reader 'cause my teacher told me so."

Another finding that supports the power of teacher encouragement as an incentive to read was that in the RS classrooms, teachers encouraged children to take books home to share with family members more often than teachers in the control group. Consequently, both the child and parent survey data indicate significant differences in favor of RS participants on the frequency of bringing books home from the classroom to share with family members.

One of the most profound findings in the research on motivation is that verbal praise and encouragement are powerful extrinsic, nontangible incentives. The findings from the RS studies support the notion that teacher praise and encouragement provide the foundation for creating a motivating classroom context for literacy learning.

Tangible Incentives Should Approximate the Desired Behavior

In the interviews we conducted with RS children, we were surprised with their response to the question "What did you like best about the RS program?" We had expected that students would focus on getting the reward (a book of their choice) for meeting the challenge of reading 21 books. However, the children overwhelmingly responded that they liked reading and having lots of books available. Responses such as, "I liked reading the books," "I liked having lots of good books," and "I liked reading with my buddy" suggest that the children valued reading and books as a result of participation in the RS program.

One unique feature of the RS program is that the incentive for reading 21 books is choosing a book for personal ownership. In the RS program the incentive is linked to the desired behavior—reading. As mentioned, the reward proximity hypothesis (Gambrell, 1996) posits that the relation between the incentive or reward and the desired behavior may be an important variable in increasing motivation. Basic to this hypothesis is the assumption that incentives demonstrate the value system. If tokens or candy are used as incentives it is likely that children will value the tokens or candy; if books are the currency or the incentive, it is likely that children will perceive that reading and books are of value.

The proximity of the reward to the desired behavior may be as important as whether the reward is expected or unexpected (Lepper & Greene, 1978), tangible or nontangible (Anderson, Manoogian, & Reznick, 1976), or high value or low value (McLoyd, 1979). Though previous studies have employed a wide range of incentives and rewards (such as certificates, stars, rings, and tokens), few studies have employed the use of incentives that are closely linked to the desired behavior. Future literacy research is needed to explore whether using incentives that are linked to literacy increases motivation to read.

Tangible Incentives Should Be Linked to Meeting Challenging Learning Goals

The research of Ames (1992) and Deci (1975) supports the notion that motivation is enhanced when students are given incentives for accomplishing challenging tasks. The studies conducted on the RS program also emphasize the importance of linking the incentive to a specified level of accomplishment. Across two RS studies conducted with entirely different populations, we consistently found that what children were most excited about was meeting the individual challenge of reading 21 books within 10 weeks. However, before implementing this component of the program, interviews conducted with parents and teachers of first graders confirmed that the goal of reading (or having someone read to them) 21 books in 10 weeks was a challenging, yet realistic goal for the children.

Choice Provides an Important Incentive for Literacy Learning

Research abounds that attests to the motivating quality of choice in literacy learning (Deci & Ryan, 1985; Turner, 1995), as stressed in other chapters in this volume. Cognitive theorists describe motivation as a process of thought and decision making (Phillips & Soltis, 1991; Resnick, 1993; Thomas, 1985; Weiner, 1992). In this view, children do not passively respond to their environment; rather, they actively make choices and attend to salient factors in their environment. It may be easy to overlook the simple idea that providing opportunities for choice can be viewed as providing incentives to learn.

One characteristic of most reading incentive programs is that they allow for student choice. In the four programs described in the previous section, choice is an important feature. In the RS program choice is embedded in the program in three ways: children choose their reading materials; they can read independently or have someone read to them; and they select a book as a reward for meeting the 21-book goal. In the interviews we conducted with the children, parents, and teachers who participated in the RS program, choice was frequently mentioned as an important aspect of the program. In particular, parents and teachers responded that providing the children with choices was the most highly motivating feature of the RS program. What is most encouraging is that research clearly supports the notion that there is a strong correlation between choice and the development of intrinsic motivation (Paris & Oka, 1986; Rodin, Rennert, & Solomon, 1980; Turner, 1995).

Concluding Comments

Although the distinction between intrinsic and extrinsic motivation is an important one, the simplistic intrinsic-extrinsic dichotomy often has led to confusion and misinterpretation. Early studies tend to support the view that intrinsic and extrinsic motivation are antagonistic (Deci, 1971, 1972; Lepper, Greene, & Nisbett, 1973), whereas more recent studies suggest that under certain circumstances extrinsic incentives (tangible and nontangible) can enhance intrinsic motivation to learn (McLoyd, 1979; Ryan & Grolnick, 1986; Ryan, Mims, & Koestner, 1983). Current theory and research suggest that learners can be autonomous even when offered incentives to learn, if choice is a feature of the learning context.

Incentives that reflect the value of the desired behavior can be used to enhance intrinsic motivation, if there are opportunities for self-determination in the ways that goals are achieved and if the incentives are offered for accomplishing challenging learning goals. The appropriate use of incentives can lead learners to engage in reading and can lead to the internalization and integration of the value of reading. When incentives are linked to the desired behavior and promote engagement in the desired behavior, motivation can become self-determined and can foster high-quality learning. Further, appropriate incentives offered for goal-oriented, challenging reading performance can enhance intrinsic motivation to read.

References

Anderson, R., Manoogian, S.T., & Reznick, J.S. (1976). The undermining and enhancing of intrinsic motivation in preschool children. *Journal of Personality and Social Psychology, 34,* 915–922.

Ames, C. (1992). Classrooms: Goals, structures, and student motivation. *Journal of Educational Psychology, 84,* 261–271.

Bandura, A. (1977). *Principles of behavior modification.* New York: Academic.

Brennan, T.P., & Glover, J.A. (1980). An examination of the effect of extrinsic reinforcers on intrinsically motivated behavior: Experimental and theoretical. *Social Behavior and Personality, 8,* 27–32.

Cameron, J., & Pierce, W.D. (1994). Reinforcement, reward, and intrinsic motivation: A meta-analysis. *Review of Educational Research, 64,* 363–423.

Codling, R.M., & Gambrell, L.B. (in press). *The motivation to write profile: An assessment tool for elementary teachers* (Instructional Resource). Athens, GA: National Reading Research Center.

Codling, R.M., Gambrell, L.B., Kennedy, A., Palmer, B.M., & Graham, M. (in press). *The teacher, the text, and the context: Factors that influence elementary students' motivation to write* (Reading Research Report). Athens, GA: National Reading Research Center.

Csikszentmihalyi, M. (1975). *Beyond boredom and anxiety.* San Francisco, CA: Jossey-Bass.

Csikszentmihalyi, M. (1991). Literacy and intrinsic motivation. In S.R. Graubard (Ed.), *Literacy: An overview by fourteen experts.* New York: Farrar, Straus & Giroux.

Csikzentmihalyi, M., & Csikszentmihalyi, I.S. (1988). *Optimal experience.* Cambridge, England: Cambridge University Press.

Deci, E.L. (1971). Effects of externally mediated rewards on intrinsic motivation. *Journal of Personality and Social Psychology, 18,* 105–115.

Deci, E.L. (1972). Intrinsic motivation, extrinsic reinforcement, and inequity. *Journal of Personality and Social Psychology, 22,* 113–120.

Deci, E.L. (1975). *Intrinsic motivation*. New York: Plenum.

Deci, E.L. (1992). The relation of interest to the motivation of behavior: A self-determination theory perspective. In K.A. Renninger, S. Hidi, & A. Krapp (Eds.), *The role of interest in learning and development* (pp. 43–70). Hillsdale, NJ: Erlbaum.

Deci, E.L., & Ryan, R.M. (1985). *Intrinsic motivation and self-determination in human behavior*. New York: Plenum.

Deci, E.L., Vallerand, R.M., Pelletier, L.G., & Ryan, R.M. (1991). Motivation and education: The self-determination perspective. *Educational Psychologist, 26*, 325–346.

Dewey, J. (1938). *Experience and education*. New York: Collier.

Fargo, G.A., Behrns, C., & Nolen, P. (1970). *Behavior modification in the classroom*. Belmont, CA: Wadsworth.

Fawson, P.C., & Fawson, C. (1994, May). *Conditional philanthropy: A study of corporate sponsorship of reading incentive programs*. Paper presented at the 39th Annual Convention of the International Reading Association, Toronto.

Gambrell, L.B. (1996). Creating classroom cultures that foster reading motivation. *The Reading Teacher, 50*, 14–25.

Gambrell, L.B., Almasi, J.F., Xie, Q., & Heland, V. (1995). Helping first graders get a running start in reading. In L.M. Morrow (Ed.), *Family literacy connections in schools and communities* (pp. 143–154). Newark, DE: International Reading Association.

Gambrell, L.B., Codling, R.M., & Palmer, B.M. (1996). *Elementary students' motivation to read* (Reading Research Report No. 52). Athens, GA: National Reading Research Center.

Gambrell, L.B., Palmer, B.M., Codling, R.M., & Mazzoni, S.A. (1996). Assessing motivation to read. *The Reading Teacher, 49*, 518–533.

Karnoil, R., & Ross, M. (1977). The effect of performance relevant and performance irrelevant rewards on children's intrinsic motivation. *Child Development, 48*, 482–487.

Kohn, A. (1993a). Why incentive plans cannot work. *Harvard Business Review, 71*, 54–63.

Kohn, A. (1993b). *Punished by rewards: The trouble with gold stars, incentive plans, A's, praise, and other bribes*. Boston, MA: Houghton Mifflin.

Lepper, M.R. (1981). Intrinsic and extrinsic motivation in children: Detrimental effects of superfluous social controls. In W.A. Collins (Ed.), *Minnesota symposium on child psychology* (Vol. 14, pp. 155–214). Hillsdale, NJ: Erlbaum.

Lepper, M.R., & Cordova, D.I. (1992). A desire to be taught: Instructional consequences of intrinsic motivation. *Motivation and Emotion, 16*, 187–208.

Lepper, M.R., & Greene, D. (1978). Overjustification research and beyond: Toward a means-ends analysis of intrinsic and extrinsic motivation. In M.R. Lepper & D. Greene (Eds.), *The hidden costs of reward: New perspectives on the psychology of motivation* (pp. 109–148). Hillsdale, NJ: Erlbaum.

Lepper, M.R., Greene, D., & Nisbett, R.E. (1973). Undermining children's intrinsic interest with extrinsic reward. *Journal of Personality and Social Psychology, 28*, 124–137.

McLoyd, V.C. (1979). The effects of extrinsic rewards of differential value on high and low intrinsic interest. *Child Development, 50*, 1010–1019.

Moore, S.A., & Fawson, P.C. (1992, December). *Reading incentive programs: Beliefs and practices*. Paper presented at the 42nd Annual Meeting of the National Reading Conference, San Antonio, TX.

Montessori, M. (1967). *The discovery of the child*. New York: Ballantine.

O'Leary, K.D., & Drabman, R. (1971). Token reinforcement programs in the classroom: A review. *Psychological Bulletin, 75*, 379–398.

O'Leary, K.D., Poulos, R.W., & Devine, V.T. (1972). Tangible reinforcers: Bonuses or bribes? *Journal of Consulting and Clinical Psychology, 38*, 1–8.

Paris, S.G., & Oka, E.R. (1986). Self-regulated learning among exceptional children. *Exceptional Children, 53*, 103–108.

Piaget, J. (1952). *The origins of intelligence in children.* New York: International Universities Press.

Piaget, J. (1971). *Biology and knowledge.* Chicago, IL: University of Chicago Press.

Phillips, D.C., & Soltis, J.F. (1991). *Perspectives on learning.* New York: Teachers College Press.

Resnick, L. (1993). Toward a cognitive theory of instruction. In S.G. Paris, G.M. Olson, & H.W. Stevenson (Eds.), *Learning and motivation in the classroom* (pp. 5–38). Hillsdale, NJ: Erlbaum.

Rigby, C.S., Deci, E.L. Patrick, B.C., & Ryan, R.M. (1992). Beyond the intrinsic-extrinsic dichotomy: Self-determination in motivation and learning. *Motivation and Emotion, 16*, 165–185.

Rodin, J., Rennert, K., & Solomon, S. (1980). Intrinsic motivation for control: Fact or fiction. In A. Baum, J.E. Singer, & S. Valios (Eds.), *Advances in environmental psychology II.* Hillsdale, NJ: Erlbaum.

Rogers, C. (1963). The actualizing tendency in relation to "motives" and to consciousness. In M.R. Jones (Eds.), *Nebraska symposium on motivation* (Vol. 2, pp. 1–24). Lincoln, NE: University of Nebraska Press.

Ryan, R.M., & Grolnick, W.S. (1986). Origins and pawns in the classroom: Self-report and projective assessments of individual differences in children's perceptions. *Journal of Personality and Social Psychology, 50*, 550–558.

Ryan, R.M., Mims, V., & Koestner, R. (1983). Relation of reward contingency and interpersonal context to intrinsic motivation: A review and test using cognitive evaluation theory. *Journal of Personality and Social Psychology, 45*, 736–750.

Skinner, B.F. (1953). *Science and human behavior.* New York: Macmillan.

Thomas, R.M. (1985). *Comparing theories of child development.* Belmont, CA: Wadsworth.

Turner, J. (1995). The influence of classroom contexts on young children's motivation for literacy. *Reading Research Quarterly, 30*, 410–441.

Weiner, B. (1992). Motivation. In M.C. Alkin (Ed.), *Encyclopedia of educational research: Volume 3* (pp. 860–865). New York: Macmillan.

School Change and Literacy Engagement: Preparing Teaching and Learning Environments

Carol Minnick Santa

A s educators, we want students to leave our classrooms continuing as readers, writers, and learners. This means that students not only are independent in these areas but also have internalized continuing literacy passion—a desire to read, write, and learn throughout their lives. However, researchers tell us that few students leave school with a passion to read and write on their own. Too many lack the literacy skills needed for continued learning. They are not equipped as consumers, critics, and producers of knowledge. They are not *engaged* in literacy activities. What can we do to change this situation?

Every school is blessed with a few teachers who know how to create environments that researchers have documented as supportive of reading engagement. In these classrooms, we see children deeply involved in learning. These children read extensively for pleasure and for researching their own inquiries (Allen et al., 1991). Teachers have created environments where individual choice is honored, where students have voice and ownership in their agendas, and where they feel comfortable taking risks and exploring topics of interest (Guthrie, McGough, & Bennett, 1994; Oldfather, 1993, 1994). These classrooms have integrated content areas where children have time and permission to become absorbed in deep learning (Guthrie et al., 1996). Thematic studies and large concepts form the core of the curriculum. Children and teachers share an "honored" voice (Oldfather & Dahl, 1995) because the classroom climate is one of respectful cooperation. The teacher is not the sole source of truth and authority; rather, the authority for knowledge is shared among children and teachers.

In some situations, an entire school supports an engagement perspective, although these cases are rare. In most systems, only a few teachers create environments different from the status quo. Yet, the issue of reading engagement is far too important to occur inside one or two classrooms. It must become a part of entire schools and districts. For this to happen, every aspect of a school's culture must be conducive to an engagement perspective. This requires changes in the sociology and curriculum of schools so that teachers are not only supported but also challenged to create contexts where children can become deeply involved in reading and learning. Two complementary forces must converge: the principles derived from work in school change and principles from research on engagement pedagogy.

In my school system, we have been making deep changes in literacy instruction, all designed around a central goal of reading engagement. We have been able to make changes because of the way our school district operates: none of this could have happened if administrators and teachers had not already been participants in a learning community. Even within this healthy, inquiry environment, our efforts have taken a long time, and there have been difficulties.

My district demonstrates principles that are essential for school innovation and change. We also have incorporated within our philosophy of teaching and in our curriculum features that researchers have defined as important for reading engagement. The combination of these two domains has been critical for creating learning contexts that support reading engagement.

In this chapter, I use my school district as an example of how principles of school change and research in reading engagement can play a critical role in transforming teaching and curriculum. First, I examine some general principles of school change in the following section.

Principles of School Change

The first principle of school change is that it is inevitable; it is a way of life. "Today, the teacher who works for or allows the status quo is the traitor. Purposeful change is the new norm in teaching" (Fullan, 1993, p. 14). Effective teachers are on a perennial quest of questioning and self-renewal. Educators must seek change and learn to appreciate its vitality. Teaching is a learning process, and the inquiry never ends (Joyce & Calhoun, 1995).

Second, educators need to understand what change feels and looks like. Just as we help our students become more metacognitive about literacy processes, we need to become more aware of change. We need to recognize it and embrace it, so that we can pass it on. Change is messy and filled with tension—healthy tension. Recognizing what it is and what it does will help us and our colleagues become more tolerant of tension and better agents of change.

Third, change begins with a personal commitment, with something that we feel passionate about. We became teachers because we wanted to make a difference with young lives. Important changes begin with commitments dealing with this moral purpose. We vision a better future (Patterson, 1993) that begins with the articulation of this vision and the capacity of people to create and pursue visions (Fullan, 1993; O'Neil, 1995).

A fourth principle of change is that it is not linear. The route and destination are discovered through the journey itself. Change is akin to writing: a writer begins with a few ideas—tensions to resolve—but does not know the exact direction and tempo until the writing begins. The destination changes with incessant revision. It is only after printing out the final draft that the progression can be defined.

This view of change is different from neat, top-down management plans, in which the "top" decides on global tasks that need to be accomplished and defines step-by-step ways to carry them out. Does change really spread from the top? Do most of us begin with a detailed outline and rigidly follow it when we write? Changes that work usually do not keep to the original blueprint; change is not that simple.

Fifth, change involves a combination of individual and collaborative work. Change usually begins with the individual voice; we articulate visions that we value. It is important to have individual voices. If everything is done through collaborative group work, the voice of the individual can be lost. Fullan (1993) also warns that groups are more likely to deal with "fadism" and "uncritical uniformity." Sometimes groups pursue issues that do not really matter. Thus, in any change effort Fullan recommends the encouragement of individual voices. Personal change leads to organizational change. Often the people least willing to speak up in a group are those who have the most innovative and important questions. Questions are formed by a combination of what we feel is correct and knowledge gleaned from research and outside experts. When our beliefs are confirmed by research, we can be more articulate.

Change also involves collaboration for good ideas to converge. Change demands opportunities for teacher talk so that personal ideas and visions become clearer. There is a ceiling effect to how much we can learn if we keep it to ourselves. Change gathers momentum with enough voices.

Sixth, change happens when common sense is corroborated with outside knowledge from research or experts. In my school district, teachers and administrators distributed research reports and articles defining factors leading to reading engagement. Research that supports "hunches" about what should work helps persuade skeptics who are more comfortable with the status quo.

Seventh, change flourishes with a balance of bottom-up and top-down strategies: "Neither centralization nor decentralization works.... Centralization errs on the side of control, decentralization errs toward chaos" (Fullan, 1993, p. 37). With concensus above and below, change happens. Too much decentralization leads to a lack of focus, leaving teachers too bogged down with management issues and less opportunity to deal with things of importance—like teaching. Guidance from the top helps, yet the top cannot become too controlling. Change flourishes in a healthy top-down, bottom-up balance. Each side needs the other.

Finally, instructional change occurs when learning environments are healthy for teachers. Change happens in environments where teachers feel safe to take risks, to carry out what they believe, to collaborate with colleagues, and to make decisions. Important work takes place when teachers collect, analyze, and reflect on data. School renewal is not a formula, but an environment for inquiry (Joyce & Calhoun, 1995; Joyce, Wolf, & Calhoun, 1993).

Centers of inquiry are the same kind of learning environments we want for children. As Corno and Randi stress in Chapter 3, we cannot teach students to be continuous learners, engaged readers, and effective collaborators if we do not work in school communities that have these same characteristics. Children's reading engagement and learning as inquiry cannot happen unless schools become places where teachers consume, critique, and produce new knowledge (Fullan, 1993; Joyce, Wolf, & Calhoun, 1993; Sagor, 1995).

Principles of school change parallel issues of reading engagement. Unless these principles are incorporated within a system for teaching, the goal of reading engagement will remain within the boundaries of only a few teachers. We have integrated these principles with knowledge about reading engagement to make drastic changes in our district's literacy program.

Context for Change

Our school district serves about 5,000 children in a blue collar, low- to middle-class community. We are a kindergarten through grade 12 district with five elementary schools, a middle school, and a high school.

Our management team consists of a superintendent, business clerk, special education director, and principals. Except for my part-time position as language arts coordinator, we have no mid-management employees. Our superintendent is a passionate proponent of teacher decision making; he believes that educational decisions are best made by those closest to students—teachers. To operationalize this philosophy he has turned curriculum budgets over to each school, which means more funds in individual teacher budgets. The superintendent constantly challenges us to deal with inquiries arising from teachers, the school board, students, and the community. In our monthly administration meetings, we focus primarily on instructional issues: Should we have year-round schools? How can we combine curriculum areas at the high school? How can we get parents more involved in the instructional program? We circulate professional articles and books. Our superintendent knows that creating learning environments for administrators is a precursor for creating similar environments in schools.

In much the same way, principals in our district strive to create a learning environment in their school—an environment that encourages risk taking (Reitzug & Burello, 1995). Faculty meetings focus on instructional issues. Professional articles abound in faculty lounges and often are discussed at faculty meetings. A portion of each principal's budget is allocated to inservice professional development. Principals often use these funds to hire substitutes so that faculty can work on collaborative projects.

Our district is committed to the idea of having teachers in charge of curriculum. Curriculum decisions are handled by K–12 curriculum committees comprising teachers and administrators and led by a teacher facilitator. The curriculum committees make decisions about overall instructional philosophy, instructional materials, and assessments for each major curriculum area. The committee members are given release days from teaching for some of their committee work, and they also work on their own time before and after school. Having teachers as the curriculum leaders and decision makers has been critical to our change efforts. Teachers who chair curriculum committees are highly respected among their colleagues as exceptional teachers.

Through collaboration with the University of Montana, various graduate classes are held in our district, which allows easy access to many teachers. These courses cover topics such as multiage classrooms, first-grade reading intervention, content reading and study strategies, and teachers as researchers.

One of the most successful graduate courses taught in the schools has been the focus on teachers as researchers, or systematic, intentional inquiries carried out by teachers (Santa & Santa, 1995). The class is one way to cultivate and support teacher research. In this class, the teachers and I apply a general problem-solving strategy to teaching and learning investigations. We help one another sharpen questions and define problems through professional reading and brainstorming sessions. Participants receive group feedback to refine their research plans. Each participant tries his or her project and returns to the group to report and obtain more feedback. The year-long class concludes with teachers supporting one another through drafting and revising articles on their projects, which they send to be published in professional journals. The capacities to suspend disbelief, take risks, and experience the unknown are essential to learning; when teachers understand how inquiry works, they become better facilitators of inquiry in their own classrooms.

An atmosphere of inquiry at the management, teacher, and classroom levels is a priority. Such an atmosphere constitutes an overall attitude that Oldfather and Dahl (1995) terms the "honored voice." Although Oldfather speaks of honored voice as a classroom condition, it can be thought of more broadly as part of a school and district condition. Honored voice is a deep responsiveness in which communities of learners invite, listen, respond to, and act upon one another's "thoughts, feelings, interests, and needs," and participants feel safe in their inquiries (p. 6).

In essence, we feel more satisfaction and involvement in our work when feeling deeply respected. We cannot expect classroom environments to honor the voices of children unless teachers receive the same honor. Similarly, engagement in literacy tasks only can occur in classroom climates deeply responsive to children's ideas, opinions, and feelings. Intrinsic motivation is fostered in a climate where teachers' and children's ideas are valued. Because of a supportive and respectful context, we have been able to make substantial changes not only in our language arts program but within all curricular areas.

Questioning Current Practices

The initial force behind our change effort was a deep concern that our students were reading infrequently. How could we change our language arts curriculum so that students spent more time reading at school and at home? As with any important change effort, our quest began with a personal commitment of a few teachers who questioned the status quo. They began voicing their concerns: our children are hardly reading; they only read three to four stories per week out of their basal readers; students spend more time doing worksheets than reading.

The situation was not much better in the content areas. Teachers had separate times each day for reading, science, and social studies. Curriculum was defined by what was in the textbook, and teachers did their best to cover as much as they could. Practically no integration occurred, and students had little time for reading and writing during school because there was too much content to cover.

Our questioning of current practices gathered momentum. I worked to keep tensions high by flooding teacher lounges with articles and by bringing up issues about reading engagement in our management meetings. A major catalyst was the report *Becoming a Nation of Readers* (Anderson et al., 1984), which documents that children spend far more time doing skill sheets than reading. Principals had their faculties read and discuss this work as part of faculty meetings. The conclusion from each school was the same: we had to make some drastic changes in our language arts program.

Many teachers began to feel uncomfortable with their traditional basal instruction. They also had other concerns: How could they make time for students to read with so many content areas to cover? If they did not have students do worksheets, how would they perform on end-of-unit tests?

These concerns were raised in the K–12 language arts committee responsible for curriculum decisions in this area. As chairperson of this committee, I facilitated a change effort that has led to a focus on reading trade books, interdisciplinary teaching, and a different view of assessment. The committee's progression has been far from linear; we address problems and issues as they arise and figure out ways to move forward. Even though new problems and tensions continually arise, I can reflect on our process. I realize that the same progression would be impossible in other settings, yet many of our ideas could be adapted.

Articulating a Vision and Developing a Philosophy

Because of the concern about language arts instruction among district teachers, our committee decided to uncover what teachers thought about literacy teaching. What were their current theories? What were their passions and moral commitments?

This process was quite helpful for several reasons. First, teachers have few forums in which to articulate what they believe. Second, personal theories directly influence our work even when we are not aware of them; sometimes we do not know what we believe until we have to tell someone else. Third, we cannot grapple with changing current theories until we know our current stance. Discussing personal theories became important not only for individual teachers, but also for the district as a whole.

The committee asked teachers to reflect about what they termed vital for children's reading and writing. We initiated discussion by asking teachers to respond to a survey developed by the committee (Santa, 1991), which asked teachers for information about their current reading program. The survey included queries about the use of basal readers, trade books, skills teaching, and assessment, and about whether they felt satisfied with their current program. Then, we asked teachers what their goals were and what kind of reading program they would consider to be ideal.

During the several weeks set aside for teachers to complete the survey, I collected input from children by conducting a simple study. I asked children in elementary classrooms what they would like to see in a language arts program. In one hand I held a new basal anthology, in the other a library book. I asked the children, "How should we spend district money? Should we spend it on purchasing new basal readers or should we spend it on trade books?" Children's opinions were clear: they always voted for books and willingly volunteered reasons. They talked about how difficult it was to become really interested in reading from the anthology. They said they would read a lot more if they could read library books at school. In fact, most related how much more they read at home than at school because they could read literature at home.

Hearing children talk about why trade books were more interesting to read and how their reading habits at home differed from those at school fostered our change effort. Teachers who felt bound by traditional systems began to think harder about their own philosophies of teaching.

After compiling data from the teacher survey and from the children, I sent a summary to each school. These summaries became the topic of faculty discussions, and tensions about change began to mount. The committee wanted to ensure that everyone had an opportunity to voice ideas, particularly those who infrequently spoke up in groups. We also wanted to make sure that principals were involved. To accomplish this, we asked principals to interview their teachers. This not only gave every teacher an opportunity to talk through ideas, but it also allowed principals to hear teachers' views.

The committee compiled the principals' notes and examined them for common themes. Three trends emerged. First, teachers expressed concern that students were not reading very much, as mentioned earlier. Children did not choose to read on their own either for learning new information or for pleasure. Teachers also questioned their reliance on basal anthologies and skill sheets.

Second, teachers worried about assessment. Those primarily using a reading workshop approach wanted a way to evaluate their children's learning. Similarly, teachers who still used basals did so because they feared students might miss key skills. Because the basal scope and sequence had always constituted our curriculum, teachers did not know what their expectations for children would be without them.

Third, teachers wanted to spend more time in class having students choose books to read on their own, but they simply had too much content to cover. They did not have time to give students opportunities to read. They suggested that we should simplify our curriculum and integrate content areas.

The committee summarized these trends into a draft philosophy about teaching. During the next two months, teachers held grade-level meetings to discuss and modify the draft. I circulated professional articles addressing such issues as extended reading, assessment, and integration of curriculum. During faculty meetings teachers discussed ideas and built consensus about beliefs and future directions about literacy teaching.

Notes from these collaborative sessions, information from the surveys, and conclusions were combined into an overall goal and philosophy statements. This summary is presented in the following excerpt.

Goal: Children deserve to read for enjoyment and for gaining knowledge. Students deserve opportunities to learn skills and strategies for accomplishing reading and writing tasks as part of in-depth studies of topics and themes.

Philosophy:

- Children need extended time each day to read self-selected literature. They also deserve time to read at home. Therefore, the only homework for language arts will be home reading.

- The core of the language arts program should be trade books. Students deserve experience with common literature and with reading extensively from self-selected books.

- Reading instruction must be incorporated within realistic situations and integrated with content areas.

- Science, social studies, and language arts should be combined into cross-curricular themes.

- The primary response to reading should be writing and student generated discussion.

- Children deserve systematic instruction in reading comprehension.

- Although emphasis should be on "real" reading and writing, children deserve to have an understanding of sound-symbol relations as a tool for writing and reading.

- Assessment should help students understand their own growth and should be tied closely to instruction.

Agreeing about our beliefs led to new issues. Because combining curriculum areas was a way to gain time and create richer learning environments, teachers began to question their attempts to cover content texts. They asked, "Should we instead select a few areas to teach in depth as part of integrated blocks of study?" Teachers also asked questions about assessment: "Why not decide on what is really important for students to learn, and then use these areas for assessment targets?" "Maybe we don't need to identify multitudes of discrete skills at each level? Instead let's identify the most critical areas for students' learning."

All of these issues defined the committee's next tasks, which included developing a scope and sequence of strategies, combining curricular areas, and developing assessment.

Developing a Scope and Sequence of Strategies

The change efforts we initiated led to the development of a complete scope and sequence of literacy strategies. The language arts committee began by generating an array of strategies or targets reflecting our reading engagement goals and philosophy. This draft was sent to all teachers for their comments. After teachers had opportunities to respond individually, they made revisions during grade-level meetings. They decided during these sessions which reading strategies to emphasize at specific grade levels. Their conclusions were returned to the language arts committee to put in final order. The process for developing this document took about one year.

The final document contains three major target behaviors, outlined following, that form the basis of our language arts program.

Target 1: Commitment to Literacy—Extended Reading and Writing

It was no accident that commitment to literacy became our first target; we wanted to ensure that students had opportunities each day to select their own books to read and to write on self-selected topics. In adapting the workshop model to their classrooms, most teachers relied on the work of Atwell (1987), Calkins (1986), Reif (1991), and Romano (1987). Teachers and students also designed various ways to keep track of student progress in writing; most developed portfolio systems.

Besides developing a reading and writing workshop at school, we also initiated a home reading program. In fact, the only homework for language arts is home reading. Teachers send home with the children calendars or reading records where children keep track of their reading. Students set their own goals for the amount they plan to read at home, and students and their parents monitor these goals. Children then bring their home reading records to school and keep them in their reading portfolios.

Our commitment to make extensive reading and writing our first target is well supported by the research on reading engagement, as discussed in the first section of this volume. The central tenet of the reading and writing workshop is student choice, interest, and goal setting. All these factors honor the voices of children (Oldfather, 1994).

In classrooms that honor student voices, children have input in what happens in the classroom. Numerous studies confirm the positive relation between intrinsic motivation and the autonomy orientation of a classroom (Ryan & Grolnick, 1986). Flink, Boggiano, and Barrett (1990) found that students perform less well when teachers do not allow students choices about learning tasks. Because of this situation, Oldfather (1994) recommends that teachers examine their professional beliefs about sharing control and responsibility with students. Classrooms that foster motivation and deep learning represent a balance between choice and structure, as students and teachers collaborate on what they learn, how they learn, and how they will be evaluated.

Another tenet of the reading and writing workshop is goal setting. In our reading workshop model, students set their own goals for what and how much they plan to read both at school and at home. Students evaluate themselves based on whether they have met or exceeded their goals. In almost every case, students read more than they specify in their goals.

As discussed in the first section of this book, in a review of research relating to achievement goals, Wigfield and Guthrie (1995) note that the kinds of goals (ego involved or task involved) influence performance and achievement. Ego-involved goals deal more with appearances and competition where children try to outperform others. With task-involved goals, children select outcomes that they can accomplish. Children who select task-involved goals tend to choose challenging tasks and are more concerned in monitoring their own progress toward these goals than with competition. Task-involved children are more likely to maintain motivation. Moreover, when children set clear, specific goals, they usually perform better and have more positive feelings of confidence (Corno, 1993; Oldfather & Wigfield, 1996).

This work supports the idea that children should be involved in decisions about their reading. When children are involved in making decisions about what they will read and how much they plan to read, they are more likely to follow through with their commitments.

Another factor leading to increased motivation and learning is interest. When children have opportunities to select material they find interesting, they use more effective learning strategies and have better comprehension than with uninteresting material (Wigfield & Guthrie, 1995). This work further supports the importance of choice and control. Children deserve many opportunities to select books to read and topics for investigation that matter to them.

It is also clear that issues of choice and autonomy are central to children's growth as readers, writers, and learners. In classrooms where children make reading and writing choices, they read more and achieve better in reading than in classrooms that do not allow students similar opportunities (Anderson, Wilson, & Fielding, 1988; Morrow, 1992; Taylor, Frye, & Maruyama, 1990). Moreover, children who choose to read voluntarily develop positive attitudes toward reading (Greaney, 1980). In fact, reading engagement becomes an intangible goal in classrooms where children feel controlled by curriculum decisions that they have had no part in making.

Target 2: Comprehending, Studying, and Evaluating Ideas

Target behaviors that focus on comprehension and study strategies fall into three categories: (1) using main ideas, (2) applying study strategies, and (3) recalling, comparing, analyzing, and evaluating ideas. Also included are research, library, and report writing skills. These strategies are practical and within the context of interdisciplinary studies. For example, main idea instruction centers on organizing strategies (such as concept mapping and note taking) and expository writing in which students develop paragraphs and expository papers.

By the time students reach grades three and four, teachers begin explicit teaching of study strategies. Teachers demonstrate and have students practice selective underlining and various note-taking systems such as two-column notes and content frames. By the upper elementary grades, children know a variety of methods to organize and learn content information. In addition to the more creative writing prevalent during writing workshop, they learn to write reports and essays. With the third category of strategies (recalling, comparing, analyzing, and evaluating ideas) students sequence ideas, analyze narrative using story structures, debate and write about issues and opinions, compare and evaluate ideas, and lead their own discussions about literature and content.

Our emphasis on strategy use is supported not only by research in comprehension (Pearson & Fielding, 1991) but also by literature on motivation. Strategies such as those dealing with rehearsal, organization, and elaboration foster active engagement and result in higher levels of achievement (Weinstein & Mayer, 1986). Strategy use and motivation are completely interrelated. When students feel competent in using strategies, they tend to be more engaged in learning tasks. Knowledge of strategies increases students' confidence to succeed with tasks (Schunk & Rice, 1987). Further, students who feel competent about applying strategies such as summarizing, outlining, and note taking appear to set higher academic goals and have more self-confidence than students lacking confidence in strategy use (Zimmerman & Martinez-Pons, 1988).

Target 3: Word-Study and Sentence Skills

The third target behaviors that form the basis of our language arts program include work with phonics, vocabulary development, and sentence conventions. Children in kindergarten through grade two receive fairly explicit instruction in phonics, which includes practice reading and spelling words with particular phonics elements. Words come from the literature children are reading and from word lists developed by teachers. In addition, for each thematic study, students develop their own lists of unknown words for vocabulary study. They learn concepts of these words by expanding definitions through word mapping, writing, and oral activities.

Finally, usage, mechanics, grammar, and sentence skills are taught through children's own writing and sentence editing. Each day as part of a whole-class activity the children edit a sentence for mechanics and usage. These revisions and those that occur as part of writing workshop provide a realistic way for teaching and evaluating how well students have learned punctuation, usage, and sentence conventions.

Developing our scope and sequence of strategies was critical to the evolution of our curriculum. The teachers realized that the reading comprehension and writing strategies in our list were far more useful to students than those in any prescribed program. Students actually learned how to learn, how to lead their own discussions, and how to respond to their reading through both creative and expository writing. Moreover, teaching from basals really did not make any sense any more. These strategies made more sense within rich thematic studies where students used multiple novels and library resource materials for their investigations.

Combining Curriculum into Thematic Studies

We began the process of curriculum integration by examining our social studies and science curriculum. Covering material in the science and social studies textbooks seemed to be teachers' major concern. We questioned this assumption: teachers might be covering the text, but were students really engaged in learning? Through conversations during faculty meetings and teacher surveys we decided that less is more. Why not cover less content and provide students with rich, in-depth studies relying primarily on hands-on activities, library materials, and fiction and nonfiction books? Teachers responded through surveys and questionnaires about the cross-curricular themes they were currently teaching or those they wanted to teach. From here, we began defining several science and literature and social studies and literature themes at each grade level.

For example, in science we decided that one of our themes would be on the general topic of life science. For each grade level, we defined the topic more specifically so that students would have opportunities each year to extend their knowledge. For instance, in grade one the focus is on pet animals; in grade three the theme is insects and arachnids; and in grade six it is large mammals. For each grade, we have purchased multiple class sets of fiction and nonfiction books on the thematic topics. The thematic studies usually last about a month.

We have continued to define a variety of science and social studies themes. In the primary grades, our entire science, social studies, and language arts program is combined. At the middle grades, teachers still teach some science and social studies topics separately, but in most situations they are combined. Over the last 10 years, we have replaced all textbook expenditures with the purchase of fiction and nonfiction books that extend the thematic studies.

Language arts skills such as note taking, researching and writing reports, and giving oral presentations are taught as part of thematic studies. This means that there is no need for a separate language arts time because strategies are taught as the tools for learning and responding to the content of the thematic studies. Moreover, teachers save time not having to race from one subject to another, and they have time each day for students to participate in reading and writing workshop. Thus, our students can read extensively in school not only as part of the thematic studies, but also during reading workshop.

Integrating curriculum into rich content studies is supported by research on reading engagement. It is hardly a surprise that the exploration of challenging content and issues is more motivating to students than reading from textbooks or doing skill sheets. For example, Miller, Adkins, and Hooper (1993) found that third graders had more intrinsic motivation for complex assignments than for simple assignments. In fact, simple assignments such as copying and writing single words or sentence fragments prompted work avoidance (Turner, 1995).

The strongest support for the motivating power of integration comes from work by Morrow and Guthrie. For instance, Morrow, Pressley, and Smith (1995) did an extensive study of integrating curriculum in science and literature with third-grade classes. The investigation included three conditions. The first experimental condition was fully integrated. Instead of reading from their basal readers and science texts, the children read high-quality literature about the science topics in their textbooks. The second experimental group used trade books for language arts rather than the basal reader, but had a separate time for science when they read from their science textbook and completed supporting worksheets. Children in the control group used the basal reader and science textbook as their primary reading material. The children in the first group did significantly better on all literacy measures than children in the other two groups. The first group also performed better than the other two groups on a test of science concepts. Moreover, as indicated on a follow-up survey, children in the first group had better attitudes toward science than those in the other groups.

The work by Guthrie and his colleagues (Guthrie, McGough, & Bennett, 1994; Guthrie et al., 1996) investigating the Concept-Oriented Reading Instruction (CORI) in science, discussed in Chapter 7, is another example of strong support of the motivating power of integrated instruction. Children experiencing combined language arts and science instruction in the CORI classrooms read more frequently and widely than students in the same school in a basal nonintegrated program. Students in the CORI classrooms also scored higher on measures of intrinsic motivation (curiosity, aesthetic enjoyment, and social challenge) than did the basal students who were higher in extrinsic responses (grades, work avoidance, and personal recognition).

Developing Assessment

The final component of our change process deals with assessment. Previously described are some aspects of assessment that occur as part of the home reading and reading and writing workshop components of our language arts program. In these situations, children are basically in charge of their own assessment, where they set goals and collect their writing and various reading records in their portfolios.

For the thematic studies, teachers and students evaluate performance with products that students keep in portfolios such as notes, concept maps, paragraphs, and reports. Students select examples of these products for their portfolios along with comments on why they think they represent their best work.

Over the past several years, teachers have students lead their own parent conferences (Santa, 1995). About a week before conferences, students organize their portfolios and make decisions about work they plan to highlight with their families. The children accompany their parents to the conferences and tell them about their work. Teachers have found that, with this method, they can hold several conferences simultaneously, as they move from one child-parent group to another as a facilitator.

Although such child-centered and child-controlled assessment has not been directly studied by researchers investigating factors conducive to reading engagement, some implications can be drawn from research that supports this form of assessment. Having children take charge of their own assessment creates an environment of deep respect for children's voices. The assessments also center on task- rather than ego-involved goals, which Wigfield and Guthrie (1995) note are more likely to maintain motivation.

Although most of our assessment focuses on helping children and their parents understand the growth of individual children, we also are in the process of examining overall achievement through program assessments. For evaluating district goals, we are developing cross-curricular measures for evaluating writing, study strategies, reading comprehension, and listening. We do know that there has been a dramatic increase in the use of the library and in the total number of books children read. Teachers also report that more than 90 percent of their students meet their school and home reading goals.

Final Reflections

It is not enough to teach children to become readers and writers; we want children to leave our schools with the continuing desire to read, write, and learn. Our task is to pursue this vision so that it becomes a reality. It is not enough for reading engagement to occur only within a few classrooms in a school. All children deserve to be in a school situation where they have an opportunity to become passionate learners, writers, and readers.

Most school situations will have to change to achieve this broader meaning of literacy. Children have little opportunity to become engaged learners with a segregated curriculum; they need large blocks of time for their explorations. Such engagement cannot happen when teachers feel pressed to teach one subject after another and when the curriculum is defined as getting through textbooks or completing a basal anthology. By combining content around major themes and issues, teachers and children have opportunities to examine topics from multiple perspectives and immerse themselves in their own inquiries.

Students will not become passionate readers unless they have time to read books both in and out of school. This does not mean excerpts of books from an anthology, but complete works. If we truly believe that reading is important, then we must demonstrate our commitment by making time in every school day for children to read the books they want to read.

Students also deserve to know learning strategies. Students who know how to do investigations, read various materials, organize information, and then report their information to others gain confidence about themselves as learners. Confident learners tend to be motivated learners. It makes sense for strategy instruction to be the basis of an integrated program.

Finally, children feel more control over their learning when they are partners in the assessment process. Effective assessment is designed to clarify each student's individual growth rather than to compare one child with another. Students deserve to participate in every aspect of the evaluation process as they set their own goals and keep track of their progress. Self-concepts grow stronger when students monitor their own successful progress toward goals.

Integrating curriculum, promoting extensive reading, applying learning strategies, and involving children in their own assessments are key factors for creating environments for literacy engagement. Incorporating such sweeping changes into the core of teaching demands healthy learning environments for teachers. The changes are too complex to be mandated from the top and too difficult for teachers to manage on their own. Both sides must work together to put personal visions about making life better for children into practice. Change occurs within centers of inquiry where teachers seek answers to questions that truly matter. Teaching engagement and literacy engagement follow the same path.

When principles of change work in conjunction with common sense confirmed by research on literacy, schools can become places of promise—places where children leave school with the passion to read, write, and learn throughout their lives. When school systems honor teachers' and students' voices, such promises have a chance of becoming reality.

References

Allen, J.B., Michalove, B., Shockley, B., & West, M. (1991). "I'm really worried about Joseph": Reducing the risks of literacy learning. *The Reading Teacher, 44,* 458–467.

Anderson, R.C., Wilson, P.T., & Fielding, L.G.(1988). Growth in reading and how children spend their time outside of school. *Reading Research Quarterly, 23,* 285–303.

Anderson, R.C., Hiebert, E., Scott, J., & Wilkinson, I. (1984). *Becoming a nation of readers* (The report of the Commission on Reading). Washington, DC: U.S. Department of Education.

Atwell, N. (1987). *In the middle: Writing, reading, and learning with adolescents.* Portsmouth, NH: Heinemann.

Calkins, L.M. (1986). *The art of teaching writing.* Portsmouth, NH: Heinemann.

Corno, L. (1993). The best-laid plans: Modern conceptions of volition and educational research. *Educational Researcher, 22*(2), 14–22.

Flink, C., Boggiano, A.K., & Barrett, M. (1990). Controlling teaching strategies: Undermining children's self-determination and performance. *Journal of Personality and Social Psychology, 59,* 916–924.

Fullan, M. (1993). *Change forces.* Bristol, PA: Falmer.

Greaney, V. (1980). Factors related to amount and type of leisure reading. *Reading Research Quarterly, 15,* 337–357.

Guthrie, J.T., McGough, K., & Bennett, L. (1994). *Concept-oriented reading instruction: An integrated curriculum to develop motivations and strategies for reading* (Reading Research Report No. 10). Athens, GA: National Reading Research Center.

Guthrie, J.T., McGough, K., Bennett, L., & Rice M.E. (1996). Concept-oriented reading instruction: An integrated curriculum to develop motivations and strategies. In L. Baker, P. Afflerbach, & D. Reinking (Eds.), *Developing engaged readers in school and home communities* (pp. 165–190). Hillsdale, NJ: Erlbaum.

Joyce, B., & Calhoun. E. (1995). School renewal: An inquiry, not a formula. *Educational Leadership, 52*(7), 51–55.

Joyce, B., Wolf, J., & Calhoun, E. (1993). *The self-renewing school.* Alexandria, VA: Association for Supervision and Curriculum Development.

Miller, S.D., Adkins, T., & Hooper, M.L. (1993). Why teachers select specific assignments and teachers' reactions to them. *Journal of Reading Behavior, 25,* 69–95.

Morrow, L.M. (1992). The impact of a literature-based program on literacy achievement, use of literature, and attitudes of children from minority backgrounds. *Reading Research Quarterly, 27,* 250–275.

Morrow, L.M., Pressley, M., & Smith, J.K. (1995). *The effect of a literature-based program integrated into literacy and science instruction on achievement, use, and attitudes toward literacy and science* (Reading Research Report No. 37). Athens, GA: National Reading Research Center.

Oldfather, P. (1993). What students say about the motivating experiences in a whole language classroom. *The Reading Teacher, 46,* 672–681.

Oldfather, P. (1994). *When students do not feel motivated for literacy learning: How a responsive classroom culture helps* (Reading Research Report No. 8). Athens, GA: National Reading Research Center.

Oldfather, P., & Dahl, K. (1995). *Toward a social constructivist reconceptualization of intrinsic motivation for literacy learning* (Perspectives in Reading Research No. 6). Athens, GA: National Reading Research Center.

Oldfather, P., & Wigfield, A. (1996). Children's motivations for literacy learning. In L. Baker, P. Afflerbach, & D. Reinking (Eds.), *Developing engaged readers in school and home communities* (pp. 89–113). Hillsdale, NJ: Erlbaum.

O'Neil, J. (1995). Our schools as learning organizations: A conversation with Peter Senge. *Educational Leadership, 54*(7), 20–23.

Patterson, J. (1993). *Leadership for tomorrow's schools.* Alexandria, VA: Association for Supervision and Curriculum Development.

Pearson, P.D., & Fielding, L. (1991). Comprehension instruction. In R. Barr, M. Kamil, P. Mosenthal, & P.D. Pearson (Eds.), *Handbook of reading research: Volume II* (pp. 815–860). White Plains, NY: Longman.

Reif, L. (1991). *Seeking diversity: Language arts with adolescents.* Portsmouth, NH: Heinemann.

Reitzug, U., & Burello, L. (1995). How principals can build self renewing schools. *Educational Leadership, 52*(7), 48–50.

Romano, T. (1987). *Clearing the way: Working with teenage writers.* Portsmouth, NH: Heinemann.

Ryan, R.M., & Grolnick, W.S. (1986). Origins and pawns in the classroom: Self-report and project assessments of individual differences in children's perceptions. *Journal of Personality and Social Psychology, 50,* 550–558.

Sagor, R. (1995). Overcoming the one-solution syndrome. *Educational Leadership, 54*(7), 24–27.

Santa, C. (1991). Cutting loose: A district's story of change. In J. Feeley, D. Strickland, & S. Wepner (Eds.), *Process reading and writing: A literature-based approach.* New York: Teachers College Press.

Santa, C. (1995). Students lead their own parent conferences. *Teaching K–8, 25,* 92–94.

Santa, C., & Santa, J. (1995). Teaching as research. *Journal of Reading Behavior, 27,* 439–451.

Schunk, D.H., & Rice, J.M. (1987). Enhancing comprehension skills and self-efficacy with strategy value information. *Journal of Reading Behavior, 19,* 285–302.

Taylor, B.M., Frye, B.J., & Maruyama, M. (1990). Time spent reading and reading growth. *American Educational Research Journal, 27,* 351–362.

Turner, J.C. (1995). The influence of classroom contexts on young children's motivation for literacy. *Reading Research Quarterly, 30,* 410–441.

Weinstein, C.E., & Mayer, R.E. (1986). The teaching of learning strategies. In M.C. Wittrock (Ed.), *Handbook of research on teaching* (3rd ed., pp. 315–327). New York: Macmillan.

Wigfield, A., & Guthrie, J.T. (1995). *Dimensions of children's motivations for reading: An initial study* (Reading Research Report No. 34). Athens, GA: National Reading Research Center.

Zimmerman, B.J., & Martinez-Pons, M. (1988). Construct validation of a strategy model of student-regulated learning. *Journal of Educational Psychology, 80,* 284–290.

Author Index

Csikszentmihalyi, M., 17, 55, 70, 75, 76, 78, 79, 81, 113, 114, 187, 191, 202, 206
Cunningham, A.E., 5

D

D'Amato, J., 175, 176
Dahl, K.L., 184, 218, 222
De Groot, E., 20, 90
deCharms, R., 86, 90, 191
Deci, E.L., 5, 7, 17, 76, 86, 87, 88, 90, 91, 92, 93, 96, 156, 157, 190, 202, 205, 206, 207, 208, 209, 214, 215
DeFord, D.E., 184
DeGroot, E.V., 86
DeLeeuw, N., 134
Devine, V.T., 207
Dewey, J., 64, 206
Diener, C.I., 185
Dilthey, W., 117
DiPardo, A., 41
Dolan, L.J., 119
Dole, J.A., 56, 138
Doyle, W., 184, 185
Drabman, R., 207, 208
Draheim, M., 102
Duffy, G.G., 56, 64, 138
Duguid, P., 136, 185, 194, 195
Dunlap, K., 162
Dweck, C.S., 5, 18, 20, 40, 159, 164, 185, 192
Dykstra, R., 131

E

Earle, J., 73
Eberstadt, F., 72
Eccles, J.S., 5, 14, 15, 16, 17, 19, 20, 23, 28, 110
Eco, U., 72
Edelsky, C., 185
Eeds, M., 80, 81
Ehri, L.C., 4
Eisenberger, R., 56
Eisenhart, M., 97
Elliott, E.S., 192
Elliott-Faust, D., 57
Epstein, J.L., 28
Epstein, S., 110

Erickson, F., 114, 170, 171, 172, 173, 176
Erikson, E., 107, 108
Evans, E., 55

F

Fargo, G.A., 208
Farmer, A.W., 42
Fawson, C., 205, 206
Fawson, P.C., 205, 206
Feldlaufer, H., 110
Fernandez-Fein, S., 27
Fernie, D.E., 184
Ferrara, R., 58
Fielding, L.G., 5, 73, 223, 227
Filler, F. C., 21
Fisher, C.W., 185, 202
Fisher, W.R., 74
Fitzgerald, J., 46
Fleet, J., 55
Flink, C., 226
Flood, J., 130, 132
Fogarty, R., 133
Fordham, S., 171
Forrest-Pressley, D., 57
Franks, J.J., 186
Freedman, S.W., 41
Freppon, P.A., 184
Frye, B.J., 227
Fullan, M., 219, 220, 221

G

Gaa, J.P., 41
Gallimore, R., 195, 196
Gambrell, L.B., 28, 88, 90, 160, 205, 206, 209, 213
Gamoran, A., 132, 162
Garcia, T., 107
Garner, R., 42, 73
Gillingham, M.G., 73
Givon, H., 56
Globerson, T., 56
Glover, J.A., 208
Goatley, V.J., 81
Goetz, E.T., 40, 73, 74, 79
Goldenberg, C., 97
Goldin, L., 195
Golding, J.M., 138
Good, T., 110

Goodchild, F., 55
Gospodinoff, K., 173
Gough, P.B., 4
Graesser, A., 138
Graham, M., 205
Graham, S., 39, 44, 56, 57, 153
Graves, D., 174, 176
Graves, M.F., 73
Greaney, V., 227
Green, J.L., 5
Greene, D., 87, 91, 205, 207, 208, 214, 217
Greene, L.C., 132
Greeno, J., 63
Greybeck, B., 108
Griffith, P.L., 4
Grolnick, W.S., 90, 91, 191, 215, 226
Guthrie, J.T., 1, 5, 14, 22, 23, 26, 28, 29, 57, 58, 69, 79, 86, 87, 88, 89, 92, 93, 99, 128–146, 152, 154, 164, 218, 226, 229, 230
Guzdial, M., 129

H

Hagen, A.S., 78, 113
Haggard, M.R., 102
Hansen, J., 176
Hanson, A.R., 45
Harold, R., 28
Harris, K.R., 39, 44, 56, 57, 153
Hart, S., 97
Harter, S., 17, 20, 28, 86, 90, 91
Hatano, G., 81
Hawthorne, R.K., 63
Hayes, D.A., 80
Hayes, K.G., 170
Hayes, M., 156
Heath, S.B., 5, 108, 114
Heckhausen, H., 56
Heland, V.J., 88
Herman, P.A., 174
Hidi, S., 69, 73, 136, 156, 192
Hiebert, E.H., 97, 185, 202, 223
Homstead, E., 130
Hooper, M.L., 229
Hopkins, K., 132
Hopkins, L.F., 81

Horn, C., 150, 154, 164
Hoyle, R.H., 131
Huey, E.B., 3, 4
Hull, G., 114
Hymel, S., 22
Hynd, C., 88
Hynes, S., 114

I–J

Inagaki, K., 81
Irby, M.A., 58
Jackson, D., 52, 57
Jacobs, H.H., 133
Jenkins, L.B., 170
Jetton, T.L., 20, 21, 73, 135
Johnsen, E.P., 42
Johnson, M.J., 41
Johnson, V., 73
Johnston, M.B., 42
Johnston, P., 163
Jones, E.D., 62
Joyce, B., 62, 219, 220, 221
Juel, C., 4

K

Kamehameha Schools Bishop
    Estate, 168, 173
Kamil, M.L., 4, 14
Kanfer, R., 53, 58, 143
Kantor, R., 184
Karnoil, R., 208
Karweit, N.L., 119
Kawakami, A.J., 181
Kear, D.J., 21
Kennedy, A., 205
Kern, R.G., 108
Kleefeld, C., 45
Klinger, E., 77
Koch, S., 78
Koestner, R., 215
Kohn, A., 205
Krajcik, J.S., 129
Krapp, A., 69, 156
Kraska, K., 58
Kuhl, J., 56, 58
Kulikowich, J.M., 5, 20, 21,
    73, 135

L

Labov, W., 114
Ladson-Billings, G., 171
Langer, J.A., 114, 170
Langman, J., 58
Lapp, D., 130, 132
Larivee, S., 37, 40
Latham, G.P., 39
Lauer, J., 18
Lavancher, C., 134
Leary, M.R., 89
Leggett, E.L., 5, 18, 20, 40, 164
Lepper, M.R., 87, 91, 205, 207,
    208, 214, 217
Lexander, P.A., 40
Lieberman, A., 62, 63
Lipson, M.Y., 42, 129, 130, 131,
    132, 185
Locke, E.A., 39
Long, D.L., 138

M

Mac Iver, D., 15, 16
Madden, N.A., 119
Maehr, M.L., 17, 18, 23
Malone, T., 87
Mandinach, E.B., 56
Manoogian, S.T., 214
Marinak, B.A., 205
Markell, R., 22
Markus, H., 107
Marsh, H.W., 28
Marshall, H., 116
Martinez-Pons, M., 16, 40, 41,
    228
Maruyama, M., 227
Marx, R.W., 20, 129
Maslow, A.H., 105
Mason, J.M., 22, 114, 171
Mathewson, G.C., 4, 21, 105
Mayer, R.E., 42, 228
Mazzoni, S.A., 206
McCann, A., 88, 128
McDermott, R.P., 97, 173
McGinnis, K., 130
McGough, K., 14, 22, 26, 142,
    218, 230
McKenna, M.C., 21
McLaughlin, J., 28

McLaughlin, M.W., 58, 108
McLoyd, V.C., 208, 214, 215
McMahon, S.I., 80
McPartland, J.M., 28
Meece, J.L., 16, 17, 20, 40, 112,
    113, 131
Mehan, H., 114, 172
Meichenbaum, D., 38
Messick, S., 56
Metz, K.E., 136
Mezynski, K., 174
Michalove, B., 218
Midgeley, C., 28, 110
Miller, G., 57
Miller, L., 63
Miller, S.D., 229
Miller, S.M., 184
Mims, V., 215
Mohatt, G., 171
Moll, L.C., 114, 195
Montessori, M., 206
Moore, S.A., 205, 206
Morales, A., 170
Morrow, L.M., 82, 88, 90, 227,
    229
Mosenthal, M.L., 14
Mosenthal, P., 4
Mount, M.D., 53, 56
Moyer, B., 107
Mullis, I.V.S., 170
Murphy, C.C., 41

N

Nakamura, J., 81
National Assessment of Educa-
    tional Progress, 129
Nell, V., 70, 72, 74, 75, 76, 77,
    78, 82
Nelson-LeGall, S., 196
Newman, R.S., 195
Ng, M., 89, 93, 99
Nicholls, J.G., 15, 16, 18, 112,
    163
Nisbett, R.E., 91, 207, 208, 215
Noddings, N., 89
Nolen, P., 208
Nolen, S.B., 86, 90
Nurius, P., 107
Nystrand, M., 71, 132, 162

Subject Index

Note: An "f" following an index entry indicates that the citation may be found in a figure, a "t" that it may be found in a table.